The Merchant John Askin

The Merchant John Askin

FURS AND EMPIRE AT BRITISH MICHILIMACKINAC

Justin M. Carroll

MICHIGAN STATE UNIVERSITY PRESS | *East Lansing*

Michigan State University Press
East Lansing, Michigan 48823-5245

Printed and bound in the United States of America.

26 25 24 23 22 21 20 19 18 17 1 2 3 4 5 6 7 8 9 10

LIBRARY OF CONGRESS CATALOGING-IN-PUBLICATION DATA
Names: Carroll, Justin M., author.
Title: The merchant John Askin : furs and empire at British Michilimackinac / Justin M. Carroll.
Other titles: Furs and empire at British Michilimackinac
Description: East Lansing : Michigan State University Press, [2017] | Includes bibliographical references and index.
Identifiers: LCCN 2016057854| ISBN 9781611862614 (pbk. : alk. paper) | ISBN 9781609175436 (pdf) | ISBN 9781628953121 (epub) | ISBN 9781628963120 (kindle)
Subjects: LCSH: Askin, John, 1739–1815. | Fort Michilimackinac (Mackinaw City, Mich.)—History. | Fur traders—Michigan—Biography. | Fur trade—Northwest, Old. | Trading posts—Michigan—Mackinac, Straits of, Region—History. | Mackinac, Straits of, Region (Mich.)—Biography. | Frontier and pioneer life—Michigan—Mackinac, Straits of, Region. | Frontier and pioneer life—Northwest, Old. | Great Lakes Region (North America)—History. | Northwest, Old—Biography.
Classification: LCC F572.M16 C38 2017 | DDC 977.4/923—dc23
LC record available at https://lccn.loc.gov/2016057854

Book design by Charlie Sharp, Sharp Des!gns, East Lansing, Michigan
Cover design by Erin Kirk New
Cover image of *Michilimackinac on Lake Huron* is based on a drawing by Richard Dillon, Jr. and published in Montréal in 1813, the print shows the place as it was in July 1812.

Michigan State University Press is a member of the Green Press Initiative and is committed to developing and encouraging ecologically responsible publishing practices. For more information about the Green Press Initiative and the use of recycled paper in book publishing, please visit *www.greenpressinitiative.org.*

Visit Michigan State University Press at *www.msupress.org*

. . .

To Maddox,
for his beautiful laugh,
his intelligent eyes,
and the joy he makes.

. . .

To Jana,
for her infinite patience,
her indomitable spirit,
and her remarkable jantics.

. . .

Contents

Acknowledgments

I WILL KEEP THIS SIMPLE AND DIRECT.

Now, as much as I would like to take sole credit for this book, I cannot. I cannot help but see my efforts in light of the loved ones who sacrificed for and supported me; the numerous colleagues and friends at Michigan State University (MSU), Indiana University East (IUE), and beyond who inspired and challenged me; the librarians, the excellent archivists, reviewers, and editors who made my research, writing, and manuscript stronger and better; and, finally, the students at Indiana University East who helped sustain my passion. Thank you all.

In particular, I would like to thank Dr. Susan Sleeper-Smith, professor of history at MSU; Dr. Ross Alexander, the dean of humanities and social sciences at IUE; and Julie Loehr, the assistant director and editor in chief at MSU Press. I could not have written this book without your generosity and support. Thank you, truly.

Jana, my dear partner and candle in the dark, read, edited, and commented on this book more times than she really cared to or imagined she ever would.

If the book has any style or quality, I owe that to her and her good taste. Thank you, Jana. (I also find it bizarre that Jana talks to me, listens to me, tolerates my idiocy, and condescends to love me. But, of course, that's an entirely different history).

All successes, I share. All failures are my own.

PROLOGUE

I Was Born at Aughnacloy in the North of Ireland in 1739

A Ubiquitous Man, the Great Lakes Fur Trade, and the British Empire

More than thirty years after his migration to the Great Lakes of North America, John Askin (1739–1815), a fifty-four-year-old British merchant living in Detroit, answered a letter from a Maryland man who claimed to be a distant relative. In the letter, Askin provided the only contemporary account of his life. "I was Born at Aughnacloy in the North of Ireland in 1739," he wrote, "[and] came to this Country in 1758, and most of my time since has been in Trade first at Albany near New York . . . & since that at a place called Michilimackinac & for these last thirteen Years past here [in Detroit]." Further on, Askin revealed that he "married in 1772 & ha[d] a large Family [and] some of my Daughters [are] married," and that he had "many other particular friends in London a Mr. Isaac Todd [and] a Mr. Willm Robertson both may be found at Messr Phyn Ellis & Englis in London."[1] With a few scratches of the pen, Askin supplied the broad strokes of his life, helping the Marylander locate him within the social, economic, political, and geographic world of the British Great Lakes region.

After years of studying Askin, I still find this letter curious—not for what his words tell us, but for what they leave out. In Askin's humble account of his life,

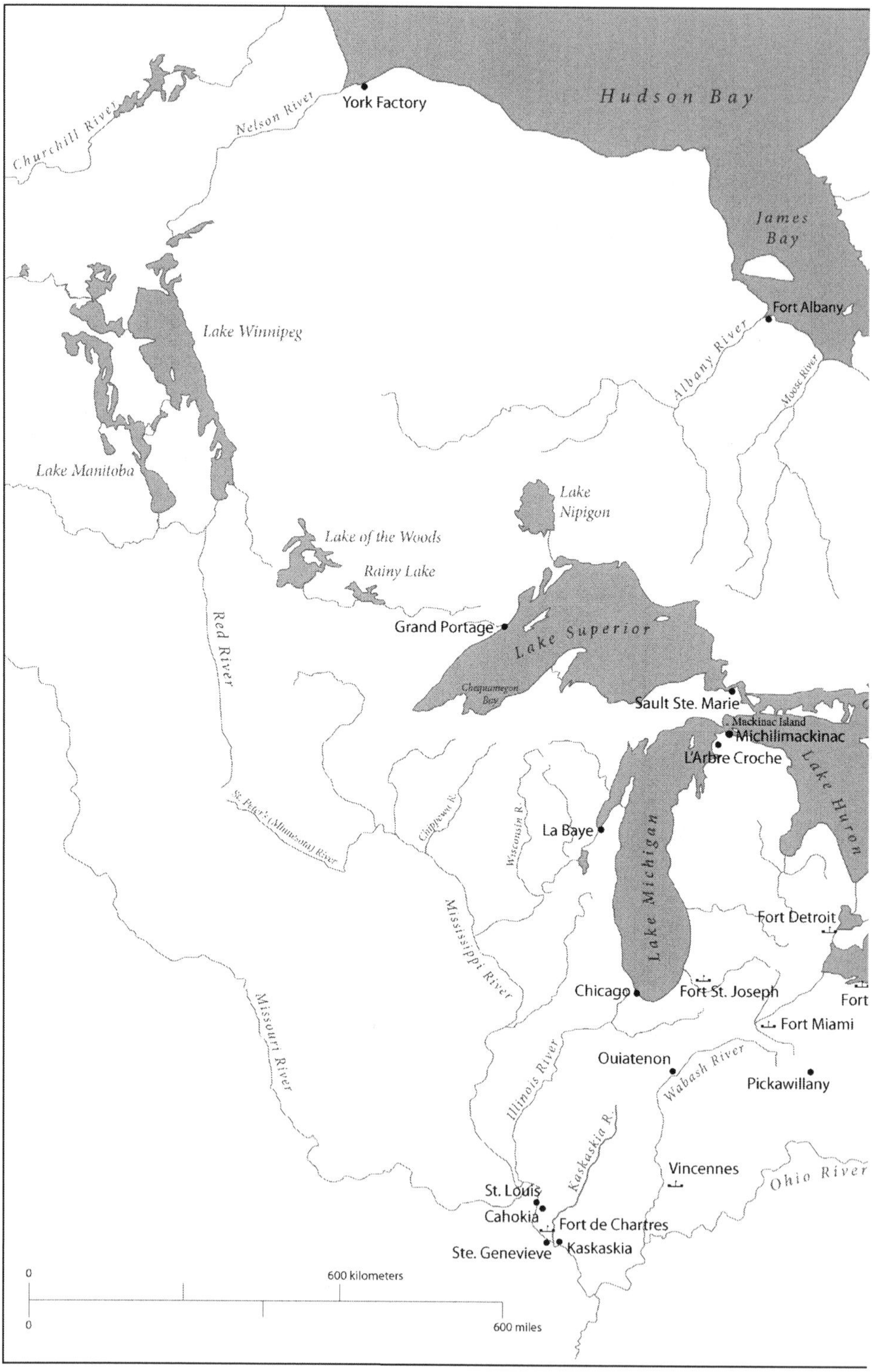

Hudson Bay
York Factory
Churchill River
Nelson River
James Bay
Fort Albany
Albany River
Moose River
Lake Winnipeg
Lake Manitoba
Lake Nipigon
Lake of the Woods
Rainy Lake
Grand Portage
Lake Superior
Chequamegon Bay
Red River
Sault Ste. Marie
Mackinac Island
Michilimackinac
L'Arbre Croche
Lake Huron
La Baye
Lake Michigan
Wisconsin R.
Chippewa R.
St. Peter's (Minnesota) River
Mississippi River
Missouri River
Fort Detroit
Chicago
Fort St. Joseph
Fort Miami
Ouiatenon
Wabash River
Pickawillany
Illinois River
Kaskaskia R.
Vincennes
Ohio River
St. Louis
Cahokia
Fort de Chartres
Ste. Genevieve
Kaskaskia
0
600 kilometers
0
600 miles

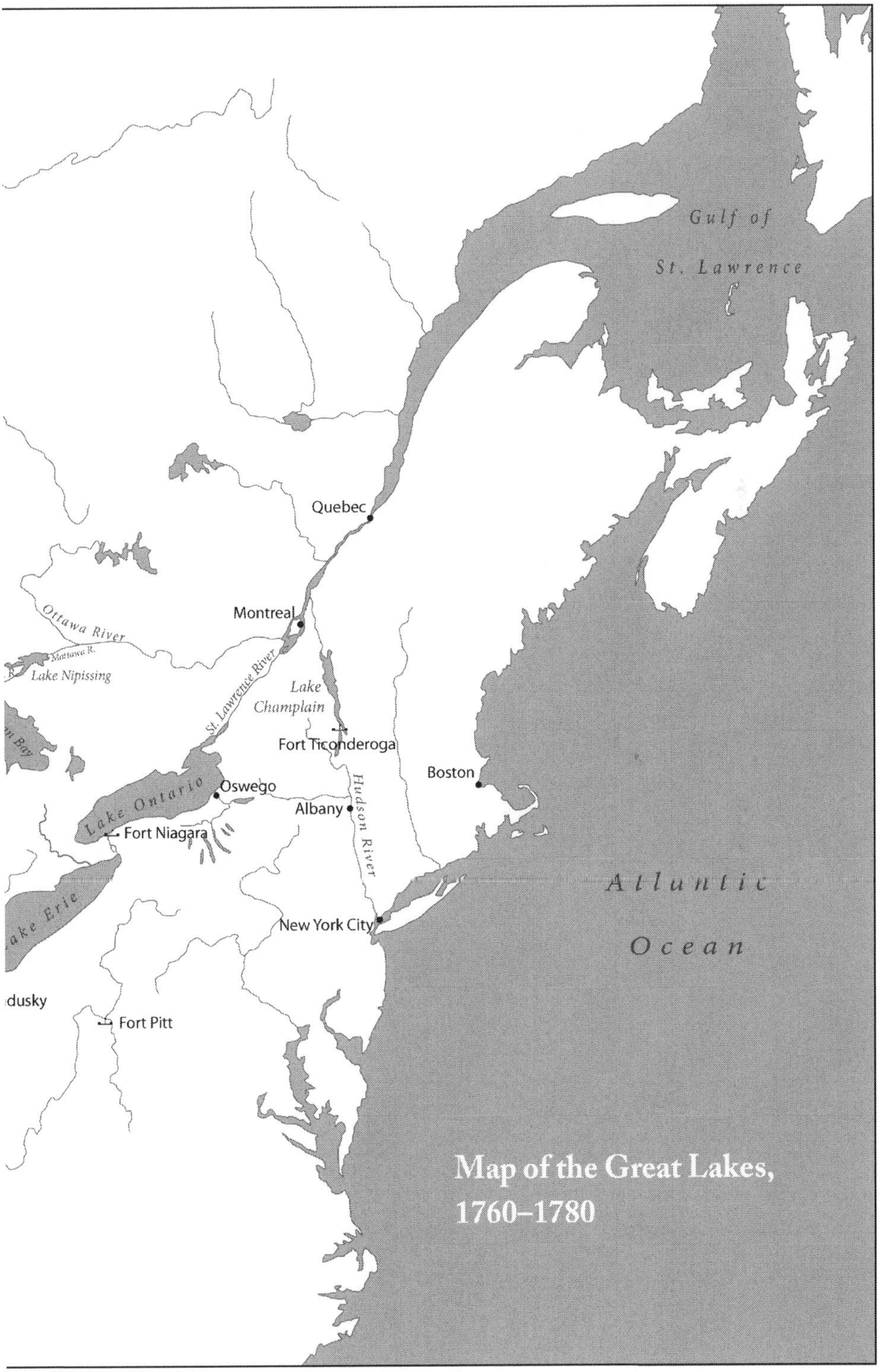

Map of the Great Lakes, 1760–1780

E. WHITE

it is hard to appreciate, for example, the decades of innovation and revitalization that defined his career as a Great Lakes fur trade merchant. In the late 1770s Askin was the premiere middleman at Michilimackinac, the community at the very heart of Great Britain's fur trade. He neglected to mention his close relationship to the British military; namely, the positions he held as a sutler during the Seven Years' War (1754–1763) and deputy commissary during the American Revolution (1775–1783).[2] In Askin's life, the one hidden in his letter, the close interconnectedness of trade and empire resulted in his greatest and most lasting successes and his most disastrous and enduring failures. Excavating these moments, how they came about, and why they matter is the central focus of this book.

Two hundred years after his death, John Askin persists as a ubiquitous but minor historical actor in many narratives of the Great Lakes, the fur trade, and the British Empire in the trans-Appalachian west.[3] I first came across Askin as an undergraduate when reading *Indian Women and French Men: Rethinking Cultural Encounter in the Western Great Lakes*, written by my future dissertation adviser, Susan Sleeper-Smith, professor of history at Michigan State University.[4] She wrote:

> John Askin, a Scots-Irish trader seasoned in the New York trade, entered the Michilimackinac trade when he married in "the manner of the country" an Odawa woman at the nearby Native village of L'Arbre Croche. At Detroit, he also married Marie Archange Barthe, whose father had traded there since the 1740s.[5]

I followed Sleeper-Smith's footnote to the back of her book, where I found a reference to the *John Askin Papers*, a two-volume set of his collected correspondence, published by the Detroit Historical Society in the late 1920s and early 1930s. Sleeper-Smith drew her thumbnail sketch from the collection's introduction, a narrative of Askin's life written by Milo M. Quaife, a prominent early twentieth-century scholar-editor of Great Lakes history.[6] For Askin, Quaife's introduction and the publication of his collected correspondence ensured continued historical interest in his life, but also cemented problematic assumptions and speculations.[7]

During graduate school, with Sleeper-Smith's unending generosity, support, and insight, I undertook an exhaustive study of Askin's life. I visited archives in Detroit, Ann Arbor, Mackinaw City, and Chicago, and consulted the voluminous academic literature related to the fur trade and British Empire. My research and writing became the basis of my dissertation project, "John Askin's Many Beneficial Binds: Family, Trade, and Empire in the Great Lakes," which I successfully defended in the spring of 2011.[8]

As I toiled in archives and libraries, it became clear that, despite Askin's ubiquity, little scholarly attention had been given to clarifying his larger role in Great Lakes history, the fur trade, and the British military during the interwar period (1763–1775). In fact, the basic scholarly narrative of Askin's life had changed remarkably little since the publication of Quaife's introduction and Askin's collected correspondence. Moreover, the excellent scholarly work that has been done on Askin over the past several decades has focused, by and large, on his more extensively documented political, economic, and social life in Detroit and Upper Canada after the American Revolution (1783–1815).[9] Accordingly, an important and intriguing gap exists in Askin's life and the larger historical record, which ought to be rehabilitated from the somewhat error-prone writings of Quaife and further offers an interesting window into a pivotal moment for the British Empire in North America.[10]

Only two unpublished manuscripts exist that focus on Askin's life between 1758 and 1780. In the late 1970s, David Armour, a prolific and respected Great Lakes historian closely associated with Mackinac State Historic Parks, wrote a multichapter and intimate day-in-the-life account of Askin's family, trade, and imperial duties at Michilimackinac during the American Revolution. In the mid-1990s, historian John Gram wrote a detailed and authoritative account of Askin's life at Michilimackinac, one that focused on his fur trading and his economic vision for the Great Lakes.[11] Both Armour and Gram's accounts are well written and informative and helped me tremendously, especially as I tried to tease out the tangles of my own account of Askin's life. However, despite the high quality of their prose and research, neither adequately grounds Askin in a larger historical or historiographical context; in other words, they reveal much about him, but he remains a peripheral figure, a subject of local interest.

Since the mid-1990s, Richard White's seminal study *The Middle Ground: Indians, Empires, and Republics in the Great Lakes Region, 1650–1815*, has framed numerous studies. White employs the language of imperial centers and peripheries, but centers and peripheries that are fast and loose and somewhat unhinged from each other. He writes that "at the center are hands on the levers of power, but the cables [which connect the empire together] have, in a sense, been badly frayed or even cut. It is a world system in which minor agents, allies, and even subjects at the periphery often guide the course of empires."[12] These fraying connections played a pivotal role in White's articulation of the "Middle Ground," which developed between the French and Indians in the seventeenth century, born out of the violence and destruction of Iroquois invasions during the Fur Wars. These connections lasted because neither the French nor the Indians were able to militarily dominate or control the other, forcing both sides to cooperate and attempt to find understanding through face-to-face contact in the pursuit of common economic and political pursuits, though with much resultant misunderstanding of each other's cultures and expectations. This "odd imperialism," as White described it, opened avenues for new behaviors, creative responses, and unique cultural configurations.[13]

My work on John Askin developed from a growing historical appreciation of an eighteenth-century British Empire that was far from a settled concept, a centralized polity, or the result of a sustained governmental agenda. The informality and haphazardness of the British Empire would play a large role in its development and subsequent dissolution and reconstitution during Askin's lifetime. For Askin, a Scots-Irish migrant to North America, the empire was a place where he could pursue and develop his own personal ambitions. For many agents, it served as an arena where their competing demands could play out, whether it was the needs of Parliament, the demands of monopolies and nongovernmental organizations, or the various initiatives of an increasingly far-flung and multifocal colonial domain.[14] Accordingly, the British Empire was far from a constant or consistent entity, and it displayed profound uncertainties, ambiguities, and disjunctions as its agents, in London and abroad, worked to meet its hodgepodge of demands and expectations. Askin, as a sutler to the British military; a merchant connected to large trading concerns in Montreal, Quebec, New York, and London; and deputy commissar to an important fur trade post, experienced firsthand how these various constitutive elements of the empire interacted or, at times, failed to interact with one another in the western Great Lakes.

Likewise, a spate of recent works have forced historians to appreciate the degree to which British officers, diplomats, and merchants had to negotiate with and often capitulate to the expectations and ambivalences of an equally complex, multifocal, and contradictory Indian world. For example, historian Michael A. McDonnell, in his recently published *Masters of Empire: Great Lakes Indians and the Making of America*, presented the Great Lakes region as a place where the Odawa and Ojibwa dominated the straits of Michilimackinac and controlled European access to North America's interior.[15] The Odawa and Ojibwa did this through malleable ties of real and fictive kinship, decentralized and dynamic local leaderships, and interconnected families, lineages, languages, trades, and villages.[16] In other words, the Great Lakes world that John Askin encountered in the late eighteenth century was neither French nor British—it was in the hands of his Odawa, Pottawatomi, and Ojibwa neighbors. To the Indigenous peoples of the region, fur trade posts like Michilimackinac, where Askin would spend most of his life and career, were hardly sites of French or British dominance, or even indicative of Indigenous dependence, but "were often only at the edge, or at the margins, of a vast Indian country."[17] In fact, by recentering the Odawa and their history, McDonnell and others show that the Great Lakes fur trade actually highlighted, for example, French and British economic dependence on Indigenous demands, often frustrating merchants and post commands alike. Events like Pontiac's War in 1763 underscored, in particular, the pretense in Great Britain's claims to imperial sovereignty.[18]

Accordingly, the Great Lakes region, only nominally under British authority, was a place defined by the Indians of the Great Lakes, the legacy of the French alliance, the imperial unease that sparked Pontiac's War, the consequences of imperial mismanagement, and the tremendous upheaval caused by colonial rebellion. After their spectacular victory during the Seven Years' War, the British found their empire in a process of profound reinvention; it was overgrown and complex. Almost overnight, the agents of the government, the military, and the fur trade, in London and abroad, struggled with its profitability, maintenance, and security.[19] In a Great Lakes landscape, one defined by violence, disaster, uncertainty, and risk, men like Askin were required to navigate fraught circumstances both creatively and shrewdly.[20] The choices he made in terms of trade or his role as an imperial agent contributed to and shaped the day-to-day realities of the British Empire in a region defined by the knots and weaves of an Indigenous world. By paying closer attention to how Askin operated in the Great Lakes, and exploring the choices he made and the context in which he made them, we can see how he and men like him reoriented aspects of British policy as they pursued their fur trades.

Given the Janus-faced nature of the region, the following chapters explore how Askin built his fur trade between the years 1758 and 1781 and illuminate three consistent strategies he used to prosper and survive during disruptive events such as Pontiac's War, the turmoil caused by Great Britain's effort to reform the North American fur trade, and the imperial violence of the American Revolution. First, Askin maintained close and personal links to the British military, particularly with its Great Lakes commandants and by holding civilian positions like deputy commissary. These relationships and posts isolated him during periods of stress, disorder, or dislocation, and helped enable and protect his expansive trading ventures. Second, he established and solidified his position in the Great Lakes fur trade and the British military by strategically and shrewdly investing in the infrastructure of the region; investments in farms, depots, and ships made him indispensable as a trader and a boon for officials. Finally, Askin understood the value of family and kinship in the French and Indian world of the Great Lakes region, and into his home and trade he incorporated multiethnic children, French labor, British officials, and skilled labor.

By moving Askin from the periphery of historical narratives to the center of this work, these themes and chapters suggest that his life and experiences can also serve as a vista from which to view important aspects of the British Empire in North America. For example, the close interrelationship between trade and empire enabled Askin's economic triumphs, but also made him vulnerable to the consequences of imperial conflicts and mismanagement. His struggles mirror, in a microcosm, the difficulties Great Britain had in establishing its control over the French and Indian world of the Great Lakes region, and in constituting and routinizing its empire after the extremely costly and transformative Seven Years' War. The British Crown and Parliament struggled to come to terms with postwar economic realities; their efforts to reduce spending, for example, sparked fierce debates over budgets and taxes, and played havoc with efforts to establish peace in the Great Lakes.

The British inability to offer a consistent fur trade and Indian policy that addressed the extensive diplomatic expectations of its newfound Indian subjects hindered the effectiveness of local officials at important fur trade posts, such as Detroit and Michilimackinac. In fact, the ephemeral and contested nature of British authority during the 1760s and 1770s created openings for men like Askin to develop a trade of smuggling liquor, and challenge the Hudson's Bay Company's legal monopoly over the fur trade, and allowed them to boast in front of British officers of having the "Key of Canada in [their] Pocket."[21] British officials like Major Arent Schuyler de Peyster, commandant of Michilimackinac between 1774 and 1779, responded to and even sanctioned such activities as a way of fostering British authority in the Great Lakes region, especially in regards to maintaining the support of its Indian communities, demonstrating the vital importance of trade and empire working in concert.[22] Askin's life speaks to the calamitous consequences that occurred when such relationships broke down or turned bitter.

Toward the end of his career at Michilimackinac, in the early summer of 1778, John Askin asked a colleague a serious question: "Is it not as just that I a Servant of the Crown reaps a Bennifitt by government as any merchant whatsoever?"[23] In the manner of rhetorical questions, he already had an answer:

of course it was just, and certainly he would reap a benefit. The way Askin answered his own question exposed pathways, albeit fraught and imperfect, toward success, stability, and longevity for those living in the British Great Lakes region. Askin's question speaks to the collusive nature of the British Empire—the vital need for merchants, officials, and the Indian communities the merchants and officials serviced and relied on to establish effective accommodating relationships, transgress boundaries (real or imagined), and skirt or disdain regulations or orders to achieve their goals.

In the end, this book seeks not to provide a complete biography of Askin, or even offer an in-depth history of the British Great Lakes. Rather, it hopes to set one man's life against the course of an empire and, to repurpose the words of Natalie Zemon Davis, show how Askin could fashion his life "in unusual and unexpected ways."[24] In this sense, I have tried to write a narrative that encapsulates brief moments of time, knowing that if I could chart Askin's limits and horizons, I might thereby do the same for the world in which he lived.

CHAPTER ONE

Pretty Much of a Schemer

Albany, Pontiac's War, and John Askin's Bankruptcy, 1758–1764

On a humid August morning in 1763, John Askin watched his partner, James Gordon, spread out trade blankets on the bank of the Mohawk River in New York. According to Gordon,

> As rum . . . was . . . strictly prohibited my partner Askin . . . had fifteen ten gals. Cags [kegs] made as tight as possible, filled with the best of spirits, so that it might be reduced when it arrived at Detroit. These Cags were made up in Bales of Blankets, and other Coarse Clothes, to elude the discovery of them.[1]

Looking at the kegs, neatly stacked, Askin turned numbers over in his head: rum cost about three to four shillings a gallon and could be exchanged for about six to eight shillings' worth of furs. Conservatively, they could see a 50 percent return on their investment, and contraband could fetch them much more, perhaps going as high as forty shillings per gallon. First, though, the kegs had to be hidden from the prying eyes of British officials. After watching for a few minutes, Askin tipped a wooden keg on its side and rolled it forward.

The rising sun felt hot, and sweat dripped down his forehead and temples. He stopped to wipe his brow and stretch the ache from his lower back. Both men worked steadily as they readied the remaining kegs to be loaded onto three waiting boats. The plan was Askin's, and he was "pretty much of a schemer."[2]

Soon their cargo of "blankets" looked no different from the hundreds of other bundles of merchandise streaming into the western Great Lakes. Celebrating a job well done, Askin gave Gordon an enthusiastic thump on the back. Together they made their way, stomachs empty and mouths parched, to a nearby tavern. They would rest and relax before the long, arduous voyage to Detroit, where they would pursue their trade in furs.

By the end of the 1760s, the British North American colonies exported £3.4 million worth of commodities each year.[3] Half of this trade went to Great Britain, a fourth went to the slave and sugar colonies of the West Indies, while Ireland, southern Europe, and Africa split the remainder. Furs, valued at £91,000 in 1770, accounted for roughly 2.8 percent of the total exports, and roughly 5.4 percent of all Great Britain's North American imports. Although dwarfed by tobacco, indigo, rice, bread, fish, and whale-based exports, the fur trade thrived and prospered throughout the eighteenth century as an intersection between European fashion and North American Indigenous labor and diplomacy. Even with the general decline of the once-dominant British hat industry during the last half of the eighteenth century—a result of increased competition from French and North American hatters—Britain's control of Europe's supply of furs ensured the continued profitability of the trade. Furs stimulated economic growth on both sides of the Atlantic, and at fur trade centers like Albany and Montreal promoted the development of middlemen—traders and merchants who facilitated the trade and reaped, if careful and lucky, tremendous profits.

Both Askin and the British Empire worked to actualize a valuable lesson: that the social, economic, political, and diplomatic order of the Great Lakes and the Ohio Valley required a healthy, growing, and Indian-focused fur trade. The failure of Askin's trade and Great Britain's inability to secure peace with the Indians were closely linked to their inability to offer an equitable or reciprocal trade, and had profound repercussions for both empire and subject.

The five-year period that spanned Askin's earliest years as an aspiring merchant and his subsequent bankruptcy set the stage for his emigration and employment as deputy commissary of Michilimackinac and his subsequent, more successful, reentry into the fur trade.

In 1758 Askin and Gordon were newly arrived immigrants from northern Ireland who had braved a crossing of the Atlantic Ocean during the height of the Seven Years' War.[4] Starting in 1754, the empires of Great Britain and France clashed across the globe on land and sea. In Europe, following their own political and diplomatic agendas, the other great powers—Austria, Prussia, Russia, Sweden, Poland, Saxony, and Hanover—took sides with the French or British, and fought great and bloody battles. In India, oceans away, British and French trading companies, imperial armies, and local allies vied for supremacy. Hostile shots were fired in West Africa, the Caribbean, South America, and in the Philippines, and over the course of the war, from 1754 to 1763, over a million men, women, and children would die.[5]

Before long, both Askin and Gordon made their way to Albany, New York, where they found employment in the fur trade. By the mid-eighteenth century, the New York fur trade was a firmly established, multiethnic, and transatlantic enterprise.[6] Through the efforts of European hatters and furriers, beaver pelts that were trapped and cleaned in the Great Lakes by Indigenous men and women became the latest high-fashion accessories in London and Paris.[7] In pursuit of these furs and the associated profits, the partnership of Kennedy & Lyle hired the twenty-year-old Askin, while Gordon found work through a wholesaler named John Macomb, a distant relative of Gordon's father. They began their careers as clerks. Gordon was promised £1 a day for his efforts.[8]

By the time Askin and Gordon called Albany home, it was a bustling and thriving community of over two thousand Anglo-Dutch inhabitants.[9] A map of the city from 1758 shows a settlement of broad boulevards and numerous irregular buildings nestled closely to the Hudson River, protected by a fort and the long walls of a palisade.[10] Originally founded by the Dutch in 1614 as a small trading outpost, the settlement had been under British control since 1664. Albany's access to the fur-rich Great Lakes via the Hudson River and

Map of the Important Sites, Lakes, and Rivers of John Askin's New York Fur Trade, 1760–1780

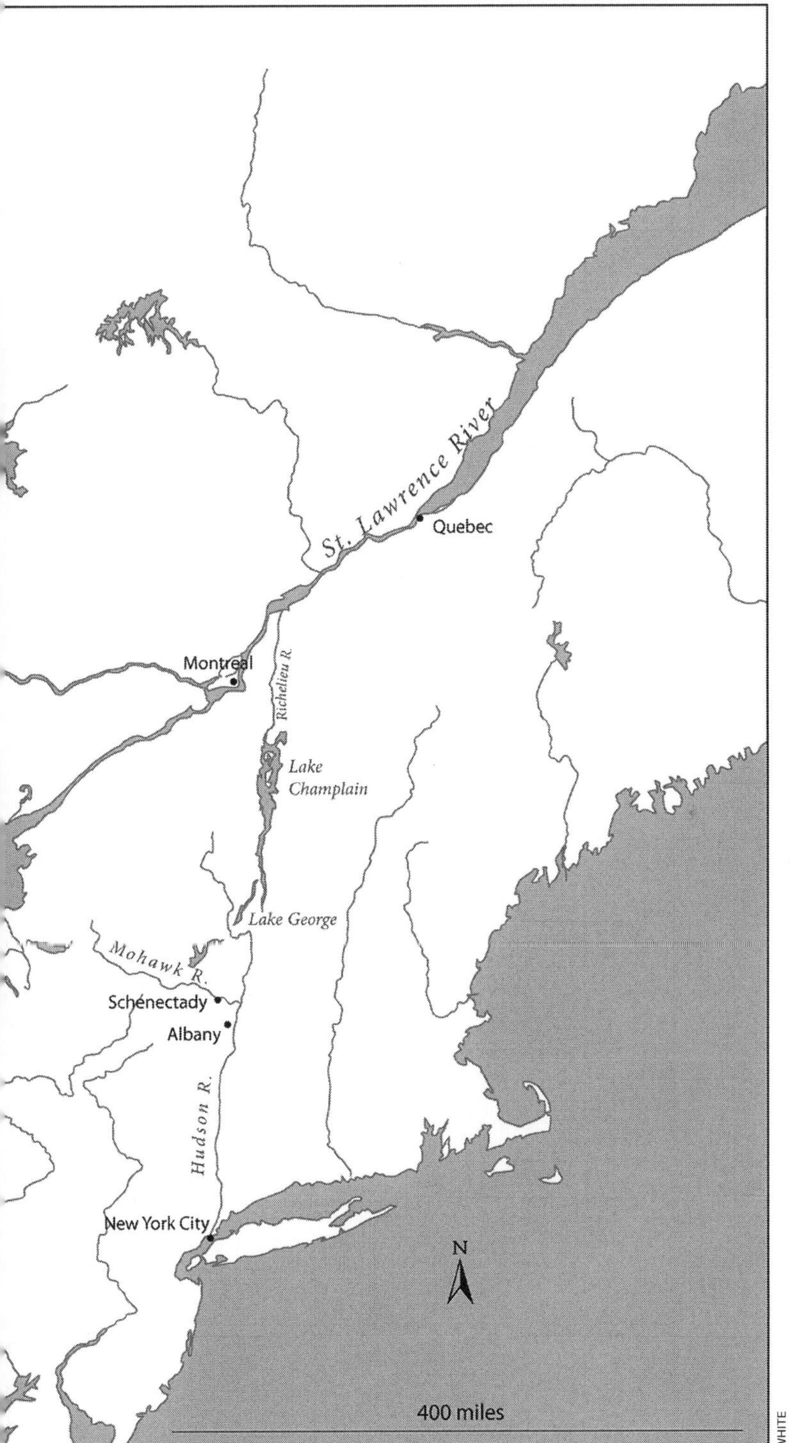

St. Lawrence River
Quebec
Montreal
Richelieu R.
Lake Champlain
Lake George
Mohawk R.
Schenectady
Albany
Hudson R.
New York City
N
400 miles
E. WHITE

the Mohawk Valley, and its vicinity to the powerful Iroquois Confederacy—long-standing British allies, consisting of the Mohawk, Oneida, Onondaga, Cayuga, Seneca, and Tuscarora—established it as a central site of Great Britain's North American fur trade. From 1700 to 1755, rabbit, muskrat, otter, raccoon, deer, and, most importantly, beaver furs represented 20 percent of New York City's exports to Great Britain.[11]

Unlike their French counterparts in Canada who traveled and wintered among their western Indian allies, often forming lasting ties of kinship in the villages in which they traded, Anglo-Dutch fur traders tended to be stationary, choosing to operate out of established posts, like Albany, Schenectady, and Oswego.[12] Indian hunters and trappers were far from naive consumers of European wares and expected traders to offer merchandise that met their exacting demands.[13] Traders who offered shoddy or subpar stock often saw their merchandise remain unsold. In this respect, Anglo-Dutch traders were able to compete with the more firmly entrenched and widespread French. The Indians of the Great Lakes were disposed to trade their lush furs with the Anglo-Dutch traders who brought cheaper, but higher-quality, British-made goods, particularly, black, red, and dark-blue stroud (a type of course woolen cloth), West Indian rum, and fine-grain gunpowder.[14] What is more, France's inability to offer satisfactory or cost-efficient alternatives to British goods and the persistent oversupply of furs in France's Parisian markets encouraged French traders to ignore imperial rivalries and smuggle their furs to Albany to fetch higher prices and better merchandise.[15]

Still, much of the hustle and bustle that Askin experienced as he went about his clerkly business for Kennedy & Lyle—keeping the account books and ledgers; providing receipts and issuing coin; overseeing shipping, packaging, and the pricing of furs; and maintaining stocks and stores—was a wartime phenomenon.[16] Since 1755, Albany, despite its economic ambivalence about fighting the French and disrupting the fur trade, benefited from its close proximity to the principal theater of the Seven Years' War in North America.[17] The long, porous borderland separating the French and British colonies that ran from the mouth of the St. Lawrence River into the Great Lakes witnessed numerous sieges and much terrible bloodshed. By strengthening the stone fortress and stockade that protected the city and adding a hospital and new barracks, the British military transformed Albany into a base of operations that supported lackluster campaigns against the French-held Fort Niagara and Fort Saint-Frédéric in 1755, and Fort Carillon and Fort Frontenac in 1758.

In the summer of 1759, as the military prepared another thrust into New France, Gordon arrived in Albany to discover that the position he expected to take was already occupied. Luckily for him, European armies were always in need of supplies. John Macomb "in conjunction with . . . Kennedy & Lisle, concluded to fit out . . . Askin . . . and [Gordon] with a boat load of Goods and sen[t] [them] a sutling [i.e., acting as sutlers] to the Army."[18] By July, Askin and Gordon were shadowing a large British army under the command of General Jeffrey Amherst, the commander-in-chief of the British military in North America, through the woods and waterways of northern New York. That summer they witnessed France abandon Fort Carillon, which had been, just a year earlier, the site of a bloody and disastrous British defeat. And several weeks later, on the southern shore of Lake Champlain, Askin and Gordon explored what was left of the smoldering wreck of Fort Saint-Frédéric, after the retreating French had blown it up.

Not far from Frédéric's ruins, in early September, Amherst began building a new fort called Crown Point. While the British soldiers toiled, Askin and Gordon found a clearing by the camp, pulled out several blankets from the back of an oxcart, and laid them on the ground. On top, they set a wide variety of items, ranging from the mundane to the luxurious: fresh fruits and vegetables, tobacco, books, extra clothes, threads and needles, sugar, and, if smuggled, spirits. Askin haggled with a Scottish officer over the price of snuff when Gordon brought him news of Quebec, a French citadel on the St. Lawrence River; outside the city, the French and British had fought a great battle and the French army had fled.

With Quebec in British hands, spirits soared across the British Empire. In early 1760, Askin and Gordon were back in Albany, where they "spent the winter making preparations for the [summer's] campaign, for [they were] engaged to supply the corps of Rangers, under the command of Capt. Robert Rogers, consisting of about 500 men."[19] They received from Amherst a permit to supply "Refreshment and Necessaries . . . Rum and Spirituous Liquors Excepted."[20] The contract was a windfall for the two young sutlers.[21]

Captain Robert Rogers was the most daring, successful, and famous provincial officer in the war. From his own purse, he recruited men from across New England and led them to prominence by skillfully ambushing Indians and the French in northern New York. Rogers cemented his fame in October 1759. He led his men deep into enemy territory and burned the village of Saint-Francis, which long served as a staging ground for Abenaki raids into New England. He earned the sobriquet *Wobomagonda*, "White Devil," and the respect and trust of Amherst.

In August 1760, Askin and Gordon trailed Rogers's men up Lake Champlain. The rangers scouted for a British army marching north from Crown Point, while at Fort Oswego, Amherst and his men began sailing east down the St. Lawrence River. The two forces planned to converge on Montreal, France's last remaining stronghold on the St. Lawrence. Cut off from France since the capture of Quebec, the governor-general of New France, Pierre de Riguad de Vaudreuil de Cavagnial, the Marquis de Vaudreuil, lacked the men and resources to mount an effective defense of the city. Instead of withstanding a hopeless and bloody siege, he surrendered Montreal to Amherst on September 8. Major fighting in North America ended.

Days after the fall of Montreal, Askin and Gordon consigned their remaining seven hundred pounds of trade goods to a Montreal merchant and made arrangements to return to Albany.[22] However, before leaving, Askin sought out Rogers, whom he had grown to know quite well, to say his farewells and, perhaps, talk a little business. Amherst had ordered Rogers west to accept the surrender of the remaining French garrisons at Detroit, Michilimackinac, St. Joseph, and Miami.[23] These communities represented the heart of France's Great Lakes fur trade, and Askin knew that Rogers would be well placed to take advantage of opportunities after the war.

In fact, before leaving Montreal, Rogers impressed upon Paul Burbeen, a clerk for Abraham Douw, an important Albany merchant, to let his employer know that "[Rogers] expected to make a Fortune" from his new orders. Leaning in to speak confidentially, Rogers told the clerk that "the French Officer that Commanded at Fort Detroit . . . promised him about Three Hundred Thousand wt. of Furs at a low price."[24] Privately, however, Rogers knew his boast was optimism laced with mounting desperation. Over the course of the war, he had spent and borrowed over £6,000 to raise, outfit, and supply his men, believing the Crown would reimburse his efforts.[25]

Rogers and his men left Montreal and arrived at Fort Niagara on October 1, where they spent the night repairing their leaking vessels. He met with merchants Edward Cole, a close associate of Sir William Johnson, the superintendent of Great Britain's Northern Indian department, and Nicholas Stevens, and over dinner with Lt. Cesar Cormick, a fellow ranger, the four men formed Rogers & Company.[26] They purchased £3,423 8s. worth of goods, and Rogers became the company's first customer, using their coffers to pay for the resealing of his ships and provender for his men.[27]

Two months later, on November 29, Rogers accepted the surrender of the French garrison, and the British flag flew over Fort Detroit. In the frigid air of a Michigan winter, as the French paraded and stacked their arms while Detroit's inhabitants and their Odawa, Pottawatomie, and Wyandot neighbors looked on, Rogers drank in the scene; he was in the middle of it, relishing the thrill of military victory and economic success. In fact, over the next several months, George Croghan, a deputy of Johnson's in the Indian Department, and Captain Donald Campbell, the new commandant of Detroit, drew upon Rogers & Company for their official duties: purchasing presents to help clear a path toward peace between Britain and its Indian subjects, and procuring supplies, food, and firewood for the newly installed British garrison.[28]

With the Great Lakes and Ohio Valley ostensibly under Great Britain's control, Sir Jeffery Amherst, the commander-in-chief of British forces in North America, his second-in-command, General Thomas Gage, and Sir William Johnson agreed to abandon several of the newly conquered French posts in hope of consolidating garrisons and reducing imperial expenditures.[29] In 1761, after regarrisoning Detroit, Amherst ordered the southern posts of Fort Miami on the Maumee River and Fort Ouiatanon on the Wabash River manned. West and north of Detroit, British soldiers settled into Fort St. Joseph, Green Bay, and Michilimackinac. Located at strategic junctures, often on riverways or straits between lakes, these posts ensured proximity and contact between the region's Indians, fur traders, and British officials.

At these posts, Amherst, Gage, and Johnson also envisioned a more orderly, centralized, and manageable fur trade. With the French defeated, they would require British and French traders and merchants to pay a fee and post a good-behavior bond to obtain a license from military officers, Indian agents, or colonial governors to trade with the Indians.[30] The license would dictate where the traders or merchants could operate and place them under the auspices of the post's commandants, who would ensure they sold merchandise at set prices and not traffic in liquor, take advantage of visiting Indians, or disobey any other orders.[31] Failure to comply with the new regulations could result in loss of license, bond, and banishment.[32] By shifting the fur trade away from Indian villages, the British leadership hoped a fair and equitable trade would develop between the British, French, and Indians of the Great Lakes and Ohio Valley, and the pretext for hostility would vanish.

That is not to say, however, that Amherst was genuinely worried about violence; he believed the Indian communities of the Great Lakes and Ohio Valley were now nothing more than conquered subjects. Under intense pressure by London officials, Amherst quickly moved to end the costly French practice of placating the Indian communities with presents. He argued that gift-giving made Indian peoples indolent, and that such items should only be given as rewards or out of dire necessity. With new regulations freeing Indians from the ills of alcohol and the wiles of unscrupulous traders, Amherst believed they would take greater initiative hunting and trapping for the furs they needed to acquire vital merchandise. At the newly reestablished posts he directed his subordinates to provide no more than trifles to their Indian visitors, and then undertook a policy of keeping Indians low on gunpowder. Writing to Johnson in August 1761, Amherst argued that keeping "them scarce of Ammunition, is not less to be Recommended; since nothing can be so impolitick as to furnish them with the means of accomplishing the Evil which is so much Dreaded."[33]

In the spring and summer of 1761, as Indians traveled to the former French posts now flying the Union Jack, they grew suspicious. Large British garrisons, more numerous than before, watched them from the ramparts, and some commandants even refused them entrance to their posts; those who did afford entry proved parsimonious with food, gunpowder, rum, metals, gorgets, blankets, and even gun repair at the post's blacksmith.[34] Johnson, with a lifetime of experience as a fur trader and Indian diplomat, generally supported Amherst's efforts, but he worried about withdrawing presents too quickly. Johnson wrote to a London official that "the French spared no labor, or Expence to gain [Indian] friendship and Esteem," and with the war barely over, and many of the region's Indian communities still hostile to the British newcomers, he nudged Amherst to be accommodating to Great Britain's "Old, as well as New Indian Allies" to "secure their friendship." Amherst read Johnson's letters carefully and then ignored the advice, claiming he could "see very little Reason for Bribing the Indians, or Buying their good Behavior."[35]

Meanwhile, having returned to Albany, Gordon trudged through muddy snowbanks, laboriously making his way to Askin's quarters to discuss dissolving their partnership. Two seasons in the sutler trade and three long years in North America had left Gordon weary and homesick for northern Ireland. He "proposed [in early 1761] that Askin should either give or take £500, [even though] by our Books our profits appeared much larger." Not wanting to force Gordon to remain longer than needed, or, just as likely, not willing to leave extra profits on the table, "Askin agreed to give [Gordon] that sum and take the burthen of setling [their] affairs on himself." However, as soon as they revealed their plans, their creditors vetoed them, refusing "to release either of [them] until [their] affairs were setled." Stuck in Albany until their loose ends were tied up, Gordon spent "the greatest part of the summer 1761 . . . unemployed," while in mid-March of the same year, as the snows melted and the new trading season began, Askin received an important visitor.[36]

Back in January 1761, Rogers had completed his orders and traveled to Philadelphia, where Amherst commissioned him as a regular in the British army and gave him command of a company of soldiers fighting Cherokee in South Carolina. The commission was a major token of appreciation, one that few colonial officers ever received. From Philadelphia, Rogers journeyed north to Portsmouth, New Hampshire, to marry Elizabeth Browne, the daughter of a local minister. By early August, less than a week after his wedding, Rogers boarded a vessel to Charleston. However, he put both commission and courtship on hold to talk to Askin about Edward Cole.

The partnership of Rogers & Company left Cole in charge of their business at Detroit, and while their efforts initially bore fruit, the fruit had begun to spoil. In fact, by the time Rogers sat down with Askin, he had not heard from Cole in months, and with his new commission placing him far from the Great Lakes, Rogers worried about his investment. On March 17, he signed a document appointing Askin "his true and lawful attorney." The instrument explicitly targeted Cole, giving Askin the power "to ask, demand, sue for, levy, recover and receive, all such Sum and Sums on Money, Debts, Rents, Goods, Wares, Dues, Accounts, and other Demands whatsoever."[37] Cole would keep Askin busy over the next couple of years.

Soon their conversation turned to the fur trade. Askin, no longer a sutler or content with being a lowly clerk, broached the subject of forming a partnership. He argued that Rogers's name and cachet would open doors for them in Detroit, Michilimackinac, and the other western posts. For his part, Rogers knew and trusted Askin's skills as a trader and merchant. Together, they formed "a comercial house in Albany, established principally for carrying on the Indian trade," and in the fall of 1761 they hired the unemployed Gordon to be their new clerk.[38]

Unfortunately, the records of Askin's life in Albany are sparse and incomplete. However, a surviving receipt book, kept between the years 1761 and 1762, does offer insight into his early participation in the Great Lakes fur trade.[39] The receipts mostly provide names, dates, places, and monies borrowed or paid, but through them it is possible to see the dimensions of Askin's network of trade.

The majority of the records detail business conducted at Albany and Schenectady. In fact, they show the end of Askin and Gordon's relationship with John Macomb and the important role Abraham Douw, the Albany merchant whom Rogers had bragged to in 1760, played in underwriting Askin and Rogers's venture. In a receipt dated June 1, 1761, Askin and Gordon drew upon an account with Douw to pay Macomb £150 in the New York currency (NYC).[40] Given the date, the payment seems to be related to the dissolution of Askin and Gordon's former sutler partnership. Macomb later received from Askin another £15 NYC in December, and after that point he disappeared from the receipt book entirely.[41] However, Douw proved a continuing presence: on May 25, Douw paid £84 18s. NYC from Askin's account; on May 26, another £105 came out; on May 29, £276 15s.; and June 22, £171 2s. 10d.[42] Over the span of two months, Askin drew upon Douw for nearly £800 NYC. Given the debt-oriented nature of the fur trade, and that 1761 represented Askin's first foray into the trade, it seems likely that these receipts represented the purchase of merchandise and the paying of old debts and, from Douw's perspective, the establishment of new ones.

The receipt book further reveals Askin's supervision of Rogers's other partnerships. In fact, the earliest records come from Edward Cole in Detroit. Three receipts dated February 10, 1761, show Cole charging Rogers & Company's account with Edward Rachaen at Albany. Cole drew "Ninety five dollars and one third . . . for Necessaries[.] Supply'd Lt. Buttes at Miami for his Majestys Use and Charge." He then asked Rachaen to pay "Mr. Lajoye" 548 dollars and "Mr. Davoine" 95 dollars for "Value [Received]." Likewise, at Niagara, Cesar Cormick, an original partner in Rogers & Company and, like Askin, a private partner with Rogers, drew upon Askin between April and June to cover the cost of portaging over the falls.[43] In mid-August, Askin took charge of "Twenty packs [of] Peltry" for Cormick and another "fifty Packs of Peltry" for Cole, all from Detroit, and entrusted them to Dutch merchant Volkert am Doun to forward them to New York City.[44] Gregg & Cunningham and John Keatin, New York City importers and exporters, sent the packs across the Atlantic to be sold in London.

In the spring of 1762, Askin undertook a tour of his business interests in North America. In the face-to-face world of the fur trade, where huge sums of money relied on the honesty, integrity, and reliability of all parties, he knew that he needed to establish a strong rapport with its important figures. In late March, he was in New York City. A receipt showed him paying £4 for room, board, and other sundries.[45] He was there discussing business with Gregg & Cunningham, making suggestions about what to order in the coming season.

Even though he was new in the trade, Askin understood that engaging the services of a respectable New York merchant meant dealing with their London factors, the men who supplied the manufactures that made the trade possible.[46] For a budding trader or merchant, these men often meant the difference between success and failure. A savvy New York City merchant selected a London firm that could, early in the new year, ship the very best quality strouds and clothes, trade guns, gunpowder, copper pots and kettles, Venetian beads, needles, traps, knives, axes, fishing hooks, and other merchandise demanded by Indians for their furs. As these items came from all over Great Britain and Europe, the cost of the goods would be debited from the New York merchant's account with a steep markup to cover outlays and a commission for the effort. Superlative merchandise supplied early in the season gave fur traders the best possible chance of acquiring a large quantity of high-grade furs. Two or three years later, the furs acquired through these goods would arrive in London in bales, casks, hogsheads, or barrels, and they would be sold to British hatters or European buyers, and the London merchant would finally make a profit.

After assembling and collecting orders, the London merchants loaded them into a ship, labeled and secured the exports, and, if asked, bought insurance for their clients in New York City. More fees were assessed. Protected by the might of the Royal Navy, the ship arrived in New York City a month later, mostly unscathed. Longshoremen unloaded the ship's cargo hold, and Gregg & Cunningham waited to take charge of their own allotment.

At a warehouse, their clerks carefully divided the newly arrived wares into outfits of merchandise necessary for the fur trade. For example, an individual outfit might contain dozens of blankets, kegs of liquor, a crate of trade goods, bags of lead shot, rolls of stroud, heads of tobacco, barrels of gunpowder, a score of kettles, and a box of knives.[47] After several days, Gregg & Cunningham checked their inventory against their account book, and began the process of labeling the bundles based on owner and location; they pulled several aside, marking them *J. A.*

Gregg & Cunningham debited Askin's or Douw's account for the goods, their commission, and other sundry fees they incurred. From their warehouse, the outfits were loaded onto a Hudson River sloop, and within a day or two docked at Albany. In early April 1762, Askin greeted the arrival of his merchandise; he would spend the spring and summer personally shepherding his merchandise to Detroit.[48] First, he paid to have the goods carted to Schenectady, about twenty miles northwest of Albany, on the bank of the Mohawk River. He then hired paddle men—British, Dutch, Iroquois, or a mixture of all three—for about £3 per day to take him upriver to Fort Oswego.[49] In the 1760s, a New York canoe could hold about fifteen hundred pounds of cargo, a third of which was for foodstuffs and equipment, with the remaining space reserved for trading stock.

At Fort Oswego, Askin stepped off his canoe and trudged through the water, feet and ankles submerged, to help pull it ashore. From there, his crew emptied the canoes and carried the goods overland to Lake Ontario. Askin then paid to have the merchandise and canoes loaded onto a schooner and taken down the lake to Fort Niagara.

A short time later, standing on the deck of the ship, Askin heard the thunderous rumble of Lake Erie emptying into Lake Ontario. At the Niagara Falls portage, Askin disembarked quickly and pushed his way through the crowd of busy laborers and their burdened carts to find John Stedman, the official tasked by Sir William Johnson to organize the movement of supplies and people around the cataract.[50] After a quick greeting and short conversation, Askin paid Stedman to have his goods carried by wagon up an escarpment and vertical rise of over three hundred feet to Fort Schloser. On the upper landing, above the falls, Askin had the merchandise once again loaded onto boats or canoes, and set off on the last leg of his journey, skirting the southern shore of Lake Erie, heading west.

Detroit was founded in late July 1701 as the brainchild of Antoine Laumet de la Mothe, sieur de Cadillac, a French explorer and former governor of Fort Michilimackinac.[51] By October of the same year, the French finished construction of the timber stockade. Cadillac then invited France's Indian allies to establish themselves by his new settlement, and within two years, villages of the Algonquin-speaking Odawa, Ojibwa, Delaware, and Miami, along with the Iroquoian-speaking Huron, took root. Cadillac imagined that Detroit, situated as it was on fertile land farmed by French settlers, surrounded by Indian allies and kin, set astride an important route to the upper Great Lakes, would only grow in importance and prosperity; it would be a bulwark against British intrusions and serve as breadbasket for the fur trade.

However, Cadillac's vision was slow to realize. In 1708, Jérome Phélypeaux, comte de Pontchartrain, the French minister of the marine who had originally supported the founding of Detroit, indicted Cadillac for corruption and abuse of authority. Over the next several decades, ineffective, autocratic, or self-interested leadership combined with the lack of imperial support left the settlement moribund. With New France's sparse colonial population of barely fifteen thousand and the promise of arduous agricultural labor, coupled with the lure of the fur trade further afield, few settlers were drawn to Detroit. In 1707, it only had sixty-three permanent French inhabitants, and less than half of those farmed. In the 1730s, the population grew to roughly 250 settlers. During this period, Detroit's inhabitants lived in simple houses inside the stockade. With draft animals, they plowed long, thin, ribbon-like strips of land that stretched from the banks of the Detroit River inland. This unique system of land use ensured every farmer access to water and transportation, and would over time turn Detroit into an important agricultural center, differentiating it from other fur-trade-focused western posts.

Over time, it became evident that Cadillac's effort to establish a multiethnic settlement ignored existing Indigenous conflicts.[52] In Detroit, enemies and allies lived side by side. In 1706, the Miami moved from Detroit after skirmishing with the Odawa. In 1712 the arrival of Fox and Mascouten Indians, long-standing rivals of the Odawa, Potawatomi, and Ojibwa, led to a Fox siege of Detroit, and a violent reprisal by the Odawa, Pottawatomi, Huron, and French. Nearly one thousand Fox and Mascouten Indian men, women, and children were killed or taken captive, and over the next thirty years Detroit would serve as a staging ground for campaigns against the Fox, Mascouten, and their allies along the western shore of Lake Michigan. In the late 1740s, Huron, influenced by the British traders and merchants in the Ohio Valley, destroyed Detroit cattle, fields, and farmhouses before the French were able to negotiate peace.

The contest for the Ohio Valley revived French interest in Detroit. Britain's flourishing Atlantic seaboard colonies boasted a growing population of around one and a half million subjects in 1750, and soon after, settlers coveting access to new lands began crossing the Appalachian Mountains to push up the Ohio River. During the 1740s and 1750s, Detroit's stockade was rebuilt, enlarged, and strengthened. Several governors of New France and commandants of Detroit developed strategies for the recruitment of permanent settlers by promising gifts of tools and food stipends. By 1750, Detroit boasted a population of 450 men, a few dozen Indian and African slaves, and a small garrison of soldiers. Surrounding the settlement, two thousand Indians lived in large villages along the Detroit River. Detroit sold more wheat than its population consumed; Indian corn, squash, and beans further diversified the fare. Its farmers fed fur traders in the upper country, and Detroit supplied food, militia, and Indian allies to France's war effort against the British during the Seven Years' War.

In early June 1762, a month after leaving Schenectady, Askin arrived at Detroit. Askin left his cargo under the care of his crew and made his way from the river to the looming stockade to look for Edward Cole. An hour or so later, Askin found him walking down Rue St. Anne and after a forced greeting and terse discussion, Cole led him to a warehouse. Shifting through packs of furs, Askin gave Cole a receipt and took possession of seventy-five pounds of leather, 150 raccoon pelts, eleven pounds of water rat pelts, three fisher pelts, two fox pelts, eleven cat pelts, and thirty-six pounds of fur "in the hair." These furs would be credited to Cole's account and set against the cost of the merchandise that the trading house of Baynton & Warton in Philadelphia provided Rogers & Company in 1761. Askin also received "as [an] advance on goods & Debts" 665 pounds of leather, twelve hundred raccoons, one hundred pounds of beaver, and eighty cat and fox skins.[53] Taking quick leave of Cole, Askin hired laborers to carry the packs down to his canoes.

Askin then sought out the homes of respectable French merchants and traders. He knew that in order to engage the fur trade as a newcomer with no ties of kinship with the region's Indian population, consigning his goods to a French merchant or to several French traders was his best option.[54] However, before handing over his merchandise Askin had to be deliberate and careful in factoring in his costs in calculating the overall value of his merchandise: wages for his crew and laborers, the cost of food and equipment for the journey, transportation and storage fees, taxes and incidentals.[55] If the price of furs in London stayed stable or, better, rose in value, Askin would receive enough furs to cover the cost of his merchandise and sell the rest to his New York supplier for a sizable profit. After careful negotiating over price and an examination of the quality of the merchandise, Askin ordered his laborers to carry the outfits to their respective French traders. These Frenchmen would bear the cost and risk of transporting them north to the upper Great Lakes, and would spend the winter trading among the Indian hunting grounds.

At Detroit, British traders and merchants like Askin came into close contact with a French and Indian Great Lakes world over a century in the making. In the early seventeenth century, the first Frenchmen who traveled to Indian country came as strangers.[56] In this context, trade between French and Indian cultures was immediate, equal, and reciprocal, as they lacked the ties of kinship to make their exchanges something more. But after the Iroquois invasions of the mid-seventeenth century, French traders called *coureurs de bois*, or runners of the wood, came west, drawn by the allure of furs and profits. Often unmarried and unlicensed, these men discovered the social and economic advantages of engaging Indian peoples on their terms, often living among the people they traded with and adopting their clothing, foods, and languages.[57] More importantly, they married Indian women. Indian women provided the ties of kinship that socially transformed the act of exchange, provided their husbands with labor, fodder, and furs for his trade, and forced the trader to become accountable to the community. Likewise, the trader's presence enhanced the prestige, power, and authority of his wife's kin, who benefited from the social and political power that his goods offered.[58] These fur trade relationships could last a season or two before the trader or his partner moved on, or they could last a lifetime. Regardless, they often resulted in children—multiethnic and cross-cultural—who grew up to become traders, merchants, diplomats, boatmen, or translators, knowing the languages, cultures, and expectations of the Great Lakes fur trade society their parents fostered.[59]

Into the French and Indian world came James Sterling, a former Irish officer during the Seven Years' War who would later become a close associate of Askin's. In the summer of 1761, he acted as an agent for the Schenectady-based trading house of Livingston, Rutherford, Duncan, Coventry and Syme at Detroit. Sterling was sharp, well educated, a culturally astute entrepreneur, and, like Askin, spoke French. He quickly established himself within the developing British and existing French fur trade communities and began to prosper. He kept a letter book from 1761 to 1765, and his voluminous and detailed correspondence with traders, merchants, and officials offers valuable insight into the nature of the early British fur trade at Detroit, and helps contextualize Askin's own efforts to establish himself within the community during the same period.[60]

In the fall of 1761, Sterling wrote to Walter Rutherford from Detroit; his letter shines light on the prevailing exchange rates and trading strategies that Askin might have employed. Sterling explained that

> it is Sometimes Necessary to give one Article very chape in order to encorage the person to trade in the main, between ye Trade with ye Inhabitants and Indians I sell one thing with another that they will I belive bring duble the prime Cost at least.[61]

Smaller trade goods like "Knives, gart[e]ring, Bed Lace, Thread" could be exchanged for more than they were worth, and Sterling warned against the "possibility of [concerning] oneself to a certain stated price."[62] At times, strouds could fetch three or four beaver skins; a blanket or match coat could cost him two beavers, two hundred wampum beads one beaver, a brass kettle six beavers, a gorget four to five beavers, and a wristband one and a half beavers. The fur trade, mediated by close ties between French traders and their Indian kin, and competition from other less scrupulous traders and merchants, meant that Sterling walked a fine line between driving a hard bargain and alienating the labor that drove his prosperity.

"I can assure you without boasting," Sterling wrote to John Duncan in early January 1762, "that I have acquired the good will and esteem of the Inhabitants [of Detroit]." Connecting his willingness "to render [him]self as agreeable as possible to [the French]" to his success in the trade, Sterling lamented that "had [his] goods arriv'd in time [he] would have carried by far the greatest Trade of any person [at Detroit]."[63] However, while British merchants like Sterling and Askin relied upon the labor, skills, and connections of the French inhabitants of the Great Lakes to pursue their trade, a miasma of mistrust and animosity lingered. Francophobia and a desire to reap the rewards of the Seven Years' War led to British efforts to oust the French from the fur trade. Likewise, French traders willingly carried British goods, but resisted British efforts to trade among their Indian kin, sometimes violently.[64] Even Sterling, ingratiating as he could be, was far from immune from animosity. In June 1762, Sterling complained to James Syme that he had to wait for clerks from New York to send goods to Fort Miami and Fort Ouiatanon, "as it is rare to get a Frenchman here that can be depended on or entrusted with goods."[65] His views were charitable in light of prevailing British opinion in the early 1760s.

In the summer and fall of 1762, however, the French were the least of Askin and Sterling's worries, as their fellow countrymen gave them their greatest headaches. By late June, Askin was back in Albany, and several weeks later, in mid-July, he paid a total of £1 16s. for the carriage of nine loads of Edward Cole's pelts over the Niagara portage.[66] These furs failed to cover Cole's debts, and in the fall, Askin ordered Gordon to travel to Detroit to collect £2,461 13s. 16d. For Gordon, this demand devolved into a two-thousand-mile tour of the Great Lakes and Ohio Valley. He left Albany and made his way to Detroit, where he learned that Cole had left "by way of Sandusky and Pit[t]sburgh" for

Philadelphia. Gordon left Detroit "about the middle of Nov'r" with "Captain Prentice of the firm of Prentice and CA lender" and traveled by boat to Sandusky. Six days later, at Sandusky, Gordon bought a horse and set off on a twelve-day slog to Pittsburgh. They arrived in Philadelphia around December 20 "after a very fatiguing and disagreeable journey."[67] He found Cole and they settled their business. When Gordon returned to Albany in mid-January 1763, Askin awarded the former sutler and clerk a promotion to silent partner in John Askin & Company.

Gordon's grueling trek spelled the end of Rogers & Company. In early spring 1763, the principal investors planned to divide the profits. On March 11, Rogers, Askin, and Cole met in Newport, Rhode Island. They examined the accounts kept by Cole and found them "settled to [their] Satisfaction." Askin signed the settlement as witness, and Rogers, Cole, Stevens, and Cormick received £975 17s. 7½p. each. From the original purchase of £3,423 worth of goods at Niagara, the partners made £3,903 after deductions, which represented a £480 profit from their venture.[68] It was a measly sum given their early access to Detroit and the Great Lakes fur trade, and reflected Rogers's inattentiveness and Cole's lack of initiative. Askin must have looked upon the affair with a sense of concern and worry. They were primed to prosper, but the partnership saw only a 12.3 percent return on their original investment, a mere 6.15 percent profit each season, and for the deeply indebted Rogers, who was being sued for back pay by his former rangers, the settlement was a mere drop in the bucket.

Meanwhile, in Detroit, Sterling spent 1762 writing letters of complaint about Robert Collbeck, the man in charge of the partnership's storehouse at Niagara. In the middle of January, Collbeck left the storehouse to go drinking with traders, and put the stores in the hands of drunken servants. Such behavior gave Sterling "reason to think I shall have a shocking Acct. in the Spring of the Goods now under his care, especially the Liquors."[69] Five months later, Sterling complained to Captain George Etherington, the commandant of Fort Michilimackinac, "My bateaux arrived [at Detroit] from Niagara . . . the Bales, Barrels, etc. wet dirty & breaken and many things defficant [deficient]."[70]

The activity of British traders and merchants like Collbeck, who, according to Sterling, kept "a Seraglio of Indian Squaws in [a drunken] Condition," were reasons why General Jeffrey Amherst and Sir William Johnson, who favored a more gradual weening, curtailed the liquor trade in the aftermath of the Seven Years' War.[71] Concerned with what the unrestrained sale of liquor might do to Britain's nascent authority in the Great Lakes, both men saw the ban as a way of checking imperial expenses and the exploitation that might lead to Anglo-Indian death, theft, murder, rape, or general animosity.[72] In May 1761, Captain Donald Campbell, the commandant of Fort Detroit, wrote to Colonel Henry Bouquet at Fort Pitt: "The Indians goe to Niagara and buy Rum, and neglect to purchase Ammunition, for their Subsistence, and then become a Burthen on the Officer."[73] As a result, Major William Walters, the commandant of Fort Niagara, "received an order from General Amherst not to suffer the Traders to sell any Rum or spirituous Liquor to the Indians on any pretense."[74]

Despite efforts to confine trade to British posts, liquor flowed west because Indians demanded it. Having put a stop to the traffic of liquor at Fort Niagara, in the spring of 1762 Walters soon had Indians "beg[g]ing that I would allow the traders to sell their people a Little Rum for their Refreshment." Their persistent demands and his inability "to convince [the Indians] that the keeping Rum from them was for their good" forced Walters to write Johnson asking for permission to sell them "a two Gallon cag of Rum when they came to Trade to carry home by way of a cordial."[75] Described as "milk" in the diplomatic language of the Great Lakes, a term that evokes the childishness of drunken behavior and the ubiquitous Indigenous language of kinship-based dependence of their former French "father" and his Indian "children," gifts of liquor denoted the seriousness of Euro-Indigenous diplomatic and trade meetings.[76] By the eighteenth century, Indian communities expected French or British officials and traders to carry and provide gifts of brandy or rum to conduct business. Likewise, traders who did not carry spirits found themselves competing with and losing furs to those who did.

Moreover, liquor offered traders who defied Amherst's deeply unpopular restrictions easy access to Indian communities and their lucrative furs.[77] Gifts of cheap liquor allowed unconnected or uninitiated British traders, loaded with overpriced, subpar merchandise, to ignore the social conventions that ensured just and equitable exchanges.[78] Even inexperienced traders knew that, as historian Richard White points out, "a drunken Indian would agree to what a sober Indian would not."[79] In sobriety, Indian peoples remembered their ill-treatment, and their humiliations chafed.

In a letter written to James Syme on June 8, 1762, Sterling, from his perspective at Detroit, saw the ban as a good thing for himself and the fur trade as a whole. Since the ban denied French traders brandy, Sterling's trade would "gain considerably by it."[80] However, his optimism required the ban to work across the region, but that was far from the case. Campbell reported to Johnson that "notwithstanding of the Number of Traders from Albany we should have little Else but Rum had it not been for Traders from Pensilvania & Mr. Sterling from New York, who are the only people that have brought any Considerable quantitys of goods for the Indians."[81]

Ironically, given the preponderance of rum smugglers operating in the Great Lakes, Sterling, whose reputation as a trader was beyond reproach, found it exceedingly difficult to acquire alcohol through official channels for official means.[82] He wrote to Syme on June 17, 1762:

> We had such a Quantity of Liquors at Niagara and Oswego [I] thought it most prudent to dispose of what I had . . . on hand before the other arrived in the Spring, never judging that Gen. Amherst would hinder, at least what was so far on the way to come up; But as I have obtained and sent you . . . Capt. Campbell's two Passes for two Batteus [bateaus] to come up with Liquors and other Necessaries for the use of this and the adjacent Garrisons, I hope you will make the best use of them, and obtain the General's Approbation.[83]

For the remainder of the year, Sterling agonized over acquiring liquor. In early July, he protested to Ensign Robert Holmes, the officer commanding at Fort Miami, "I have sent you all the Spirits I had—Liquors are very scarce . . . at the present."[84] By the early autumn, Sterling begged his agent at Niagara to forward whatever spirits could be had, particularly rum, as it was his "main chance for drawing custom."[85] Campbell's pass "did not meet with [Amherst's] approbation," and Sterling pressed Major Henry Gladwin, the new commanding officer at Detroit, for a new one.[86] In late January 1763, Sterling informed his partner that the new commandant wrote to Amherst and vouched for his character, and assured the general that Sterling would not sell it to the Indians.[87] He asked for just three gallons per French family, and with three hundred families at Detroit, he would only need nine hundred gallons. Given the scarcity of liquor in Detroit, each gallon would sell for roughly forty shillings and fetch a considerable profit, but only if Sterling could receive them.

In the spring of 1763, John Askin left Robert Rogers and Rhode Island behind to return to Albany, where he busied himself preparing for the season's new trade. Late in the evening, over candlelight, as he rushed to finish his daily correspondence, Askin made an important and risky decision. He placed an order for rum, planning to smuggle it to Detroit. If uncovered, the rum would be confiscated, the investment would never be recovered, and Askin would have to return to Albany empty-handed to endure the hostility of his creditors. If caught, his budding reputation in the Great Lakes would be ruined. Amherst, Gage, and Johnson viewed certain traders with contempt and derision. In fact, the Earl of Egremont, Charles Wyndham, the secretary of state for the Southern Department, wrote directly to Amherst from London criticizing British traders' use of "every Low Trick and Artifice to Overreach and Cheat those unguarded ignorant People."[88] While neither Askin nor Gordon left an account as to whom they planned to trade the liquor with, presumably, given their efforts to conceal the kegs in blankets, it was for the Indians and the fur trade.

It is impossible to know what drove Askin's decision to smuggle rum. Perhaps, like so many other Albany traders, he was driven by revenue, and felt little remorse about exploiting or profiting from distant Indians. Or perhaps he was desperate. Only a few months earlier, in October 1762, he and Rogers borrowed nearly £4,000 to pay off their Albany creditors.[89] It is impossible to know Askin's thoughts when he, Gordon, and their crew pushed off their three boats from Schenectady to paddle steadily up the Mohawk River. It was August 1763, and the journey to Detroit began well enough. As the rum traveled past Fort Stanwix and over the portage to Lake Oneida, through Lake Oneida to Oswego, and across Lake Ontario toward Niagara without being discovered, Askin's spirits must have started to soar. But it was too soon. Just as Askin could imagine hearing the familiar crush of Niagara Falls in the distance, their group encountered devastating information. "On our way between Oswego and Niagara," Gordon lamented, "we met a boat coming express with the News of the general Attack made by the Indians headed by Pontiacks on the Western Posts."[90]

The British leadership in the Great Lakes and Ohio Valley had known of the mounting anger of the region's Indians since the summer of 1761. In mid-June, Campbell learned of "the bad Designs of the Indian Nations against [this] place and the English in General." The Iroquois sent wampum belts and envoys to "all the Nations from Nova Scotia to the Illinois to take up the Hatchet against the English."[91] On July 3, not far from Detroit, in front of a council of Odawa, Wyandot, Ojibwa, and Potawatomi, Seneca sachems called for the assembled "to cut off the English at Fort Detroit" and "endeavor to do the same with the Garrisons at Niagara & Fort Pitt." The two Seneca cited Amherst's policies as the source of their discontent: "The English treat us with much disrespect, & we have the greatest reason to believe by their behavior they intend to cut us off entirely." Campbell attended the council the following day and carried with him the Iroquois war belts. Despite experiencing "great astonishment" at seeing their war belt in British hands, Tahaiadoris calmly reiterated "what had passed in Council . . . the day before, [and] continued repeating farther grievances agst. the English."[92]

Between July and September, Campbell's report and Amherst's orders drew Sir William Johnson with a sizable contingent of Iroquois west to Detroit to take numerous councils with the Odawa, Shawnee, Huron, Wyandot, Delaware, Potawatomi, and Ojibwa. Before setting off, Johnson wrote to Amherst, "I shall be able to Settle matters with all the Nations of Indians that way to your Excellencys Satisfaction, and the Interest of ye. Government." However,

Johnson warned that if "our Old, as well as New Indian Allies are [not] allowed Ammunition for their Livelyhood, or hunting . . . they will in such case ever be Jealous of us."[93] Still, the commander-in-chief refused to budge on presents and ammunition, and continued to underestimate the harm and hostility his policies bred among the Indians of the Great Lakes.

Unable or unwilling to locate the growing animosity in British behavior, Amherst and his British commanders blamed the French. A British merchant at Green Bay wrote, "The Indians would do very well here but for the Canadians; They spirit them up to everything that's bad against the English."[94] Concurring with the sentiment, the British commander of Detroit wrote, "I think its very Evident that our Scoundrel Enemies below, are Stirring up the Indians every where to do mischief."[95] Even when the French tried to warn the British of potential violence, they were ignored or routinely dismissed. At Michilimackinac, Charles de Langlade, the former French commander of the post and nephew of the Odawa chief Nissowaquet, repeatedly warned the British commandant, Captain Etherington, of the ire of the local Odawa and Ojibwa communities. "Mr. Langlade," Etherington responded, "I am weary of hearing the stories you so often bring me; they are foolish twaddle of old women, and unworthy of belief; the Indians have nothing against the English, and cherish no evil designs."[96]

While the French happened to be convenient scapegoats, myopic considerations allowed bad British policies to fester and mingle with the unreconciled consequences of the Seven Years' War. Amherst failed to appreciate that gifts were central to Indigenous notions of diplomacy. To accept a gift confirmed peaceful intent and provided the framework for future relationships, while to reject a gift signaled hostility and the potential for war.[97] Gifts of food, goods, repairs, and medals, freighted with diplomatic and political symbolism, mediated conflicts and ended hostilities; they redeemed and appeased fallen kin, established friendship, and showed good intent. Since the fall of Quebec in 1759, the Indians of the Great Lakes had suffered from scarcity, famine, and disease. Instead of acting as the French had acted, with succor as "fathers" to their Indian "children," the British acted as enemies acted, and their every action seemed to confirm the Indians' worst suspicions. Their new British father was there to reduce and dominate them.[98]

Avaricious traders, aggressive settlers, large garrisons, newly established posts, lack of presents, demands for the return of captives, and the continual disrespect offered by British commanders alienated and angered the Indians, and their resentments merged with the teachings of the Delaware prophet Neolin, whom British officials quickly nicknamed "Imposter."[99] He preached a message of revitalization, calling upon Indians to reject European goods and behaviors, like drinking rum, and to do so by driving the British settlers and traders out of their lands and communities. By removing the British from the Great Lakes and Ohio Valley and returning to the old ways of their ancestors, Neolin promised his adherents, the Master of Life would return the animals to provide for them and offer an afterlife free of Europeans.

On May 7, 1763, an Odawa war chief named Pontiac, along with roughly three hundred Odawa, Potawatomi, and Ojibwa warriors, entered Detroit. Pontiac grew up in the vicinity of Detroit and rose to prominence among the Odawa in the 1740s. A staunch ally of the French, he fought against the British during the Seven Years' War, and the hostility remained. Merging the revitalizing teachings of Neolin with a desire to restore the French to North America, Pontiac believed capturing Detroit would represent a major setback for the British government and its tenuous claims of sovereignty.[100]

With weapons concealed under bundles of blankets, Pontiac's warriors planned to overwhelm and capture the British garrison unaware. However, Major Henry Gladwin, the commandant of the post, had been tipped off beforehand and stationed his soldiers at the ready. The Indians retreated. A few days later, the war began in earnest. On May 10, Captain Campbell and Lieutenant George McDougall were taken captive by Pontiac during a council. In a few weeks, the number of warriors surrounding the post tripled; British supplies and reinforcements were attacked and repulsed. On July 4, Campbell, the man who uncovered the Seneca plot back in 1761, was beaten to death, scalped, and thrown into the Detroit River as recompense for the death of the nephew of Wasson, an influential Saginaw valley Ojibwa chief.

General Amherst wrote to Johnson that he could not imagine the Indians having "in their power to Execute any thing Serious against US, While We Continue to be on our Guard."[101] This sentiment proved short lived. A few days later, Lieutenant Edward Jenkins, commander of Fort Ouiatanon, wrote that the Indians "told [him] Detroit, Miamis [i.e., Fort Miami] and all these posts were cut Off, and that it was a folly to make any resistance."[102] The Potawatomi captured Fort St. Joseph on May 25, 1763. One week later, the Indian communities in Illinois Country captured Fort Miami, and then Fort Ouiatanon on the Wabash River. And on the following day, a group of Ojibwa and Sauk warriors used a game of *baaga'adowe*, the forerunner of modern lacrosse, to capture Fort Michilimackinac while the garrison watched the spirited play.[103]

Hearing the sounds of violence and the screams of pain, Alexander Henry, the first British trader to arrive at Michilimackinac after the Seven Years' War and later a close associate of Askin, ran to his storehouse window and "saw a crowd of Indians within the fort furiously cutting down and scalping every Englishman they found."[104] Terrified, he fled his trading house and begged Charles de Langlade to protect him from the Indians. The Frenchman intimated that he could do little to help. All seemed lost for Henry, until a Panise woman hid him in Langlade's garret.[105] Discovered the following morning by the surprised Langlade family, and then by the Ojibwa, Henry, along with the other British merchants and soldiers who survived, was transported to the Ojibwa's village several miles south of the fort. Once there, he waited for death, having been told by his captors they intended to "make broth" of him and the others.[106] To further the threat, an Ojibwa warrior offered Henry a slice of bread cut with the same bloody knife used to kill his countrymen.

Robert Rogers heard of the Indian attacks and offered his services to Amherst. He and 173 soldiers traveled west under the command of Captain James Dalyell, Amherst's aide-de-camp, to relieve Detroit.[107] Soon after arriving, on July 31, 1763, Dalyell led a surprise attack that went drastically awry when the 278 British soldiers were themselves ambushed as they crossed a narrow wooden bridge by some three hundred Indians. The blood from roughly 70 killed or wounded soldiers dripped into a small creek and gave the battle its name: Bloody Run. Dalyell was among the fallen.

A week later, on August 5 and 6, five hundred British soldiers under the command of Colonel Henry Bouquet marched to relieve Fort Pitt and had better success.[108] Despite heavy causalities, Bouquet's men thwarted an ambush by Delaware, Mingo, Huron, and Shawnee warriors and caused the Indians to flee. However, British success at Fort Pitt was soon marred by a defeat at Niagara.[109] The Seneca had long worked and controlled the lands surrounding Niagara Falls. After the Seven Years' War, the British, under the direction of John Stedman, dispossessed Seneca labor and transformed the portage to allow oxcarts and wagons. On September 14, over three hundred Seneca warriors ambushed a British wagon train led by two dozen British waggoneers, including Stedman. Stedman and two others escaped to warn the British army, who were themselves ambushed by the Seneca. The British suffered ninety causalities.

Askin and Gordon heard the news of the Seneca attack firsthand while at Fort Niagara. "Here we remained," wrote Gordon, "from September untill late in the Fall, and all the trading people were cooped up in . . . a low point of land between the Fort and the Lake."[110] News trickled in slowly. In November 1763, they learned that Pontiac and the Indians surrounding Detroit had broken their siege and retreated to their winter hunting grounds; the lack of gunpowder and supplies, their inability to close the fort from resupply, and the tenacity of the British garrison had taken a toll. In the Ohio Valley, the war widened into raids against Virginia, Maryland, and Pennsylvania and showed little sign of abating. However, it became increasingly clear to the Indians that the British were not going away, and their French "father" was not going to return.

Soon after, Askin and Gordon returned to Albany. While still at Niagara, Gordon "was violently attacked with the Ague and fever, which reduced [him] almost to a skeleton." Homesick, desperate, and ruined, Gordon "mustered up from the remains of [his] shattered fortune a bare sufficiency" and returned to northern Ireland.[111] A few years later, Gordon would return and participate once again in the fur trade; he would also fight alongside the rebellious colonials in the 1770s. Likewise, in May 1765, Rogers, whose prestige and connections introduced Askin and Gordon to the important military and fur trade posts of the Great Lakes, left North America as well, traveling to London to press the Crown for a civil and military command.[112] He would publish his journals and write a play about Pontiac, and the wide Atlantic Ocean provided him space to escape his creditors. A year earlier, they had jailed him in New York City; with the help of British soldiers, he had escaped. Of the three partners of Askin & Company, only Askin remained in North America.

Unable to sell his liquors or collect last year's fur returns, Askin faced his creditors and suppliers empty-handed and quite alone. In early 1764, he went to the trading houses of Abraham Douw, Gregg & Cunningham, Hymen Levy, Henry Agnew, Kennedy & Lyle, and several others to explain his current situation and attempt to borrow just a little more money to get him back on his feet and start trading again.[113] He saw stony faces, listened to terse conversations, and fielded sharp questions about repayment. Later, he estimated that he owed nearly £7,000 to these men.[114] Pontiac's War caused his trading ventures to fail; alienated from the British fur trade community of New York, he was unable to secure easy credit, and without that Askin could do little to organize the purchase of new merchandise to exchange for furs, and he lacked the means to repay what he owed. Askin was bankrupt.

He could trace his misfortunes to Amherst's destructive policies, Great Britain's inability to appreciate the French and Indian world they inhabited, and bad partnerships—costly lessons paid in blood and coin. He had only been in North America for five years. At twenty-five years of age, Askin had experienced a lifetime of ruin.

CHAPTER TWO

There Have Been Many Who Complain Much against You

Michilimackinac, Fur Trade Reforms, and John Askin's Commissaryship, 1764–1767

JOHN ASKIN, LEDGER IN HAND, DIRECTED THE RED-JACKETED SOLDIERS OF THE Seventeenth Regiment forward as they carried cargo across Michilimackinac's beach and through the fort's tumbledown sea gates.[1] He entered the first building on the right, the fort's storehouse, and instructed the soldiers to stack their loads in neat orderly rows. As the soldiers retreated from the building, Askin paused in the gloom to count casks and barrels. They had carried in forty, but one hundred still remained on the ten boats that carried them north from Detroit. A year after the collapse of his trading venture, Askin was now the bankrupt deputy commissary of Fort Michilimackinac, and hoped the position would offer him a new beginning.[2]

Just a few hours earlier, around midday on September 22, 1764, Askin had rested against the gunwale of a docked bateau and watched as Captain William Howard, a lifelong soldier and the new British commandant of Michilimackinac, greeted a delegation of French inhabitants on the shore of Lake Huron.[3] Father Pierre Du Jaunay, a Jesuit missionary among the Odawa of Arbre Croche, greeted Howard cordially and turned to introduce him to

Pierre Parent. Parent gave Howard "the Keys of the Gates" and told the British officer how he had prevented the Indians from destroying the fort after the previous year's bloodshed. Marie-Josephe Dumouchelle and Jacques Philippe Farly presented their hands next, and pointed to their homes within the fort, explaining how they "preserved a Quantity of Beaver & e. belonging to the English Traders."[4] Another Frenchman, Alexis Sejorne dit Sans Chagrin, asked for news of Alexander Henry.[5] Howard gestured toward the boats, and Sans Chagrin saw the newly redeemed Englishman among the crew looking none the worse for his captivity among the Ojibwa. Messers Chevalier, Cardin, and Bourassa stepped forward and offered their compliments and services.[6] These Frenchmen, members of large multifocal and multiethnic French and Indian fur trade families, were perfectly suited to greet the new British garrison; such men were well versed in navigating the complex negotiations among economics, politics, and diplomacy in the Great Lakes.[7]

With keys in hand and a head full of French names, Howard ordered his two companies to disembark, and he set about putting his new command in order. He surveyed the wooden palisade, kicked the wood, and saw it splinter from water rot. Fort Michilimackinac, established by the French in 1715, was built too close to the water; the waves lapped against its weathered walls. Captain Beamsley Glazier, a future commander of Fort Michilimackinac, described the conditions of the post to Gage. "This Fort," Glazier wrote, is "so bad . . . [It has] large hills and deep gullies, which are 40 yards of the west and south [of the] Bastions . . . where 1500 Indians may ly under cover from any fire from the Fort excepting Shells."[8]

Howard knew Michilimackinac required work. He walked back toward the gates, shaking his head, and before being set upon by more orderlies and inhabitants, he had time to think. Truth be told, the meeting with the French had confused him; it did not conform to the advice of his superiors. A few minutes later, he entered the fort, barked a command for attention, and began organizing the French community. He required all those present to swear an oath of allegiance to His Royal Majesty, King George III, and so they did.[9]

Meanwhile, Askin had clambered out of his boat and followed a press of people into the stockade.[10] Through the gates, he noticed to his right the storehouse, and to the left a larger, well-made building—the commanding officer's quarters. Walking down the boulevard, he came to an open plaza with a sizable well. He looked left and admired a neat row of wooden buildings with fenced-in gardens in the back. Their timber looked gray and weather-worn, and smoke billowed from their stoves and fireplaces. They were small and comfortable, and would remain so, even in the frigid cold of a northern Great Lakes winter. Some housed French merchants, while others would soon house the garrison's junior officers. Pausing briefly by the well, the large timber Catholic Church, Ste. Anne de Michilimackinac, caught Askin's eye, and he knew that was where the priest must perform his rites. Turning, he saw the landward gate directly ahead. He walked past two more neat rows of houses and then, through another set of gates, he left the fort. Beyond, Askin saw a large garden, stables, and an autumnal forest, thick with shadow. He searched the dense branches of the trees, still heavy with flashes of red and orange leaves, and felt, for the first time since landing, his isolation.

John Askin led a fragmentary early life at Michilimackinac after the collapse of his New York fur trade and Great Britain's reoccupation of the post after Pontiac's War. Askin and the British negotiated the instability of their position and authority as economic complications frustrated the development of an effective Indian and fur trade policy—the twin pillars of a functional Great Lakes world. Western commandants like Howard struggled to attain peace with the region's Indian communities, halter French and British merchants and traders, and carry out the counterproductive directives of their own commanding officers. Likewise, Askin, bankrupt and isolated, clung to his position as deputy commissary. Pressured by creditors, he kept the King's Storehouse and looked for ways to prosper while he watched other merchants, British and French, flourish by chasing furs further north. However, despite the disastrous financial situation he found himself in, Askin's efforts to supply the British garrison introduced him to the connections and capital that would one day allow him to reenter the fur trade and become a dominant middleman.

Though Detroit, Fort Pitt, and Niagara had held against Indian attacks in the summer and fall of 1763, hostility and mistrust lingered. Neither side won a decisive battle. Despite having cowed the great powers of Europe, Great Britain's military had very little to show against the Indians of the Great Lakes. A discredited General Jeffrey Amherst, whose curtailment of Indian presents in an effort to save expenditures lead to an even costlier war, returned to Great Britain to face an indignant Parliament and was soon replaced as commander-in-chief in North America by his second-in-command, General Thomas Gage.[11] Gage shared Amherst's general disdain of Indians, but believed they fought justly, and he proved more amenable to the advice of Sir William Johnson, the superintendent of Indian Affairs for the Northern Department.

Moreover, early in 1764 enough signs penetrated the fog of war to signal to the Indians of the Great Lakes and the Ohio Valley that the British planned to stay, and France, their Great Father across the Ocean, was not going to return; the Master of Life had not been appeased. It also became clear to both Johnson and Gage that the Indians, despite their want and need of British merchandise, could and would continue the war if pressed. By the spring of 1764, the British and certain Indian communities made halting and tentative steps toward peace and reconciliation, and should others prove recalcitrant, Gage was prepared for the worst.

By April 1764, Gage "assemble[d] a Body of Troops . . . to chastise the Savages who still continue[d] in Arms."[12] He put Lieutenant Colonel John Bradstreet, famous for forcing Fort Frontenac's surrender during the Seven Years' War, in command of nearly two thousand British, French, and Indian men-at-arms and provided extensive instructions. First and foremost, Gage ordered Bradstreet to secure and protect Niagara from further Seneca attacks, and then march to Sandusky on Lake Erie and stage attacks against any hostile Wyandot, Shawnee, and Delaware bands in the Ohio Valley. Afterward, Gage ordered Bradstreet to march on Detroit and sound the peaceful intent of the Odawa and their allies, but "if those Savages should again commit hostilities," Bradstreet was to "destroy and extirpate them." As for the French "who may have taken up Arms, or otherwise acted traitorously," Bradstreet should give them the "rigour and severity they deserve."[13] To truly pacify the region, Gage ordered Colonel Henry Bouquet, commander of another sizable British force, to push north from Fort Pitt. Together with Bradstreet's men, the two commanders would chastise the hostile Indians, punish the perfidious French, and secure the fur trade communities of Detroit and Michilimackinac.

However, delays thwarted Bradstreet's expedition from marching west in the spring of 1764, and he and his soldiers, Howard included, were on hand to witness Johnson's far-reaching Indian council at Niagara in July.[14] Thousands of Indians from across the Great Lakes came to Niagara, mostly representatives from neutral or pro-British Odawa, Ojibwa, Fox, Ho-Chunk, and other communities, and offered Johnson familiar complaints. For example, on July 11, 1764, Bildanwan, an Odawa chief, spoke: "We are become very poor, having no Trade or Goods, which reduced some of us to great necessity last Winter & we fear some of us may starve next, unless supplied." Johnson heard demands for powder, knives, axes, rum, and "other Necessary Articles" and responded to the assembled chiefs that they should help bring "Wicked People to Sense of their [error. As] Soon as that is done, Trade will im[m]ediately flourish." To those who came to Niagara, he prudently distributed provisions and presents like pipes, tobacco, and even barrels of rum to the assembled chiefs and headmen to bring them over to Great Britain's side.[15] He offered them traders, as well. But for "those Nations, who continued obstinate," Johnson darkly promised only a British army.[16]

On August 16, two weeks after the council concluded, Gage expressed his worries that the "[Odawa] of Detroit, [Potawatomi] or [Wyandot], or [Ojibwa] of the Bay of [Saginaw]" failed to participate, and as long as the Ohio Valley Shawnee and Delaware, "the Promoters of the War," remained unchastised, peace remained impossible.[17] However, good news leavened the bad. "Pondiac," Johnson replied to Gage, "is now with about 300 Men . . . [and] expressed his desire of making peace, finding himself deserted by so many of his People."[18] Moreover, according to Major Henry Gladwin, the commandant of Detroit, the Indians of his post seemed amenable to peace.[19] With Bradstreet and his men now gone from Niagara and marching near Presque Island on Lake Erie, under direct orders from Gage to "attack the Shawnese and Delawares," both Johnson and Gage believed lasting peace could be established, traders could be protected and monitored, and the Indians could be satisfied through a prosperous and more equitable fur trade.[20]

However, instead of striking His Majesty's enemies, on August 12 Bradstreet pursued a tentative peace treaty at Sandusky with representatives of the Shawnee and Delaware communities of the Ohio Valley. Upon reading the treaty for the very first time, Gage raged to Johnson:

> Bradstreet has taken upon Himself to Conclude, with the Shawnee and Delawares, [a treaty] which contains no Article whereby the least Satisfaction is given for the many horrid Murders committed by those Barbarians, the sole Promoters . . . and the Chief Actors in the Bloody Tragedy.[21]

Unaware of Gage's spleen, Bradstreet and his men pushed toward Detroit; they had burned no villages and fought no battles, and did little to strengthen the cause of Great Britain's arms. In a letter written in December to the Lords of Trade in London, Johnson explained that Bradstreet's efforts resulted in promises "to deliver up within a certain time all prisoners . . . as well as to stop all Hostilities, yet, [the Shawnee and Delaware] never observed to perform either."[22] Likewise, in early October, Gage wrote a pointed letter to Bradstreet: "With your Letters of Peace, I received Others giving accounts of Murders."[23] Bradstreet had, in the eyes of his commanding officers, blundered his way through the campaign.

A couple of weeks after meeting with the Shawnee and Delaware, Bradstreet sent a small expedition of French and Indians to escort Captain Thomas Morris southwest to the unoccupied Illinois Country to treat with the region's Indian communities and the French at Fort de Chartres. According to Captain John Montresor, a British military engineer who kept a diary of Bradstreet's expedition, Morris was to administer "the Oath to the Inhabitants" and make "necessary remarks . . . & proceed to New York by the way of the Mississippi."[24]

Instead, Morris—brutalized, robbed, nearly murdered, chased out of a village, and almost burned at the stake—experienced firsthand the deep anger held toward the British interlopers. In fact, Morris learned from Shawnee and Delaware envoys that their peace with Bradstreet was a ruse; they promised him they would "Send the hatchet [in October]."[25] Luckily, the Miami of the Wabash and Maumee Rivers turned Morris back before he suffered serious injury, and the fortuitous captain traveled with news of Pontiac, whom he had spoken with during a council, and of his growing desire for peace.[26]

On August 27, Bradstreet and his men arrived at Detroit. He ordered the French inhabitants of the community to take "the Oaths of allegiance and fidelity to his Britannic Majesty."[27] He relieved Major Henry Gladwin, the commandant who had held the fort against Pontiac and his allies during the summer and fall of 1763, replacing him with Lieutenant Colonel John Campbell. Continuing his flurry of activity, Bradstreet raised the local French militia and ordered a sizable contingent to follow Captain Howard and his two companies of British regulars north to Michilimackinac.[28]

Supplies for the expedition had already been set aside by Captain Montresor, and Askin was, most likely, on hand to help see the goods and men loaded onto the waiting bateaux. Howard had met with Bradstreet to learn the extent and tenor of his orders. On September 1, Howard, his men, and Askin left Fort Detroit, traveling up the river, through Lake St. Clair, to the open waters of Lake Huron.

Meanwhile, on September 5, Bradstreet met at Detroit with representatives of the Ojibwa, Shawnee, Wyandot, Odawa, and Miami. According to Montresor, the Odawa and Ojibwa were "responsible for their agreeing to the terms of Peace."[29] Bradstreet sent the proceedings to Gage and Johnson, who expressed horror at its contents. Johnson complained that in "the present Treaty I find, [the Indians] make expressions of subjection." One of the provisions, in fact, provided King George III and the British Empire sovereignty over the Indian peoples of the Great Lakes, while another required Indian communities to deliver to British officials any Indians who killed or robbed a British subject. "For some Centuries," Johnson wrote, "neither have they any word which can convey the most distant idea of subjection, and should it be fully explained to them, and the nature of subordination punishment ettc, defined, it might produce infinite harm." Blaming the wording on faulty translators or "some other mistake," Johnson "dread[ed] its consequences" as "some [British] attempts towards Sovereignty not long ago, was one of the principal causes of all our troubles."[30]

Following the treaty, Bradstreet reopened the fur trade at Detroit, and then took his men to Sandusky and waited for the Shawnee and Delaware to return British prisoners, as promised earlier. They never came. To make matters worse, he received word of Gage's and Johnson's rancor and their rejection of his diplomatic efforts. He waited there from mid-September to mid-October, threatening to attack or coordinate with Bouquet's force in the south, before returning to Niagara. However, Bradstreet's return proved disastrous; according to Johnson, storms, bad planning, and the lack of provisions scattered "his Troops & Indians, many of whom perished, & many are still behind." By November 19, after a four-month campaign, Bradstreet and his men limped into Niagara; some soldiers marched through the forest with provisions, and some survived through the generosity of the Iroquois, who fed and housed them before sending them away.[31] Bradstreet's reputation was crippled, and his career stalled.

Meanwhile, at Michilimackinac, Howard worked tirelessly to govern the complex and multifaceted French and Indian community, connected by ties of kinship and trade that stretched across the Great Lakes.[32] The small fort was surrounded by two of the largest Indian communities in the region: around five thousand Odawa and around seventeen thousand Ojibwa. For example, thirty miles southwest of Michilimackinac sat the principal village of the Odawa at Arbre Croche, while to the west was a village on Manitoulin Island, and to the south another village outside of Detroit.[33] Likewise, numerous important Ojibwa communities stretched southeast from Lake Superior all the way to Lake Erie. Villages existed at Grand Portage, Chequamegon Bay, Sault Ste. Marie, Mackinac Island, Cheboygan, Thunder Bay, Saginaw Bay, and Lake St. Clair.[34] These villages, often home to around two hundred inhabitants and led by hereditary chiefs, community elders, and war and spiritual leaders, represented the principal social and economic units of the Odawa and Ojibwa peoples and the other nations of the Great Lakes and Ohio Valley.[35] These communities, closely and historically related to each other and to the Potawatomi communities further south, had undergirded the economic and military power of the French, and served the same role under the British regime.

Migrating seasonally and coalescing in bands of various sizes given the time of year or nature of their tasks, the Odawa and Ojibwa of the upper Great Lakes harvested, hunted, gathered, trapped, and traded with kin.[36] Summer was the time of plenty and large gatherings. The Odawa gathered at Arbre Croche, where ties were renewed and marriages arranged. Men organized war, hunting, and trading parties that ranged far and wide. Summer was often a period of diplomatic maintenance; important village leaders came to posts like Michilimackinac to treat with French or British commandants and receive presents as an affirmation of friendship and allegiance.[37] These presents would then be redistributed by the village leaders to members of their community, sustaining their own trust and bolstering their authority. Women stayed closer to the villages, performing the bulk of the communities' agricultural work by planting fields of corn, squash, and beans.[38] In fact, the agricultural labor of Indian women fed the Great Lakes fur trade; Indian corn, boiled in lye and dried to create hominy, fed traders and boatmen.

Late fall and early winter was the period of scarcity, when upper Great Lakes Indian families dispersed to their hunting grounds in the northern woodlands. During these months, fish, an integral part of the Ojibwa and Odawa diet, were netted, speared, or trapped by weirs and then carefully cleaned, dried, and smoked for long-term storage. Women brought in the last of the summer crops and collected the fruits, berries, and nuts preserved during the last season. As winter came, villages broke apart, and Indian families of roughly six to eight members dispersed to their hunting grounds in the northern woods. Men hunted deer, moose, bear, and elk, and set snares and traps for rabbits, muskrats, martens, and beavers. After butchering the carcasses, the women prepared the skins by washing, scraping, stretching, drying, and then rubbing them with reserved brains to keep them shiny. Their efforts turned the perishable skins into the highly sought-after commodities that were coveted by Europeans. Winter was long and lean, and the Indians of the Great Lakes dreamed of spring and the coming maple sap harvest.

French commandants had allowed their traders to winter among the Indians at their hunting grounds. Large quantities of furs were hard to store, and most Indian communities resisted carrying their pelts over long distances to trade at remote posts. Late in the seventeenth century, for example, the French had tried to force Great Lakes Indians to travel to Montreal, but failed miserably. Long before Askin's day, the French had learned to locate their economic efforts within the Indigenous world of the upper Great Lakes.[39]

Culturally astute traders brought gifts along with their wares to establish ties of friendship and reciprocity, creating the proper conditions for future exchanges. Frenchmen fortunate enough to form marriage ties with an Odawa or Ojibwa woman found their trading efforts enhanced as a result. From an Indigenous perspective, marriage created ties and established social identities, and for the Frenchman, an Indian wife provided safety, access to furs, and a mediator within the village.[40] Likewise, the marriage ensured the woman and her kin a steady supply of European merchandise. By the end of winter French traders' canoes were brimming with furs; they returned to Michilimackinac by late spring or early summer to exchange them for the next winters' outfit of supplies.

Michilimackinac was "the [major] place of deposit and point of departure between the upper countries and the lower" for the Great Lakes fur trade.[41] Its inhabitants secured their livelihoods through the fur trade and deep relationships with the surrounding Indian communities. Charles de Langlade served as Michilimackinac's commander before its surrender to the British army in September 1761.[42] A decade earlier, he had married Charlotte-Ambroisine, the daughter of an established French trader named René Bourassa, who was born in Montreal and started participating in the western fur trade in the 1730s.[43] Bourassa's eldest son, also named René, married into the influential Chevalier family, whose branches participated in the fur trade at Michilimackinac, Sault St. Marie, Saint Joseph, Cahokia, Nipigon, and Detroit.[44] British fur trader Alexander Henry noted that the number of families at Michilimackinac corresponded to the number of houses he saw, but as a newcomer he could not have fathomed how socially, economically, and intimately bound these families were; these tangled interconnections were completely distrusted by most British commanders in the Great Lakes.

"The French inhabiting that quarter," Gage wrote to Bradstreet earlier in the year, "are reported to have behaved themselves in a scandalous and seditious manner against his Majesty's British Subjects and Government."[45] However, Howard's early encounters with the French inhabitants of Michilimackinac rapidly disabused him of most enmity and suspicion. In November 1764, for example, Lieutenant Colonel John Campbell, the commandant of Detroit, wrote to Bradstreet that Howard did not "think it proper to send any [French] Inhabitants from Michilikmackinak as he finds them of great Service there." In fact, the French, both the militiamen from Detroit and members of Michilimackinac's community, helped Howard and his soldiers strengthen the palisades with new timber and cannon, repair houses within the fort, and remove surrounding sand dunes that might provide enemies shelter or firing positions.[46] But, more importantly, the French supplied Howard with corn—"most all they had"—to supply the garrison for the winter. They promised fish and sold Howard nets, and even put themselves in danger of starvation if the supply ship from Detroit did not arrive by May 1765.[47]

Building rapport with Michilimackinac's French improved Howard's ability to negotiate the relentless and volatile demands of Great Lakes Indigenous diplomacy. Shortly after reestablishing the post, Howard encountered a Frenchman who described meeting a Sac Indian who had news of an English scalp. Howard knew that a Sac chief was at his post, and asked the chief about the scalp; he received a promise that "as soon as [the Sac] got home, [he] would inquire about it, and if the report was true."[48]

Soon after, a Frenchman who had been at Green Bay delivered a dyed-green pipe to Howard and relayed the words of a Mississippi Sioux. The pipe was not a pipe, "but a Hatchet which [the Sioux] sent down to strike against the Chippiways which they would do as long as they had a man alive." The Sioux had long fought against the Ojibwa, and Howard learned that despite their distance from Michilimackinac they had to be negotiated with or he faced being drawn into a costly and destructive war. He made inquiries and learned from his informant that the Sioux were some thirty thousand strong. "I was only to paint the Pipe read [red], and send it back," Howard informed Campbell, "which would be token enough for them to revenge the Blood of their Brothers." Then Howard learned from Michilimackinac's priest, Father Du Jaunay, that "the Ottaways [of Arbre Croche] . . . were discontented, but would not tell the reason."[49]

This news shocked Howard. The Odawa of Arbre Croche had helped the British just a year before. In fact, they had refused to participate in the sack of Michilimackinac. Through the intervention of Charles de Langlade, nephew of Nissowaquet (their principal chief), the Odawa had saved the captured Captain George Etherington and several other British soldiers and traders from the Ojibwa and the Sac.[50] Etherington appointed de Langlade commandant, and with the help of Henry Bostwick, a British trader still at the fort, they triaged efforts to reestablish peace, protect inhabitants, secure British goods, and dole out presents, especially to Etherington's protectors, the Odawa.[51] In early August 1763, they reminded the British that their efforts had "Cost [them] a great deal of Trouble" and protected the British from "Enemy Indians, superior to us in Number—Yet we thought no Danger too great to Save them."[52]

Luckily for Howard, the Odawa came to Michilimackinac with strings and belts of wampum. "The first was a welcome to the place," Howard wrote to Campbell, "the Second to whipe away the blood that was spilt of their Brothers the English." Howard "had no wampum but spoake with some presents," and they promised to return "in the Spring . . . and disperse a Cloud." Not having wampum on hand at Michilimackinac—the ceremonial strings of beads or beads woven into belts, which played central roles in Great Lakes diplomacy by lending authority to the speaker's words and demonstrating their honest intent—demonstrated the lack of foresight by the British military. Little wampum combined with a dearth of presents forced Howard to ask Campbell "to prevail on the Genrl. to send me some presents for the Indians without which, it will be difficult for me to keep the Indians in temper."[53]

British officials on both sides of the Atlantic—men shocked by the embarrassing events of Pontiac's War—became receptive to new policies aimed at ensuring peace in North America and gaining fiscal relief after nearly a decade of continual warfare. Before the Seven Years' War, Great Britain carried a hefty national debt of more than £73 million; the war nearly doubled it.[54] In London, the Board of Trade, a committee of influential men tasked with overseeing Britain's colonial administration, struggled to devise efficient and cost-effective policies the empire could afford to implement. As a result, the men came to rely heavily on the advice and consultation of Sir William Johnson.[55]

Working from his desk in November 1763, Johnson wrote a lengthy report for the Board of Trade claiming that British leaders had failed in the aftermath of the Seven Years' War "to cultivate a proper understanding with the Indians . . . without considering, that it is in their power . . . to lay waste and destroy the Frontiers." He inked his quill, paused to contemplate his next lines, and then leveled a serious critique: "Confidence in our scattered numbers and the parsimony of our people, who . . . would not expend five pounds to save twenty" is what caused Pontiac's War. Contrasting the British with the French, Johnson argued that the French "loaded [the Indians] with favours, and employed the most intelligent Agents, of good influence, as well as artful Jesuits amongst [them]," whereas the British fostered the belief among Indians that the empire meant to "enslave" them and "invade their properties." In his report, he articulated an expansive vision of Anglo-Indian North America that relied on boundary lines, land sale reforms, better and more numerous Indian agents at frontier posts, good interpreters, and strong missionary work—costly reforms, he admitted, but they would "secure [Indian] fidelity for the future."[56]

For Johnson, the key to British success in the Great Lakes required first the relief of festering tensions. To do so, officials needed to employ imperial authority to control sites of the fur trade and therein police the contours of cross-cultural encounters and economic exchanges. Johnson argued that it was "the utmost consequence, that the Indian Trade be carried on, under the Direction and inspection" of the superintendence of Indian Affairs.[57] Given proper resources, he could ensure that the myriad processes of the fur trade could be carried out in a just and equitable manner. In letters, he provided the outlines of a system that transformed former French trading posts into western-style "Albanys"—fortified and secured places where Indians could travel to trade among accountable traders—rather than allowing unscrupulous men into Indian country to cause havoc. No longer given unfettered access to the North American interior, French and British merchants and traders would be required to apply for temporary licenses, pay a substantial bond for good behavior, and submit their intentions to Indian agents and newly empowered Indian commissaries at prescribed and selected posts like Michilimackinac, Detroit, or Green Bay.[58] Traders caught without a license would "forfeit their goods, pay a fine of ten pr. cent their prime cost to His Majty. and suffer six Months imprisonment."[59] By offering a centralized, bureaucratic, legitimate fur trade, Johnson, Gage, and others hoped for greater imperial control that would reduce costs in the long term.

In the eyes of Johnson and Gage, these reforms seemed to offer the added benefit of developing a free trade. Both men believed French traders and merchants conspired to deny their British counterparts access to the region's bountiful furs.[60] By restricting exchange to British-controlled posts, Johnson and Gage hoped to neutralize the long-standing ties of kinship and cooperation between the French and Indians that had blocked British fur trade efforts before Pontiac's War through murder, robbery, or intimidation.[61] Forced to travel to British posts, Indians would quickly discover the advantage of trading their furs for cheaper and better-quality British goods, and would choose accordingly.

In private deliberations the Board of Trade endorsed many of Johnson's reforms. However, within the convoluted matrix of London politics and the economic realities of the post–Seven Years' War empire, the matter of cost obstructed official plans. For example, Johnson recommended a fur tax as a way of paying for the reforms, but the Board of Trade demurred, claiming that it would be unenforceable, which delayed any effort until a permanent source of funding could be found. Under the administration of Prime Minister George Grenville, Parliament advocated the enforcement of preexisting trade laws and the implementation of a direct tax on the British colonies in North America.

Easily implemented and potentially lucrative, Grenville's government hoped to raise revenue for the upkeep of the North American colonies, especially the costly frontier military outposts, in a manner the Atlantic colonists found agreeable, and even delayed debate to accommodate and solicit for other ways of raising money. In the spring of 1765, after receiving no other recommendation, Parliament passed a revenue bill called the Stamp Act, which represented a fundamental departure for Great Britain's relationship with its Atlantic colonies.[62] Historically, Parliament had indirectly taxed its North American colonists since the mid-seventeenth century. Now, colonial importers would be required to import specially prepared, pretaxed paper with an embossed stamp from Great Britain to be used and resold for use as legal documents, diplomas, newspapers, pamphlets, playing cards, and other everyday items.

Few members of Parliament could have predicted the colonial reaction to their effort to raise revenue. From Boston to New York, Philadelphia to Charleston, colonials from all walks of life united in protest against what they saw as unfair and illegal taxation. They resorted to speechmaking, lobbying, protests, riots, intimidation, and violence. Colonial agents in London, such as Benjamin Franklin of Pennsylvania, attacked Great Britain's rationale for taxation and the need to maintain frontier garrisons. In early 1766 in front of members of Parliament, Franklin claimed that Great Britain fought the Seven Years' War and Pontiac's War for its own benefit, not for the colonies. The parliamentarians who listened to Franklin's diatribe expressed shock and anger at the absurdity of the colonials' shameless efforts to reject the cost of defeating the French, even as they benefited most directly.[63] In the summer of 1764, Grenville's administration fell. The government of the Marquis of Rockingham repealed the Stamp Act in the spring of 1766 before being ousted from power. As Great Britain and its colonies skirmished over taxation, its Indian and fur trade policy remained in limbo.

In light of the imperial and colonial wrangling over taxation and finances, Johnson and Gage failed to secure the revenue to properly supply Great Britain's Indian allies with diplomatic presents. For example, at Niagara in 1764 Johnson handed out £25,000 NYC worth of presents to the Indians of the Great Lakes.[64] Yet, less than a year later, Gage complained to Johnson, "I find the officers

Command[ing] At Detroit and Missilimakinak already talk of drawing Bills on acct. of Presents for the Indians." In light of "strong Letters from the Treasury," Gage worried that unless restrictions were set, "the officers will be clothing entire Nations."[65] He needed Johnson to reduce expenses as much as possible, but the legacy of the French and Indian alliance and Pontiac's War meant gifting had to be maintained and the costs had to be borne by the British people.

Back at Michilimackinac, throughout the spring and summer of 1765, Howard bore the stress of managing his post in the face of vacillating Odawa and Ojibwa hostility and disappointment. The French and Indians of the Illinois Country, who had embraced Pontiac and his anti-British stance even after he and his allies gave up their blockade of Detroit in 1763, challenged British control of the region and had been among the very last to negotiate peace. During the summer, Minweweh, the Ojibwa chief of Mackinac Island, the community who had sacked Michilimackinac in 1763, was in the Illinois Country and took presents from French traders.[66] The Ojibwa even threatened to attack Michilimackinac again. Luckily for Howard, George Croghan, the deputy of Sir William Johnson, met with the Indians of the Ohio Valley, Great Lakes, and Illinois Country in Detroit, and concluded a peace that allowed British soldiers and traders to occupy Fort de Chartres on the Mississippi River. In mid-September 1765, Croghan met with Minweweh and his men, and the Ojibwa leader confessed being swayed by Pontiac and French efforts to keep the British from reentering the country, and explained that he now desired peace.[67]

The Indians who came to Michilimackinac in the summer of 1765 complained bitterly to Howard about the lack of trade and set the stage for the opening of the fur trade beyond British posts. In a letter to Sir William Johnson on June 24, 1765, Howard noted that, during a council with Indians from Lakes Superior and Michigan, "they represented [the] Miserable Scituation they had been in for want of Trade, and begged I would send some Traders to them, and asked for Mr. Caddot [Jean-Baptiste Cadot]."[68] Afraid of giving offense or turning the assembled Indians hostile, Howard promised to send French and English traders among them with goods. Given the restrictions, he feared

Johnson's and Gage's reaction, writing, "hope I shall not be found fault with for what I do." In the same letter, he hedged his bets by pointing out that "My Account does not come to a fourth part as much as Capt. Elthringtons did, who had not a fourth part as much the Indians as I have had."[69] Howard handed out two passes, and then waited for Johnson's response.

Meanwhile, on July 5, 1765, upon hearing of Howard's actions, more than two dozen mostly French traders demanded the same privilege. In their petition, the traders explained:

> We have already very Severely felt the Calamities of the Late Indian war, in which many of US have Lost the greatest part of Our property, and now a Peace is Concluded and the Bonds of Friendship renewed. . . . We hope we shall not again draw their Resentment upon us by preventing Traders among them as they have so far singly desired it.[70]

Moreover, they feared losing the furs and custom of the Indians to the French of the Illinois Country, who would travel up the Mississippi River to supply their wants and needs. Beyond self-interest, they framed their demands as benefiting the British economy as a whole. "[Canada] now imports from England annually about £140,000 Sterling and if she is deprived of so great a part of her Exports as £90,000 which in former Years this Trade has produced, she must . . . sink under the Weight of her distresses."[71] The traders suggested that recent efforts to limit the fur trade to established posts would provoke the hostility of the Indians and lead to the bankruptcy of merchants and ruin of the colony.

Despite being sympathetic to their arguments, promising to "say every thing he Could in [their] favour," Howard refused to honor their request. He had already overstepped the line, and did not want to "Run the Risque of being Broke with disgrace for disobedience of Orders."[72] Instead, he suggested the traders send their petition to Johnson in New York. As a gesture of goodwill and fairness, he offered to rescind the two permits in the interim.

Johnson, however, refused their entreaties. Pointing to "his Majesty's late Instructions, the Steps taken by the Governors . . . , the nature of your Permits, and the Sentiments of the Commander in Chief," he offered the petitioners a familiar argument. He continued to harbor fears about Indian allegiance, and worried that "our Goods might . . . prove an Irresistible Temptation to some Indians, Robberies, and Murders might ensure, wch. must involve us in a fresh War."[73] Upon hearing of the request, General Thomas Gage, hostile to French traders, viewed their complaint to Howard as an attempt to "Worm the English Traders entirely out of the Trade, for there is nothing so vile and bad which they will not Attempt, to keep the Trade in their own Hands." Perceptively, he warned Johnson that if the traders, French or British, gained unfettered access to Indian country, "there will be an End, and a total One, of our Regulations, and the Posts and Forts will be of no more Consequence."[74]

Curiously, despite refusing the petition, Johnson gave Howard a limited discretion to send out traders. He explained more explicitly in a letter to Gage that "nothing but the absolute necessity of affairs should induce [Howard] to suffer any person to leave the Post."[75] By establishing necessity as a hallmark of overstepping the post-only trade restriction, Johnson empowered Howard to take matters into his own hands.

At Michilimackinac, Howard read Johnson's letter, intuited his broadened latitude, and quickly charted a path toward ameliorating the complaints of his traders and fulfilling the requests of the Indians. In early fall, Howard issued passes to a handful of French and British traders, whom he deemed men of quality and substance, and gave them special permission to winter among the Indians of Lake Superior who were in great want of supplies.[76]

News of the passes spread quickly. On September 17, 1765, Lawrence Ermatinger, a Montreal merchant who supplied goods to Forrest Oakes at Michilimackinac, wrote a letter of complaint to Johnson:

> we became Adventurers . . . and expected that we should receive the same advantage as many others of his Majesty's Subjects did, but contrary to our Expectations, some have been permitted to go out of the Fort to Winter, while others are deprived of the benefits of his Majesty's Proclamation which says that the Trade shall be as free for one as for another.[77]

Merchants and traders denied passes by Howard remonstrated. In fact, in mid-November, Johnson forwarded letters from Thomas Walker, another Montreal merchant, to Gage, claiming they "contain[ed] heavy charges against the Conduct & partiality of Captain Howard . . . & insinuating pecuniary Motives for it."[78] Both Gage and Johnson thought Howard was innocent of such charges. Still, his actions put them both in an awkward position, especially as they tried to maintain their "New Method" of trade.[79] An official inquiry took place, and found Howard not guilty.

However, by then the commandant of Michilimackinac had elected to retire from the British military. In late October 1765, Howard wrote to Campbell in Detroit that "bodily Infirmities contracted in the services . . . tendered [him] incapable of commanding any longer."[80] He served until he was replaced in August 1766, returned to England, and died shortly after.

John Askin, as Michilimackinac's deputy commissary, heard the news of Howard's retirement directly. Over the last year, they had worked together to ensure the garrison received adequate supplies and provender. It was a constant struggle, one that rivaled Howard's other diplomatic exertions. As early as October 1764, shortly after arriving at Michilimackinac, Howard contemplated returning to Detroit, worrying that he lacked the provisions to keep the garrison from starving over the winter. Thankfully, the French community offered Howard their excess corn. However, he explained to Campbell that with their present stores he "could support 60 Men till the 15 of May every body Included, at 8 Ounces of Pork, half a Pound of Bread and a Pint of Corn [a] Day." If the supply ship arrived later than May 20, Howard warned, they "must quit the place and the Inhabitants will starve if the corn is not replaced."[81]

On May 31, 1765, Campbell, the commandant of Detroit, informed the commander-in-chief in a letter to Gage in New York that "Capt. Howard has demanded more provisions may be forwarded for his Garrison." As deputy commissary, Askin discovered that the garrison's flour was rotten, and that Michilimackinac had only "rotten Pork" to subsist on.[82] New supplies were forwarded, but five months later, in another letter to Gage, Campbell reported:

> Captain Howard informing me that the provisions (particularly Pork) He formerly Reported to be sufficient to serve his Garison 18 months On Examination finds to be all damaged and unfit to be Issued to the Troops, and if a Supply is not immediately sent him that his Garison will be in want of provision about the middle of Janry.[83]

Yet again, in another effort to forestall the starvation of Howard's men or the abandonment of his post, Campbell organized a dangerous and costly resupply expedition to the north. Shortly after, Askin, no doubt tiring of delivering bad news about provender to his superior, met the five boats "loaded with provisions" by Michilimackinac's wharf, and directed their movement into the storehouse.[84]

During his first year at Michilimackinac, Askin learned that life as an eighteenth-century commissary could be precarious, even during times of plenty. During the summer and fall, for example, supplies forwarded north from Detroit arrived sometimes putrefied or inedible, and expected goods could be lost or pilfered along the far-flung shipping route.[85] Poor packaging and preservation efforts, long chains of custody and inspection that began in faraway Ireland, and simple mishap made most criminal inquiries useless. Difficulties multiplied in the late fall as the temperature dropped in the upper Great Lakes, and the waters became rough and dangerous. Rivers froze over and lakes iced up—especially dangerous to wooden-hulled vessels—occasionally leaving the community secluded from the larger British world. In a journal Askin kept in 1774, he noted that on April 28 the waters surrounding Michilimackinac became "passable in Boats," but a day later, he flatly observed, "Some Ice returned."[86] In the Great Lakes, weather changed quickly; it was one of the few things that could be counted on.

For a few shillings a day, the twenty-five-year-old debtor supervised a tangled web of supply lines that sustained and preserved the isolated garrison.[87] Being in charge of the provisions, Askin quickly learned the names of the three score gruff British soldiers who surrounded him. Every week, these men came to him at the storehouse to collect food for their "messes"—a cluster of six or seven soldiers who organized their daily meals and ate together.[88] Askin doled out their rations. Each day, a soldier was entitled to one to one-and-a-half pounds of flour or bread, half a pound of salt pork (beef was rare in the Great Lakes), a quarter pint of peas, one ounce of butter, and one ounce of rice.[89] He was extra careful in this duty, as the soldiers paid for their own fare. Three-quarters of their eight-pence-a-day wage went to food, and mistakes or malfeasance by the commissary could result in abuse, or much worse. Askin, at their mercy, did not want to cause upset.[90]

However, if trouble did spark, Askin's easy charm, a hallmark of his personality, saw him through most danger and also helped him develop an easy rapport with the roughhewn residents of the garrison and the surrounding French inhabitants.[91] Called "Paddy" by his friends, he was fond of a bawdy joke, a good drink, a friendly jest, and a vigorous dance. He was also a family man.

As early as April 1762, Askin paid fourteen shillings a week for the services of a wet nurse. He recorded the birth of his daughter Catherine "below Albany in May 1762."[92] It seems these records are related. In late September 1765, Askin noted that Charlotte "was born at Michilimackinac." A year later, during a trip back east, Askin records the birth of Marianne at Fort Stanwix on December 12, 1766, and a son named Lewis was born at Detroit on February 14, 1767.[93] Another daughter named Madeleine was born around the same time. According to a family friend, she was "the Daughter of a Pawaneese [*sic*] slave taken in war, by a respectable Merchant [named Askin] near Detroit who has since married a white woman."[94] A boy, John Askin Jr., was also born. He would become a fur trader, British official, and Indian leader. It is impossible to know if they all survived; some disappeared completely from the historical record, but their existence would have made Askin's home a bustling place.

When the 1765 spring thaw came, Askin made his first official visit to Detroit to oversee the transfer of new supplies to Michilimackinac.[95] With a merchant's careful eye, Askin enumerated the number, weight, and variety of cargo (gunpowder, shot, flour, pork, and rum) and loaded the items on a wooden-hulled vessel called the *Victory*.[96] As he prepared the ship for its voyage up the St. Clair River, he encountered a merchant named John Porteous, a Scotsman who also entered the Great Lakes fur trade through New York.

They developed an instant rapport and left Detroit together. They arrived at Michilimackinac in mid-June, with Porteous continuing on to the Odawa village of Arbre Croche.[97] Over the next several years, Askin began showing up in Porteous's journals and letters, and James Sterling, who employed Porteous, soon caught wind of the young commissary. These New York merchants increasingly saw Michilimackinac, the center of the upper Great Lakes fur trade, as vital to their own prosperity. For Porteous and Sterling, Askin could serve as an important new point of contact for their merchandise, and so they brought him into their fold.[98]

In fact, Sterling's letter book during this period showed increased attention to the trade and supply of Michilimackinac and, as a result, its deputy commissary John Askin. Soon after the reestablishment of the British presence in the region, Sterling wrote to John Duncan that he intended to send "an assortment [of goods]" to the post and even received promises from Commodore Patrick Sinclair, the captain of the schooner *Gladwin*, to help. "The first opening of the Trade there will be very valuable," he enthused; "there are vast Quantities of peltry and no goods there."[99] Over the next several months, from November 1764 through February 1765, Sterling ingratiated himself slowly north, first through Sinclair, and then with the help of Michilimackinac's Jacque Philippe Farly, who provided Sterling excellent advice on how to assemble goods for Michilimackinac's fur trade. Likewise, writing to Lieutenant Magill Wallace at Michilimackinac, Sterling promised that he "shall be able to furnish you [with goods] as well, if not better, than any one who may come here."[100]

However, as before Pontiac's War, Sterling saw his efforts stymied by the lack of supplies and inefficient movement of his goods across the Great Lakes. Sterling detested the loss of a potential opportunity or advantage. With the arrival of peace and the opening of the fur trade, competition exploded and New York–connected merchants, men like Sterling, would experience Anglo-French competition from Quebec and Montreal. In fact, many New York merchants supported Sir William Johnson's efforts to constrain the fur trade to established posts like Michilimackinac.[101] Such restrictions, they hoped, would deny French and British traders at Quebec and Montreal their great advantages, namely, the ease of travel and transport of their supplies into the Great Lakes, and their intimate connections and ties of kinship to the Indian communities of the region. Even with restrictions in place, Sterling and his colleagues had to negotiate the growing pains of an increasingly transcontinental fur trade and develop the contacts that would pull them out of the confines of their pre–Seven Years' War trade.

In this context, the first concrete references to Askin enter into Sterling's letter book. An economic relationship with the deputy commissary of Michilimackinac made perfect sense for Sterling, as it would serve as another vital conduit in which to direct supplies and thus profit from the British military. In his first letter to Askin, Sterling was tentative and somewhat awkward. "I don't know whether you chew, smoake, or Snuff," Sterling asked on April 13, 1765, "but I have taken the Liberty to send you a Barrel Tobacco on Board the Gladwin." If Askin did not want it, then he should exchange it for peltry. If that would not do, then he could sell it to Sinclair for his soldiers, or to Howard for the Indians. "In short, you'll do wt. it as you think proper."[102] It is hard not to view this cautious request as a prelude to something more. By early fall, Sterling apologized to Askin for not being able to supply him rum and other requested materials, and treated him as an extension of his own efforts.[103]

Yet, in late September 1765, Porteous arrived at Michilimackinac and delivered a letter Sterling wrote to Askin. In it, Sterling begged the commissary to "come down to [New York] to settle [your] affairs, as there have been many here who complain much against [you]."[104] Some of the creditors even suggested that he should be arrested and carried east. Askin found the letter disturbing, and by the New Year he began keeping "An Account of My Debts & such Effects as I have to Dispose Of."[105] He owed nearly £7,000—a staggering sum for a mere commissary. He lacked the means to come close to repaying his debt.

However, being indebted did not stop Askin from taking stock of the fur trade and the role he could eventually play in it. He realized that French and British merchants and traders would need merchandise as they pushed further inland from the Great Lakes in pursuit of good beaver pelts. Through

Sterling and Porteous, he knew he had the perfect position to supply the needs of the fur trade, but presently, he lacked stable access to adequate capital and the required infrastructure to participate fully. Limited for the time being to Michilimackinac, Askin pursued smaller investments focused on bolstering local productivity, with an eye toward the future. These efforts were especially evident when an old Jesuit farm fell into Askin's hands.

In the late seventeenth century, French Jesuits founded a Roman Catholic mission for the Odawa. Later, in the 1740s, the Jesuits built a farm near their mission at Arbre Croche, on some of the only arable land close to Michilimackinac.[106] Before his captivity, Alexander Henry described the farm as being "situated between the village and the fort" and noted that the Odawa "grow maize for the market of Michilimackinac."[107] During the Seven Years' War, and as Jesuits came under attack across Europe, the order abandoned their mission and the farm fell into disuse. Askin acquired it around 1764.[108] While his means of acquisition remain unknown, Askin became closely associated with the parcel of land. In 1766, Jonathan Carver, a British explorer, published a map noting the location of "Askin's farm."[109]

The farm proved to be a sound investment. In the late eighteenth century, the average diet of a British soldier in the Great Lakes consisted of bread, salt beef or pork, peas, rice, and butter; these rations were issued by their commissary once a week.[110] The bland fare kept the soldiers fed, but its weak nutritional value left them vulnerable to disease. Soldiers who endured a prolonged period without vitamin C, for example, developed lethargy, shortness of breath, bleeding gums, and, at worst, nerve damage or death. Soldiers at frontier garrisons like Michilimackinac, from lowly privates to commissioned officers, looked for ways to supplement their meager diets. They turned to hunting, fishing, maintaining their own gardens and livestock, or bartering with Indian communities. Judging by the diary Askin kept of a later farm at Michilimackinac, he understood the value of this insatiable local market; accordingly, he grew buckwheat, potatoes, oats, parsnips, squash, cucumbers, onions, spinach, peas, and rye.[111] Askin profited from his position as commissary and his role as a farmer by selling to soldiers and officers.

The farm, located near a beautiful and placid crescent lake, would never displace the role of Indian corn in the fur trade, or offer true food security to the garrison of Michilimackinac, but it certainly enhanced Askin's position as deputy commissary and provided him additional security during a period when certain merchants clamored for his arrest.[112] Sterling's letter, delivered in September 1765, had never left his mind. Askin knew he would have to travel to Albany and Schenectady to meet with his creditors. He worked diligently over the winter, taking inventory of his estate with an eye toward an extended journey. He kept his inventory in his memorandum book, and the value of his estate must have looked paltry when set against his tremendous debts. He was busy about this work when, in late January or early February 1766, he, like many others, first heard the news of Michilimackinac's new commandant.

Howard's replacement brought controversy. Both Gage and Johnson were livid: "Where Capt. Howard has charged . . . Hundreds [in expenses]," wrote Gage, "This Man will charge Thousands, unless prevented."[113] In a different letter, Johnson pursued a more diplomatic tone, complaining that the Crown should have "made a better or more adapted appointment."[114] Major Robert Rogers, the new commandant of Michilimackinac, had fled to England in 1765 to escape his debts and prison. In London, he published his journals, wrote a popular play about Pontiac, and, most importantly, used his connections to garner his new appointment in the Great Lakes.[115] Both Gage and Johnson feared giving Rogers free rein of the post, worrying that he would use it for his own private ends, especially as he had both means and motive. "He made a great deal of Money during the War," Gage noted, "which was squandered in Vanity and Gaming, and is some Thousands in Debt here."[116] Together, they coordinated an effort to limit his authority, and hoped that the appointment of "a Deputy Agent for Indian Affairs [at Michilimackinac]" under the direction and orders of Johnson would curtail his ambition. They knew of Rogers's earlier trading efforts while in the king's service, and felt that leaving power in the hands of "himself & Freinds" would prove too tempting.[117]

Gage and Johnson shadowed Rogers's journey across the Great Lakes. Their animosities were born out of the intense rivalries, jealousies, and suspicions that transfixed the British in the late eighteenth century. On January 10, 1766, Gage sent instructions to Rogers, denoting the limitations of his authority at Michilimackinac. "I can't recommend too strongly to you," Gage warned, "the strictest economy in the small expenses that may unavoidably be incurred at this post now put under your command." He required Rogers "to pay the strictest attention and obedience" to Johnson in regards to Indian Affairs at his post.[118] Writing to the superintendent of Indian affairs in early February, Gage promised that "if you find he will not do, that Complaints are made, and that the King's Affairs are going into Confusion, thro' [his] bad management . . . I shall certainly then remove him from Missilimakinak to some other Post, where he can do less Mischeif."[119]

In the summer of 1766, during a flurry of activity, Askin began putting the King's Storehouse in order, and started making lists of the debts he owed and accounts that needed to be settled. On July 27, he created "An Account of My Debts & such Effects as I have to Dispose Of," which revealed sundry debts to French and British merchants and traders at Detroit and Michilimackinac. Askin owed John Porteous and Henry Williams, agents of the New York fur trade in Detroit, the most money: £355 6s. 11d. and £85, respectively.[120] To settle these debts, he was willing to sell his farm and stock for £250, a female Indian slave for £50, a bateau for £6, a silver watch, a canoe, guns, corn, saddle, compass, lace jackets, and books. By liquidating his estate, Askin hoped he could return to New York and negotiate with his major creditors for forbearances and additional loans.

As Askin labored to put his affairs in order, Major Robert Rogers and his wife Elizabeth made their way to Michilimackinac. They arrived on August 10, 1766, and Rogers took command of the garrison. He met Askin soon thereafter to receive the deputy commissary's report on the state of the King's Storehouse. There is no record revealing the exact nature of this first meeting. The former partners seem to have met cordially and without rancor, putting past differences or recriminations aside. In fact, upon learning of Askin's imminent departure, Elizabeth, a clergyman's daughter, pressed him for a favor, asking him to write to her mother and have her send her letters care of Askin.[121]

On August 25, Askin traveled to Michilimackinac and met with Richard Galloway, a sergeant of the garrison, to deliver a "Quantity of Provisions" to feed the troops.[122] For Askin, this was his last official duty as deputy commissary. They walked to the storehouse and, once inside, Askin pointed out the firkins of butter, barrels of salt pork, rice, peas, and biscuit that would feed the soldiers; he left the sergeant alone to take his own account. From there, he went to find William Maxwell, a trader and British soldier. When he found his fellow Irishman, Askin presented Maxwell with the keys to the King's Storehouse.

No longer encumbered by official duties, Askin turned his attention to getting his family and luggage on a ship bound for Detroit. He watched as laborers carried his three large trunks, two smaller trunks, and one case onto the ship. On the strand, waiting for his family, Askin checked the gun he carried and fiddled with his new and fashionable swordstick, a walking cane that concealed a long, thin, blade.[123] The clatter of wagon wheels, the thud of hoofbeats, and the joyous noise of people calling his name drew his attention, and Askin saw his family arrive. He led them aboard the ship, smiling, talking, and soothing the fears of his youngest children. Strong winds bore them south over the blue waters of Lake Huron, leaving Michilimackinac behind for nearly a year.

Once disembarked, Askin and his family enjoyed Detroit for several months as he settled his business and took pleasure in the hospitality of its merchant community. Throughout snowy November, Askin and James Sterling met and discussed the state of the fur trade and their plans for the future, and, no doubt, considered what waited for Askin in New York.[124] Before setting off, Askin left some of his luggage in the care of Hyacinthe Reaume, an old French cobbler and fur trader, and then, by boat, the family embarked for Fort Niagara.[125] Their journey ended in early February 1767, at which point Askin and his family settled into a Schenectady home. As he had so many times before, Askin began preparing another accounting of his debts for his creditors: Greg & Cunningham, Hymen Levy, Henry Agnew, Kennedy & Lyle, Abraham Douw, and the many others.[126]

On February 24, Askin stayed up late, working in the quiet of his house. When all was reconciled, Askin wrote that the "amt. of all I owe I believe to be . . . £6948 2s 91/2d."[127] He stoked the dying fire and made his way to bed. The years between 1764 and 1767 had been far from prosperous. Askin had been fortunate to be deputy commissary at Michilimackinac even as the Crown struggled to bring peace, prosperity, and order to the Great Lakes. Now, as he stood poised on the cusp of settling his debts, he had a chance to rehabilitate his reputation and establish himself as a prominent middleman. Drifting slowly to sleep, he imagined himself back at Michilimackinac, engaged in the fur trade. Then, rolling over, he imagined something worse: recalcitrant creditors, the walls of a debtor's prison. He fell asleep knowing that, one way or another, tomorrow, everything would change.

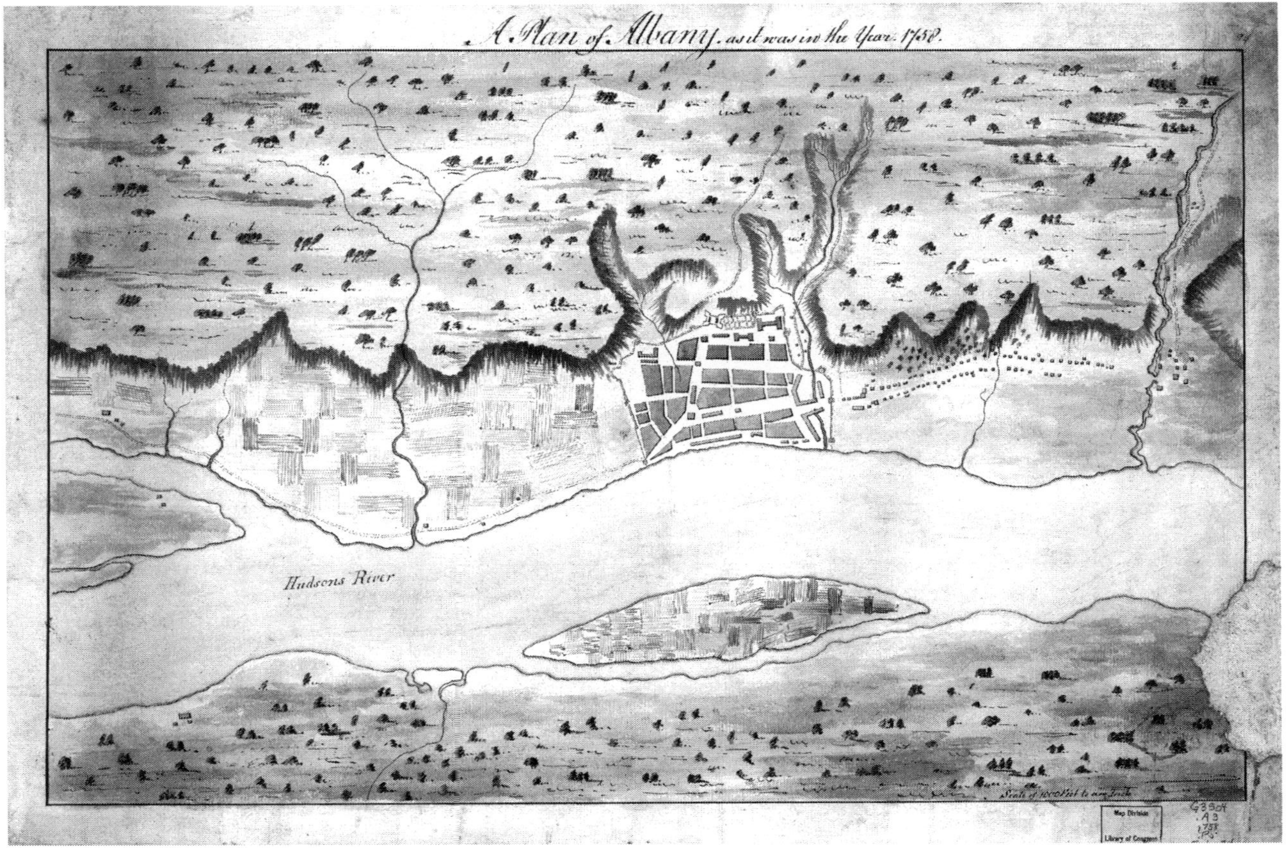

"A Plan of Albany, as it was in the year 1758."

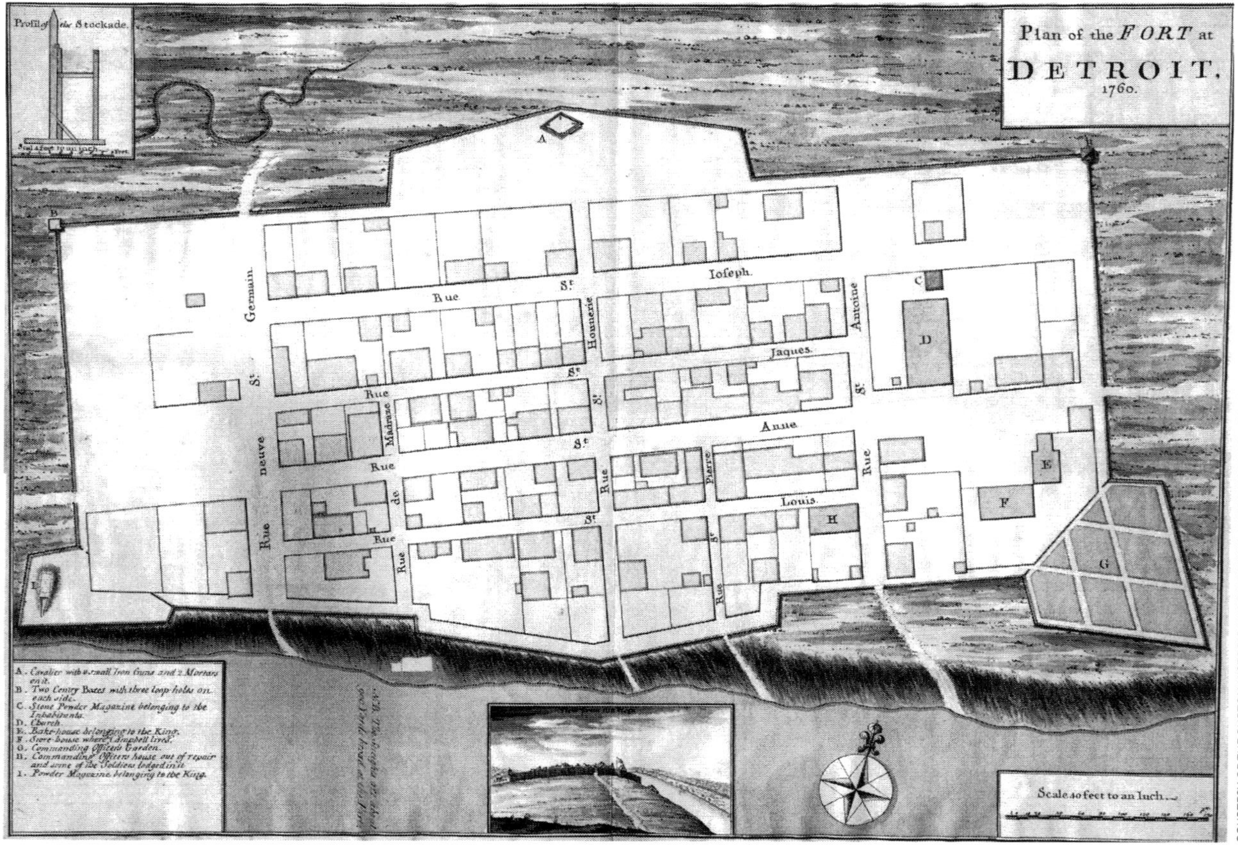

"Plan of the Fort at Detroit, 1760."

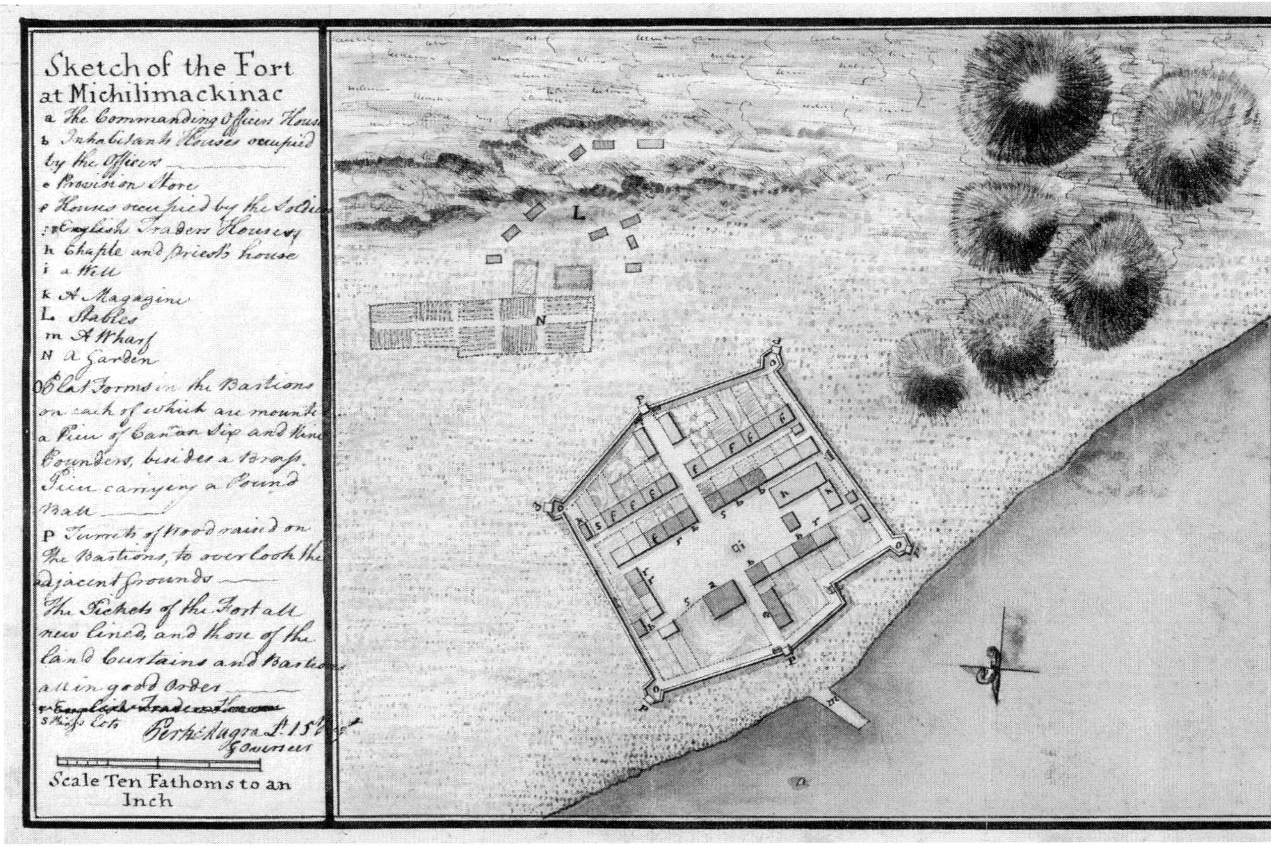

Lieutenant Perkins Magra, "Sketch of the Fort at Michilimackinac, 1765."

Sir William Johnson.

General Thomas Gage.

Major Robert Rogers.

COURTESY OF THE BURTON HISTORICAL COLLECTION, DETROIT PUBLIC LIBRARY.

Major Arent Schuyler de Peyster.

COURTESY OF MACKINAC STATE HISTORIC PARKS COLLECTION.

Merchants' Commemoration of de Peyster's Service at Michilimackinac.

CHAPTER THREE

Sound as a Roach and as Full of Intrigue

Michilimackinac, the Hudson's Bay Company, and John Askin's Fur Trade, 1767–1774

In March 1767, winter began to abate. It still snowed, but after each fall the white melted away into runoffs that pooled in shallows, giving the drowned landscape a look of desolation. As spring came, John Porteous, a western agent for the New York trading concern of Phyn, Ellice, and Company, worried about his friend, "poor [John] Askin."[1] The erstwhile deputy commissary of Michilimackinac had traveled east to settle his affairs and debts, but was having a difficult time of it. In particular, he struggled to satisfy the obstinate demands of a man named Abraham Douw, a long-established Dutch ship captain and merchant from Albany with durable connections to Sir William Johnson.[2] Porteous complained:

> I'm much concern'd about poor Askin who has been here these two weeks, but cannot bring his affairs to bear[;] this Douw has been very Crusty to him when he came down & gave him several reasons to Suspect his laying a Snare for him which has made him keep here ever Since, he has tried various methods to enduce Mr. Douw to come into reasonable terms but all are hitherto vain.[3]

It seems fitting that Douw would prove intransigent. Seduced by Major Robert Rogers's tale of the mountains of furs at Detroit in the heady days of 1760, he invested deeply in the partnership of Askin, Rogers, and Gordon, and after Pontiac's War he watched as they returned from Niagara empty-handed. Now, Askin was back, and Douw wanted to extract payment and achieve satisfaction.

It is hard to imagine what Askin thought when confronted by the pig-headedness of his previous investor. Certainly, he did not expect any kind of approbation, but the idea that Douw would stand in his way must have been galling; his return to New York had been arduous, and now, during meeting after meeting, he had to deal with onerous and seemingly endless negotiations. According to Porteous, Douw demanded preferential treatment that came "at the expence of the other Creditors." Askin refused.

After several weeks of intense encounters, Askin finally resolved his disputes with his New York creditors, and James Sterling and John Porteous paved the way toward his reentry into the British fur trade. Both men worked for Phyn, Ellice, and Company, which began operation at the end of the Seven Years' War with the activity of John Duncan, an established British merchant, who attempted to construct a storehouse at Niagara.[4] Pontiac's War and the complaints of Albany merchants, who claimed that the structure gave him an unfair advantage, hindered Duncan's efforts. Undeterred, in 1764 he formed a partnership with James Sterling and supplied the Detroit-based merchant merchandise to be exchanged for furs. Within a year, Sterling engaged Porteous to serve as his clerk, tasking him to travel to fur trade posts like Michilimackinac to sell goods, buy furs, and collect debts. However, forced to compete with French and British merchants from Montreal and Quebec, whose placement on the St. Lawrence River provided easier access to the upper Great Lakes and its bountiful supply of furs, Duncan lacked the capital to finance any significant expansion. By 1767, Duncan prepared to retire from the fur trade. His partnership with Scottish merchants James Phyn and Alexander Ellice provided the funds to build an expansive trans–North American fur trade consortium based in New York. Sterling and Porteous, who had already begun to move supplies and engage the Lake Superior trade through Askin as early as 1765, saw a significant role for him.

Eventually this opportunity led to Askin's economic rehabilitation and his growth into an important Great Lakes middleman, a role he played during the late 1760s and early 1770s in the development of what would eventually become the North West Company. The slow collapse of Sir William Johnson's and General Thomas Gage's fur trade and Indian policies corresponded with Askin's financial ascendency in trade. In a letter to Henry Seymour Conway, the British secretary of state for the Northern Department, Johnson summed up the troubled state of the British Great Lakes. "The weakness of the power of Governt," he complained, "the disorders amongst the people, the present extent & sentiments of our Indian Allies, and the want of powers in my Commission" made it impossible for him and many others to serve the British Crown in an effective or efficient manner.[5] However, for the "low designing Traders" Johnson and Gage so often reviled, these developments were for the better—and especially so for Askin.[6]

With a surer economic footing, Askin stood poised to participate and exploit the unpredictable world of the Great Lakes. Great Britain's reassessment of its western policies resulted in a chaotic lull that provoked a tremendous surge of economic activity, legitimate or otherwise. Trading consortiums at Montreal and Albany competed against each other and worked to develop new connections and points of contact within western posts. During the late 1760s, Askin built upon his tremendous experience as a sutler and commissary to serve as a middleman for an extensive multiethnic trading partnership geared toward exploiting the fur-rich regions above Lake Superior.

Phyn, Ellice, and Company, with its shifting partners and numerous associates, was typical of the fur trade toward the end of the eighteenth century and played a vital role in relocating Askin in the wider world of the Great Lakes fur trade. Formal and informal relationships helped characterize a complex and circuitous network of exchange that tied Indian hunters, French traders, British intermediaries, large-scale wholesalers, and London-based financiers into relationships defined by mutual obligation.[7] Stationed at

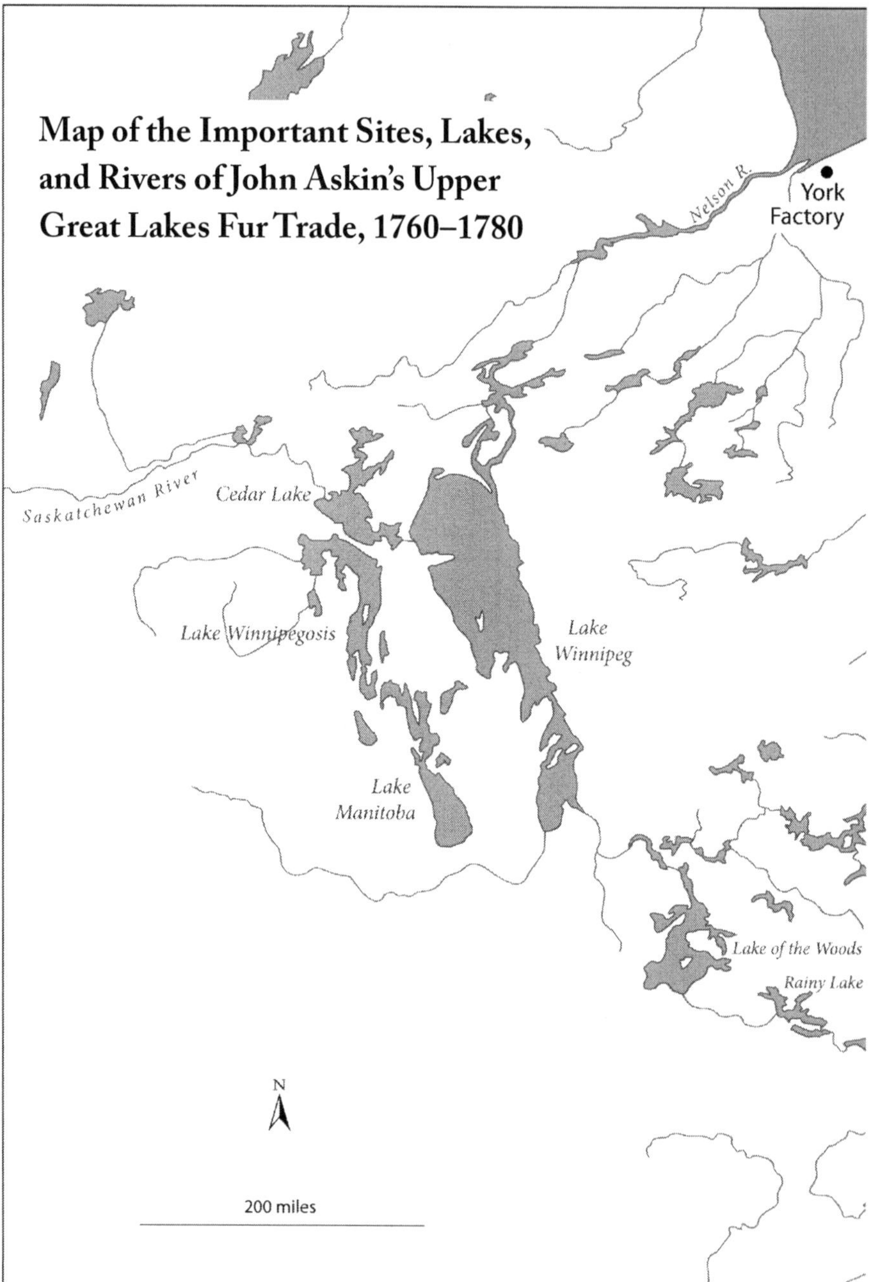
Map of the Important Sites, Lakes, and Rivers of John Askin's Upper Great Lakes Fur Trade, 1760–1780
Nelson R.
York Factory
Saskatchewan River
Cedar Lake
Lake Winnipegosis
Lake Winnipeg
Lake Manitoba
Lake of the Woods
Rainy Lake
N
200 miles

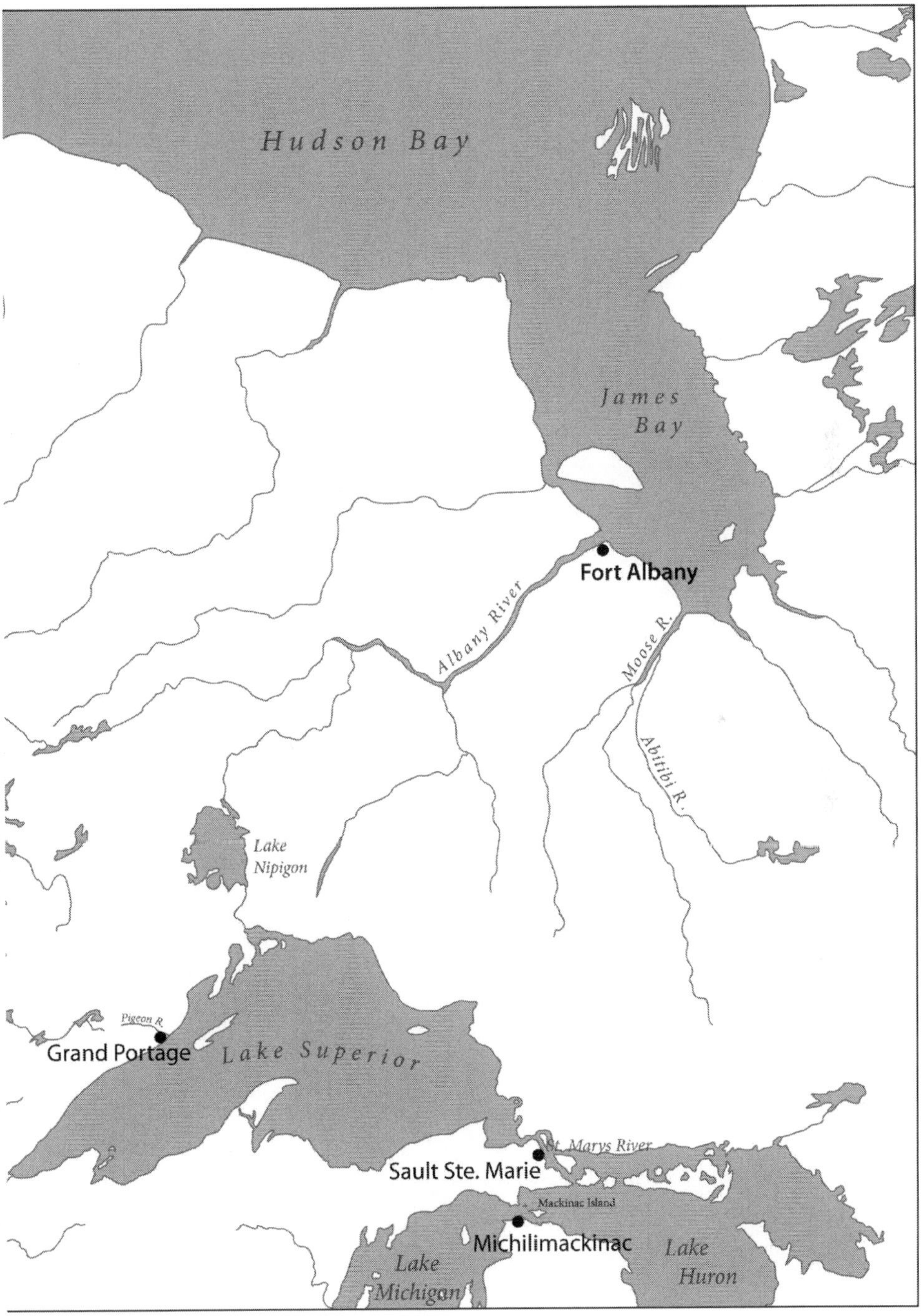
Hudson Bay
James Bay
Fort Albany
Albany River
Moose R.
Abitibi R.
Lake Nipigon
Pigeon R.
Grand Portage
Lake Superior
St. Marys River
Sault Ste. Marie
Mackinac Island
Michilimackinac
Lake Michigan
Lake Huron

E. WHITE

influential posts, middlemen forwarded goods to traders in the northwest, collected their returning furs, and shipped them east toward the marketplaces of Europe. In the contemporary parlance, they were jacks-of-all-trades: buyers and sellers, inspectors and appraisers, packers and shippers, as well as credit lenders and bill collectors, whose intimate knowledge of the local political, social, and economic landscapes ensured the trade functioned.[8] With the trade expanding further northwest, such men became increasingly important under the British regime as they coordinated the laborious and fraught exchange process. It could often take years for an investment to see a return, during which period political or economic developments in Detroit, Montreal, New York, or London could turn a lucrative venture into a disastrous one, as Askin could certainly attest.

Most fur trade transactions existed as a series of debits and credits within some middleman's ledger book. Large-scale trading consortiums at Montreal or Albany, like Phyn, Ellice, and Company, imported large quantities of manufactures and textiles from the developing industrial centers of Great Britain and Europe, generally under the condition that wholesalers would collect a percentage from every item sold in North America.[9] Before early summer saw the return of French and British traders and Indian hunters and trappers from their trading posts or winter hunting grounds, middlemen at western posts purchased yearly "outfits," a large collection of assorted goods, on credit with fixed interest from the larger partnerships.[10] French labor, contracted and insured by the middleman, shipped the supplies up the St. Lawrence and across the choppy waters of the Great Lakes, or carried them through the Ottawa River, Lake Nipissing, the French River, and into Georgian Bay. Upon the arrival of the goods-laden canoes, the middleman further separated the shipments into smaller, individual allotments.

In this way, Alexander Henry, after his captivity among the Ojibwa and his return to Michilimackinac in 1764, secured a supply of merchandise on credit for twelve months from an established merchant, allowing him to hire a crew of laborers and winter among the Ojibwa community of Chequamegon, on the southern shore of Lake Superior.[11] Luckily for Henry, he developed a relationship with a Frenchman named Jean-Baptiste Cadot, who helped clear the path for the British merchant to trade among the Ojibwa.[12]

Cadot, born in 1723, came to the upper Great Lakes—to Michilimackinac and Sault Ste. Marie—in the 1740s as an engagé.[13] Soon after, he married Athanaise, a relative of the influential Ojibwa chief Madjeckewiss, and together they raised a family. By the end of the Seven Years' War, his position among the Ojibwa had grown considerably, and from his farm at Sault Ste. Marie Cadot sought to smooth tensions between his kin and the newly arrived British garrisons. In this capacity, he befriended Alexander Henry. Following a fire at Sault Ste. Marie in the winter, they transported the burned commander of the British garrison, Lieutenant John Jamet, down to Michilimackinac. After Pontiac's War and Henry's redemption, Cadot, who was now a point man for the British military and Indian Department with a strong rapport with Howard, Johnson, and Rogers, partnered with Henry in 1765. In fact, Cadot was instrumental in convincing Howard to hand out passes to French and British traders and merchants, and he and Henry were among the very first to take advantage.

At Chequamegon, Henry found the Ojibwa impoverished by the disruptive violence of successive wars, which had cut off their access to both French and British merchandise. Henry, invited to a council meeting, commented that "the men [of the village] declared that unless their demands were complied with their wives and children would perish; for that there were neither ammunition nor clothing left among them."[14] Though desperate for supplies, the Ojibwa were far from bound to Henry and his terms, as they provided the extractive labor that made the fur trade workable and his efforts profitable. Additionally, more than a century of participation in the transatlantic economy had made them savvy and demanding consumers. A successful trader tried to anticipate their needs and, more importantly, their wants, or he faced the ruin of unexchanged goods. At Michilimackinac, Henry carefully purchased black ceremonial shrouds, colorful blankets, calico shirts, chintz shawls, petticoats, broaches, strong needles, thimbles, rum, brandy, trade guns, gunpowder, gunshot, scalping knives, fishhooks, hatchets, copper kettles, and numerous other manufactures desired by the Ojibwa men and women.[15] Desperate to establish a trading relationship, Henry advanced community goods equating to three thousand beaver skins, and settled in a "comfortable house," as the Indians traveled to Fond du Lac, where they would hunt and trap throughout the Great Lakes' long winter.[16]

Warmed by the flame of his winter fire, Henry dreamed of spring and hoped the Ojibwa would return in the coming icy months of the new year laden with enough pelts to cover the supplies, credit, and interest he had advanced; his own reputation and economic success depended on it. At Chequamegon, he carried the compounding expectations of the middlemen, merchants, wholesalers, and financiers who relied upon his efforts, and the efforts of many like him, to prosper and persist. They found the proof of his achievement in the furs he collected and the low-riding canoes that carried them back toward Michilimackinac.

That ambitious and connected men like Henry and Cadot now had access to both British credit and the Indian communities of the upper Great Lakes impressed upon Askin the need to follow suit. In the spring of 1767, the season's first furs began to arrive at Albany and Schenectady, and Askin prepared to leave northern New York. In his archive and papers, he left no account of the negotiations he held with his creditors, or how he satisfied the demands of Douw, but he managed to settle temporarily.[17] In fact, two years later, in March 1769, he secured an agreement and license from his creditors to pursue his trade for twelve months without fear of "Trouble, . . . wrong, Damage or Hindrance" being done to "his Body, Goods, or Chattles."[18] It seems likely that he left Albany and Schenectady in March with a similar short-term agreement. His debts continued and, certainly, he still had to repay them, but now he possessed some means to do so. New lines of credit and new sources of merchandise made him an attractive middleman, and his experience attuned him to the special difficulties of exchanging furs and moving supplies so far north.[19] Askin's return to Michilimackinac marked the beginning of a personal period of furious economic investment and social development that continued unabated until the end of the colonial rebellion, attesting to the success of his New York negotiations and his ambitious vision of the British fur trade.

Indeed, the letter book of John Porteous sheds some light on Askin's activity during the summer of 1767, revealing his continual engagement with the rum and liquor trade and his willingness to use it as his reentry point into the Great Lakes' fur trade. It seems that Askin left New York with the expectation of receiving a large order of New England rum. For example, in an August letter to Robert Ellice, the younger brother of Alexander, John Porteous upbraided him for "not taking care to forward Mr. Askins things to Fort Erie he has not a worth about them since they left your place."[20] Later, on September 27, Porteous wrote to Askin that his goods had arrived in Detroit. He took special care to explain to Askin the care that went into securing his spirits from theft and leakage. That Askin would turn to rum and spirits during the period directly after his rehabilitation is far from unique, and demonstrates the degree to which the liquor trade policies and restrictions proposed by General Thomas Gage and Sir William Johnson after Pontiac's War proved unsuccessful in face of British, French, and Indigenous demands. That Askin and his rum would get caught up in the summer of 1767 in a larger imperial controversy at Michilimackinac, one that threatened the authority of both the fort's commandant, Major Robert Rogers, and Benjamin Roberts, one of Johnson's Indian commissaries, would have been less unique and harder to imagine.[21]

Major Robert Rogers arrived at Michilimackinac on August 10, 1766, and went to work. "The Indians," the commandant wrote to Johnson, "have mostly all visited me, and it gives me no small Concern that I have been under an unavoidable necessity of giving them so much." Like Howard before him, Rogers had to contend with the lingering effects of Pontiac's War and the unwillingness of the British to bear the true cost of maintaining peaceful relationships with the Indians of the upper Great Lakes. He borrowed from local Michilimackinac merchants to finance his diplomatic efforts; he sent his accounts to Johnson with the hope Johnson would "excuse the larg[e]ness" of it.[22] By mid-September, Rogers organized an expensive expedition to the northwest to search for the elusive and mythic Northwest Passage to the Pacific Ocean.[23] Just one month later, Lieutenant Christian Daniel Claus, an agent for the Indian Department, wrote to Johnson that the new commandant "gave a general permit to all Traders to go wintering, for which he is vastly liked and applauded."[24] By November, as winter settled in, and the winds buffeted the fort with ice and snow, Rogers oversaw what he called "a peaceable Garrison" and maintained "a good understanding with the Indians."[25] His experiences during the Seven Years' War, both as a successful ranger and a frontier diplomat, proved invaluable, helping him navigate the complicated interconnections between the fur trade and Indian country.

Rogers hoped that these earlier efforts had helped set the stage for the opening of the Great Lakes fur trade and the establishment of a new civilian government at Michilimackinac. He had begun to conceive of a plan of action for the Great Lakes that would challenge the assumptions that underwrote Johnson's and Gage's Indian and fur trade policies. Namely, he argued against efforts to confine trade and traders to centralized posts, claiming distance alone kept the "Indians from the West of Lake Michigan or from the South and West of Lake Superior" from trading with Michilimackinac. He estimated that the British would "Lose the Trade of near thirty Thousand Indians" and drive them into the hands of the French and Spanish empires if the restrictions continued. Beyond "greatly curtail[ing] & lessen[ing] our Trade," denying Indians a constant supply of merchandise further risked "exciting [their] Enmity rage and brutal Revenge," thus repeating the violence and disruption of Pontiac's War. Rhetorically, Rogers asked if Michilimackinac "is not the largest Channal of the Furr and Peltery Trade in North America?" and "Ought not the Government to pay a particular Attention to that Post upon which the Security of an immense Teritory and a most profitable Trade so greatly depends?" Rogers saw the value of acting as the French acted, and engaging the Indians on their own terms, especially those "long accustomed to expect Traders Annually with Supplies in their respective Countries."[26]

Rogers sent his plan directly to London, over the heads of both Johnson and Gage, and his efforts represented a broadside to their fur trade policies. In fact, upon hearing of Rogers's efforts, Johnson wrote to Lord Shelburne, the secretary of state, calling the commander of Michilimackinac "a needy man, of bad circumstances, and worse principles."[27] But little did Johnson know that circumstances at Michilimackinac would do more to undermine Rogers's efforts in the Great Lakes than a hostile letter to a British official could ever accomplish.

Meanwhile, cost proved to be the overriding flaw in Rogers's fur trade proposal and current administration of Michilimackinac. In trying to maintain peace between the various Indian communities of the Great Lakes, the commandant planned to bring representatives to the post every year, and through gifts and reciprocity forge peace and economic prosperity in the region. This required gifts and between August 10, 1766, and July 3, 1767; Rogers borrowed tremendously to achieve his aims. For example, the principal merchants and traders of Michilimackinac—men such as Stephen Groesbeck, John Farrell, Gershon Levy, George McDougall, William Bruce, James Sterling, as well as Askin—lent Rogers £5,792 5s. NYC. This extraordinary sum went to Indian presents. Other expenses, including the cost of flour and meat, wood, a bateau, and barrack and fort repairs, amounted to an additional £856 3s. 4d.[28] Soon the merchants would demand repayment, and Rogers's drafts would come before Gage and Johnson for final approval—and they would see how far he had strayed from their original orders.

"You will be so good," Gage wrote to Johnson in May 1767, "when the [new Indian] commissary gets to Missilimakinak, to [have him] acquaint Major Rogers to incur no more espences."[29] A former lieutenant in the military, Benjamin Roberts traveled west with specific orders and duties as an Indian commissary. A year earlier, in January 1766, Johnson wrote to Gage about the necessity of employing an Indian commissary at Michilimackinac "under the Superintendent & bound by his Orders . . . and oblidged to transmit regular Reports from time to time of all Transactions" as a way of limiting Rogers's authority.[30] Indian commissaries, a prominent aspect of Johnson's and Gage's fur trade policy, were tasked with "the entire Management of Trade, & Indian Affairs."[31] In fact, men like Roberts exercised tremendous authority over traders, smiths, and interpreters, as well as over Indian diplomacy and the liquor trade.

However, the relationship between the military commandants of the western British posts and these new Indian commissaries proved fraught. In fact, in October 1766, before traveling to Michilimackinac, Roberts was the Indian commissary of Niagara; in a very patient letter to Captain John Brown, whom Roberts had quarreled with, Johnson admitted, "I am not ignorant of ye. Difficultys under which both labour" but pointed to "his Majestys Intentions" and "letters . . . from the Lords of Trade" and stressed the need that commandants and commissaries had to work in concert or risk "the Whole Plan defeated."[32] Roberts carried to Michilimackinac a long and storied legacy of quarreling with post commanders. He arrived in early July 1767 to see thousands of Indians from across the Great Lakes camped along the sandy beachfront outside the weather-beaten stockade.

For several weeks, Rogers had been working to establish peaceful relationships with the communities of the upper Great Lakes, taking council with representatives from the Sauk, Fox, Ho-Chunk, Ojibwa, Odawa, Potawatomi, and Sioux. "I was no Stranger," Rogers said to the assembled headmen, "to the unhappy differences between the Chippewas and Western Indians and to the Attempts that had been made to draw others into the Quarrel." He urged them to resist the overtures and "the perfidious Conduct of the French and Spanish traders" along the Mississippi River, and promised to send traders among them to supply their needs.[33] Removing hostilities, reaffirming friendships, and establishing new bonds required the giving of gifts, and so Rogers borrowed nearly £500 from local traders.[34] "Clearing the Path & Brightening the Chain of Peace" was a costly endeavor, and Rogers risked official condemnation to establish the security of his post and the prosperity of its fur trade.[35] Sidelined, Roberts walked among the crowds and took note of the gifts being passed out.

After the council concluded, Rogers gave the new Indian commissary his "Journal of Indian Affairs," and asked him to send it to Johnson. He hoped his "Accounts passed with the General [Gage], that the Persons I had the Goods of may Receive their pay."[36] Instead, Roberts mocked Rogers in his letter to Johnson, writing: "perhaps you can decypher [it. Some] of us were puzzle[d] about what Language it is Hebrew or Arabac."[37] Throughout July, Rogers and Roberts maintained an uneasy peace, especially as they struggled with the ambiguity of their commands and their own domineering personalities.

On August 19, long-simmering tensions erupted. In the gloom of dusk, one of Rogers's men helped load "40 to 42 Kegs" of rum onto the deck of a small transport, and hid the liquor on an island across from Michilimackinac.[38]

The following day, Roberts, on the lookout for smuggling, had the cargo seized and returned to the post, where, on the sandy beach of Lake Huron, Rogers had him arrested and "Carried Like a C[riminal through] the Fort Guarded by Soldiers with f[ixed bayonets] and Cast into his House."[39] It had begun as an argument over who held jurisdiction over the rum, but devolved into bitter recrimination and posturing of rank and authority. Humiliated in front of the entire community, Roberts smoldered with rage, and fired off a letter to Captain Frederick Spiesmacher, Rogers's second in command, claiming the commandant of Michilimackinac held "Secret Correspondance with the Enimies of Great Brittain, & forming Conspiracies."[40]

In the quiet of midnight, Roberts, still locked in his room, wrote a short letter to Daniel Claus, Johnson's son-in-law, explaining why he had proved so adamant about trying to take charge of the contraband rum from Rogers and keeping it out of the king's own storehouse. Roberts feared the deep-seated corruption of the past and present deputy commissaries at Michilimackinac and their collusion with Rogers. "Some [of the kegs]," Roberts wrote in his letter to Claus, "might be proved belong to Mr. Maxwell[,] Others to Mr. Askin."[41] With the ink dried, and the wax set and sealed, Roberts waited for the morning to come to again confront Rogers.

Once again, rum proved potentially problematic for Askin, and while the former deputy commissary was away from the fort, comfortably ensconced at his farm, it is unlikely he imagined himself so easily implemented in the growing quarrel between Rogers and Roberts. It is telling, though, and perhaps indicative of a close relationship between Rogers, Maxwell, and Askin, that Roberts would so easily cluster them together as conspirators. Moreover, given Askin's career-long association with the rum and liquor trade, it is just as likely that some of the more unsavory aspects of his reputation preceded him, and Roberts, finding contraband, easily could have imagined Askin's helping hand in it. Regardless of how Roberts came about his suspicions, Askin became tangentially connected to one of the most controversial episodes in the history of British Michilimackinac.

The following day, Roberts sent the letter on its way toward Albany and Schenectady. Soon its content would be known by the merchants, traders, and officials that Askin had spent months negotiating with to secure his reentry into the fur trade. News of possible fraud and the accusation of smuggling could upset his efforts before they even took shape. On the morning of April 22, Askin traveled from his family farm by the village of Arbre Croche to the confines of Michilimackinac to serve on an official court of inquiry. Sitting alongside prominent traders including John Porteous, Benjamin Frobisher, members of the far-flung Chevalier family, and William Maxwell, Askin heard the events of the proceeding days recounted in detail by an irate Benjamin Roberts.[42] His participation in the council suggests both a growing stature and regard at Michilimackinac, yet little did Askin know of Roberts's recriminations or the way he connected Askin to Major Rogers.

Over the next several days, tempers cooled. The commandant and the Indian commissary apologized to each other and, for a while, the post returned to an uneasy peace. For Rogers, though, the respite proved short-lived. In late August the expedition he had organized to search for the Northwest Passage returned to Michilimackinac, destitute and empty-handed. They had given out all of their merchandise, but brought back no peltry. Rogers had borrowed a tremendous sum of money to finance the venture, and profited nothing from the risk. Compounding his escalating debt, neither Gage nor Johnson seemed compelled to pay his wage or even honor his official accounts. The weight rested heavily on his shoulders.

In mid-September, Roberts approached Rogers and asked if he could use the post's only forge for the Indian Department. The commandant agreed, but only permitted a few days' use. Roberts then demanded permanent ownership. A few days later, on September 22, Captain Spiesmacher wrote plaintively to Johnson: "I am sorry to inform You that Majr. Rogers has again Confin[e]d Mr. Roberts and is Determen'd to Sen[d] him from [Michilimackinac]." The argument turned rancorous when Roberts sought "to lessen [the commandant's] Athorety, by telling him on the publike Parade, that he did not look on him as his Commanding officer, nor would [obey] orders of his."[43] In early October, Roberts left the post and traveled south for Detroit, and reiterated to any of those who would listen that Rogers was traitorous and unfit for command.

Meanwhile, in New York, Johnson and Gage read the deposition of Nathaniel Potter, Rogers's personal secretary, testifying about conversations he had with his former employer and the acrimonious dissolution of their relationship. "In July," Potter testified, "Major Rogers had a private conversation . . . in which he explained his designs . . . [and] said he was much in debt to several Traders whom he was unable to pay and that this gave him great uneasiness." According to Potter, Rogers spoke of his grand designs for Michilimackinac, and promised that if they were denied, he would "retire to the French towards the Mississip[p]i and enter into the[ir] Service." He planned to profit from them by "stir[ring] up the Indians against the English." When Potter expressed outrage over the plan and refused to discuss the idea further, Rogers "flew into a violent passion and swore that he wou'd never pay [him] a farthing" and "kill him" to keep him quiet.[44] Potter's testimony and a letter written to Roberts by an Englishman in French service sealed Rogers's fate. Later, under further scrutiny, Potter's allegations proved suspect, potentially motivated by unpaid wages and conversations with Benjamin Roberts.[45] But in early November, Gage wrote to Johnson that "It is not Necessary to say more about Major Rogers," and sent a warrant west to arrest Rogers.[46] Captain Spiesmacher directed soldiers from the garrison across the snow-covered parade grounds of the fort, and placed Rogers, their former commandant, under arrest.

Spiesmacher chained and confined Rogers in December 1767. It seems that during this period Askin often visited the newly confined commandant and his wife, Elizabeth. Later, during Rogers's trial at Montreal in October 1768, Joseph Ainsse, a fur trader and interpreter, recalled visiting Rogers and seeing "one [John] Askins" and being told by the major that "he was glad to see [Askin]," but worried that "Captain Spiesmacher might suspect some mischief to be hatching" if Askin visited more than "once or twice a Week."[47] Their conversations were friendly and open; their length and candor were consistent and sympathetic to the point of causing serious suspicion.

Indeed, Askin's visits went beyond the social: they centered on gaining executive control over Rogers's property, and he may even have gone so far as to enlist the help of Ensign Robert Johnston, a soldier in the garrison with access to the imprisoned, in his plans.[48] Considering the amount of credit the merchants of Michilimackinac extended Rogers during his tenure as commandant, many creditors demanded access to his property as a means of potential repayment, but Askin went above and beyond the others with the hopes of getting his £1,500 loan repaid first.[49] Allied with Stephen Groesbeck, an Albany-based trader whom Rogers also owed a sizable sum, Askin and Groesbeck illicitly gained, perhaps with the help of Ensign Johnston, written authority to sell Rogers's effects to pay off his debts.[50] Both men, according to Spiesmacher, "[Rogers's] two principal creditors," recouped their losses, and through sale of property were able to cover some of the paper script Rogers used to pay the soldiers of the garrison.[51] During the winter of 1767 and the spring of 1768, Askin traveled back and forth from his farm to the fort and pondered how close he came to being caught in Rogers's mire yet again.

As Rogers quarreled with Roberts in the fall of 1767, Askin penned a letter to Johnson. "I thought it my duty," he wrote, "not only to Justify myself to you, but also to present my living there being look'd upon either detrimental to the Public or Trade."[52] Askin heard of Roberts's accusation, perhaps from Roberts himself, who, a day earlier, wrote a letter to Daniel Claus clearing Askin of any wrongdoing in the rum-smuggling affair.[53] "For should any Malicious means be taken to remove me from [Michilimackinac]," Askin wrote, "it would not only very much hurt my Circumstances, but [put] it out of my Power hereafter to do Justice [to my] Creditors."[54] In the spring of 1768, with Rogers and Roberts gone, and Captain Howard across the Atlantic never to return, Askin witnessed firsthand, and at times tangentially, the vagaries and vulnerabilities of British officials in the upper Great Lakes. Charges of corruption, favoritism, and greed leveled by a consortium of self-interested French and British traders and merchants constrained Howard, while clashes of personality, petty jealousies, and imperial politicking resulted in Rogers's arrest for treason. Cleared in Montreal of treason, but mired in debt, Rogers returned to London and, suffering from alcoholism, died alone in 1795, alienated from his wife and child.[55] In later years, during the colonial rebellion, Askin would have reason to think back on these events and consider the lessons they might have offered, but, in the interim, he felt very lucky that Rogers's fall did not carry him down as well.

For Askin and his fellow fur traders and merchants, as disruptive as Rogers's command of Michilimackinac was, it corresponded to the functional end of Johnson's and Gage's fur trade policy efforts. On August 7, 1768, Gage wrote to Johnson that in London "The Noise and Complaints of Indian Expences have been so great, that the Reform made in that Department does not surprise." During this period, Parliament continued to struggle with the tremendous debt accrued during the Seven Years' War, and colonial efforts to resist paying imperial expenses shifted the burden and cost of regulating the fur trade away from North America. In response, Parliament devolved control over the trade back to the governments of each colony and gutted the core of Johnson's and Gage's efforts. "The only Posts now to be maintained are Missilimackinac, Detroit, & Niagara with Forts Pitt and Chartres," Gage reported, and noted, "The two last yet under Consideration whether to be abandoned or not." Gage further reminded Johnson that "The Commissarys for the Trade ought certainly to be removed, as soon as the Service will permit." After years of trying to control and regulate the activities of French and British traders and merchants, Gage wiped his hands of them: "They are a vile Race, and we shall see soon how finely the Provinces will manage them."[56]

Freed in the short term from the caustic effects of his debts and no longer restrained by the remaining vestiges of Gage, Johnson, and the imperial plan, Askin turned his attention beyond Michilimackinac to the lands above Lake Superior, where the Hayes River flowed north to eventually join Hudson's Bay. Not far from the river's mouth, near the estuary where fresh water became salty and pods of beluga whales sometimes ventured to play, stood York Factory, a palisaded outpost of the great trading concern of the Hudson's Bay Company.[57] Built in the early eighteenth century, the fort had developed a bowed and bent aspect, as the shifts and swells of permafrost forced its timber structure into awkward angles, requiring frequent repairs. Still, in late spring, as saws cut timber into broad boards and heavy hammers rang, Indian hunters and trappers came downriver, their canoes heavy with pelts; they camped along the riverbanks, ready to exchange. For all involved, York was a place of economic prosperity, and with British victory during the Seven Years' War, many members of the Hudson's Bay Company believed its wealth would only grow larger. Then, from the south, trespassers—men like Askin—came with goods and stayed to trade.

In late August 1772, Andrew Graham, a Scotsman by birth and master fur trader of York Factory, wrote to the principal men of the Hudson's Bay Company, relaying some very troubling news. "Your Trade at York Fort & Severn is greatly diminished," he wrote, and "the Keskochewan [Saskatchewan] Indians Who are the Support of it [are] being intercepted by the Canadian Pedlars."[58] These interlopers had built their trading houses inland, closer to where "the whole body of the Natives build their Canoes." The Indians soon learned they could "Purchase Ammunition & other Articles" and "procure Tobacco & other Necessarys so near." They exchanged their best pelts with the southern traders, and then carried "the refuse" north to the bay. Poorer-grade furs meant poorer profits, forcing Graham to investigate. From a disgruntled workhand he learned all about the upstart company of French and British traders and merchants destroying his post's trade. "The Company . . . consists of Messrs. Blandeau [i.e., Maurice Blondeau] at Montreal & Keshew his Brother, George McBeath, Todd, & Thomas Corry at Michilimackinac, John [Askin] at Emissions, 9 miles above that Fort & another French Gentn." He noted that "They all have much influence over the Natives," Graham pointing to "Corry & [Askin]," in particular.[59]

Months later, far away in London, the governors, leaders, and, perhaps, even the select important shareholders of the Hudson's Bay Company sat down to read about an obscure fur trader named John Askin. Askin, according to Graham, "was a great Fur trader above Albany Town, where he became Bankrupt, & afterwards came to Canada where he carries on a large Trade, not less than

500 packs of Furrs annually, where mustered from all Parts."[60] If Graham can be trusted, then by 1772, Askin handled nearly forty-five thousand pounds of furs each year, worth about £12,500–£22,500, depending on the market in London. Askin would see a sizable profit from the sale of these furs; it would be debited against his accounts in Schenectady or Montreal and would go toward the purchase of the next year's supplies, the complex process beginning over again. By singling out Askin, Graham made a larger point about not just the size and profitability of the Michilimackinac merchant's enterprise, but the fact that the furs were "mustered from all Parts," meaning that Askin's furs and profits could have gone to or benefited Graham's Hudson's Bay employers in London.

In the three years since Major Robert Rogers's humiliating ouster, Askin had slowly become an important and dynamic figure in the British fur trade. In late May 1768, for example, John Porteous wrote to Sampson Fleming, the commissary of Detroit, his letter capturing Askin's playful and expansive mood during the beginning of what would be a very prolific period in his economic life. "Askin," Porteous wrote, "is now the greatest Buck imaginable as Sound as a Roach and as full of Intrigue as ever."[61] He began investing time, energy, and capital into Grand Portage, a long-established overland route connecting Lake Superior to Pigeon River.[62] By passing the rocky and riotous waterfall at the mouth of the river, Indian hunters and trappers, followed by French traders and canoe men, used the route to gain access to the fur-rich interior of Canada.

During his stint as deputy commissary, Askin watched as other traders and merchants applied for trading permits or defied Johnson's policies to take advantage of the vast fur-rich countryside around Lake Superior. In their efforts, he saw an opportunity to streamline the movement of merchandise and pelts across the upper Great Lakes. In 1768, he cleared a large swatch of land at Grand Portage, and on it he built a trading depot.[63] The depot allowed him to send supplies necessary for a productive trade to French and British traders in exchange for the lush pelts coming downriver. During this time, he began supplying merchandise, forwarding goods, and making new connections with men like Forrest Oakes, Maurice Blondeau, James McGill, Isaac Todd, George McBeath, and William Edgar.[64] As men of both local and regional importance, they began to include Askin in their schemes. Beyond augmenting his position as an intermediary, his investment represented the first of a series of trade-related internal improvements that would characterize his career over the next decade and allow him to maintain his independence.

The conflict between Rogers and Roberts proved quite illustrative for Askin. He watched from the sidelines as the commandant and Indian commissary squabbled over access to and then control of a blacksmith shop at Michilimackinac in September 1767.[65] After Rogers's ouster, Askin stepped into the void when he saw a chance to profit. The former commissary purchased blacksmith tools and established a smithy at his farm, and hired its services out to the commandant of Michilimackinac and the British military.[66] In general, the work performed by the smithy corresponded to common agricultural demands: the crafting of hoes and axes, spears and traps, fur trade necessities, and salient aspects of Indian diplomacy, such as the repair of weapons. Askin's smithy would bring him a small but tidy profit.[67] Moreover, his investment reveals his keen eye for uncovering and exploiting local advantages, even as larger and fundamentally more transformative economic developments loomed stark on the horizon.

In 1769, plans began to materialize and develop at Quebec for an extensive Anglo-French trading venture centered on Lake Winnipeg, a body of water within the bounds of the Hudson's Bay Company's monopoly on northern trade.[68] For Askin and his partners, it was a transgressive idea rooted in memories of the French Empire, and reflective of deep ambitions and imperial uncertainty. In the summer of 1670, King Charles II chartered and then granted the company exclusive fur trade rights over the lands surrounding the rivers and lakes draining into the bay. Stretching south almost to Lake Superior, the company developed a centralized system of trade, establishing posts along the coastline of the bay, forcing Indians to travel north to exchange their furs for British and German manufactures. However, this left the Canadian interior open and vulnerable to southern encroachment.

These small Hudson's Bay posts became continuous sites of imperial contestation between the French and British Empires.[69] Between 1682 and

1713, for example, small French raids captured York Factory, Fort Severn, and Fort Albany on multiple occasions, only to have them fall back into British hands the following year, as spring and summer brought fresh thaws and renewed transatlantic access. While extensive military conflict proved indecisive, continual invasion and conquest meant prolonged disruptions for the company's trade, revealing its monopoly to be both costly and somewhat ephemeral until the removal of the French after the Seven Years' War.

Developing the fur trade near the Hudson Bay was a costly, difficult, and complex endeavor in the seventeenth and eighteenth centuries. Controlled by a governor (often a member of the British royal family), a deputy governor, and a guiding council of seven of the thirty-two shareholders, the Hudson's Bay Company nominally claimed and controlled the ice-packed region and its acres of permafrost.[70] However, artic weather, an insufficient agricultural base, long distances, expensive sea voyages, military expenditures, steep labor outlays, and Indigenous requirements created tremendous financial and institutional overhead costs for the Hudson's Bay Company. Its leaders struggled to keep costs associated with the fur trade down throughout the late seventeenth and early eighteenth centuries, and implemented a series of top-down policies uniquely grounded in the region. For example, they instituted complex price controls and exchange rates, established fixed labor costs, and demanded ever greater efforts to make their North American posts self-sufficient.

These developments gave rise, for example, to the establishment of the "Made Beaver" (MB), a preferred pelt, somewhat similar to the French *castor gras*, which was well worn, with the protective outer hairs rubbed off. Trade goods and other furs, like squirrel or marten, were given a value relative to the MB—in the 1730s, a pistol could be worth a total of four MB, two shirts would trade for one MB, and eight knives would fetch one MB.[71] The Hudson's Bay Company established elaborate pay schedules for all of its employees, from the governor of the posts to imported laborers, such as carpenters; the cost of each layer of administration could be projected into an uncertain future.

The Hudson's Bay Company first entered the fur trade with the populous Cree communities living along the Hayes River in the late seventeenth century, and, over time, the merchants learned details of the Cree's enemies—the Chipewyan—who lived to the southwest beyond the Churchill River.[72] They gradually expanded their mercantile efforts outward. South around Lake Winnipeg, the British encountered the Ojibwa communities pushing north from Lake Superior, while to the west, along the Saskatchewan River, they learned of the Siouan-speaking Assiniboine. Hostility between the Algonquian-speaking Cree and the Athabaskan-speaking Chipewyan communities defined much of the Hudson's Bay fur trade and diplomatic efforts in the early to mid-eighteenth century. Meanwhile, French pressure from the Great Lakes challenged British efforts in the interior, especially as they established posts at Lake Winnipeg, Lake Nipigon, and Lac des Prairies. Instead of directly challenging the French from the south by sending traders among the region's Indians, the Hudson's Bay Company encouraged Indian hunters and trappers to come to their posts when winter withdrew.

The Hudson's Bay Company not only relied upon Indians for their furs, but also as vital intermediaries, labor, and marriage partners.[73] Both Cree and Assiniboine traded British goods to Plains Indians for buffalo. However, given long-standing hostilities between the Cree and the Chipewyan, trade went alongside diplomatic efforts to establish peace and create a region where Indian parties could travel north without the fear of war parties, raids, or captivity. The coming of the Indians to the posts in the spring and summer, by canoe or foot, provoked a flurry of activity, as the exchange of furs for European wares required solemn ceremony, gifting, and affirmations of continued friendship. The governors, deputy governors, and the chief factors of the posts treated the Indians with generosity and largess, not simply because their trade relied upon them, but because in a world where agricultural production was limited or nonexistent, shared survival required cooperation.

By the 1750s the Hudson's Bay Company had helped establish a relative peace among the region's Indians, and with the Seven Years' War diverting French imperial attention to the St. Lawrence River Valley and disrupting the Great Lakes fur trade, the company seemed poised to finally make good on its monopoly and rebound from French competition. The furs collected by the

Hudson's Bay Company declined from nearly seventy thousand in 1738–1739 to about forty thousand in 1746–1747 in face of competition by French traders sweeping out from Grand Portage into the waters above Lake Superior. With French control removed after the Seven Years' War, Indian traders could not exploit the rivalry between French and British traders, playing one against the other while demanding more merchandise for their furs.[74] Given the top-down structure of the Hudson's Bay Company, rigid and less responsive price controls for its North American posts and the removal of the more culturally adept, decentralized, and dynamic French fur traders from the south offered the potential to alleviate serious competitive pressure on its inflexible structure. However, as the chief factors of the Hudson's Bay Company posts would soon discover, any reprieve would prove short-lived, and any effort to open new lands to the fur trade would be frustrated by southern men like John Askin and his Montreal-based trading partners.

Graham pinpointed the cause of the Hudson's Bay Company's difficulties in the late 1760s and early 1770s, writing to his superiors in London that many of the "Canadian Pedlars" below York Factory often wondered why the company "lay along the Sea & did not penetrate Inland." With the interior open and vulnerable, Askin and his partners took full advantage, building an incredible network of exchange in the process. According to Graham, theirs was a far-flung enterprise, traveling over "113 carrying places, & pass[ing] thro' different Nations of Indians who are often very unruly unless their extravagt. Demands are complied with." Outfitted by a merchant in Quebec, the valuable merchandise traveled northwest, taking, in some areas, "twenty & forty days to pass thro'." Shepherded by the able hands of Maurice Blondeau in Montreal, John Askin at Michilimackinac, and Thomas Corry by Lake Winnipeg, the goods were secured in "a decent kind of a House, Stockaded round, . . . with thirty Men." Corry's efforts proved invaluable. In fact, during his first year in the north the newly arrived Scotsman worked to entice Wappenssew, an influential Indian headman who first "came [to trade at] York Fort in 1755," to the cause of the southern partnership. In his letter, Graham flatly noted: "They have succeeded" and "no favour is refused." Consequently, Wappenssew "induce[d] the Indians to resort [to Corry] . . . Convoy[ed] the large Canoes up & down to Michillimackinac," and protected the partnership from hostility.[75]

With Corry wintering in the north, and luring away the Hudson's Bay Company's Indian clientele, Askin busied himself managing his depots at Michilimackinac and Grand Portage, ensuring the back-and-forth movement of goods and furs for the partnership. After years of exclusion from the trade, he was now in his element, and, in the absence of stringent imperial oversight, had resumed old behaviors. Hundreds of miles to the north, at York Factory, Graham brooded over Askin's activities and the nature of his "influence over the Natives." In order to stanch the hemorrhaging of sales and sell off York's "overplus," Graham had sent "some Tobacco with strict orders" to headmen like Wappenssew, demanding they come to his post next season to trade. "They will obey me," he reasoned, "if [Askin's] New England Rum does not prevail."[76]

Askin's return to the rum trade on the heels of controversy at Michilimackinac and his failed efforts to smuggle liquor during Pontiac's War helped ensure the partnership's success below Hudson's Bay. Rum, brandy, and other spirits represented an "ideal exchange item," one that fetched, even diluted with water, large quantities of furs.[77] Portable, cheap, and disruptive, the liquor was acquired by Askin at Quebec and Albany, and forwarded north to Corry, who dispensed it liberally.[78] Working in concert, Askin and Corry proved tremendously successful, inducing "tribes unknown at [York Factory to leave] their former Country" and move closer to "the Canadian Settlements for the conveniency of Trade."[79]

At Michilimackinac, Askin watched as the last of the summer traders packed their canoes with merchandise and supplies and boarded their vessels to paddle off into choppy blue waters, heading north toward Grand Portage. A month later, in the fall of 1771, he left Michilimackinac and returned to northern New York, following the familiar route back to Schenectady and Albany, where he would spend the winter. He had come back east to settle his accounts. The thirty-two-year-old merchant met with his creditors, and they "for ever Quit Claim unto the said John Askin his Heirs Executors & Administrations all

. . . Accounts Sum & Sums of money Judgments Executions Extents Quarrels Controversies Trespasses Damages & Demands whatsoever."[80] It was a singular moment. The repayment of his debt attested to the sheer profitability of competing for furs in the far north, and Askin's successful prosecution of it established him as a valuable trade partner.

In fact, before returning to Michilimackinac, Askin formalized his relationship with Phyn, Ellice, and Company with a formal contract and generous line of credit. In a letter to John Porteous, both James Phyn and Alexander Ellice wrote that they met with Askin and "shewed [him] every civility," and he promised to give them the "preference of his business." The furs he would gather from across the Great Lakes and beyond would soon make their way to Albany and Schenectady. As a result, they began preparing to send him a large quantity of "bulky articles & few fine goods" and extended him a line of credit: twelve months at 125 percent, fifteen months at 129 percent, and eighteenth months at 133⅓ percent.[81] They also "hoped to be Comissioned for your Liquors [and] conditions shall be as low as any," and given Askin's historical reliance on alcohol and spirits, easier access to New England rum certainly was a boon.[82]

With deals done, Askin departed for Michilimackinac. Empowered by the role he played as the middleman at Michilimackinac for the Hudson's Bay area trade and his contract with Phyn, Ellice, and Company, Askin, more than anyone else, understood and appreciated his enviable middleman position as a conduit between merchants and traders in Quebec, Montreal, Albany, and Schenectady. The return voyage gave him time to think, explore new angles, and, ultimately, prepare to further entrench himself at Michilimackinac.

Askin's return to New York to settle his debts was, in some ways, prompted by Thomas Corry's strong desire to withdraw from the fur trade. Two seasons at Lake Winnipeg had made Corry a very wealthy man; he now wished to leave the Hudson's Bay region and retire to Montreal. The partners planned for Askin, presently traveling north through the lower Great Lakes, to leave Michilimackinac and replace Corry. By the summer of 1772, Graham at Hudson's Bay had caught wind of Askin's imminent arrival and some of the plans surrounding his tenure. "[Askin arrives] this fall," Graham informed his superiors, "intend[ing] to build a proper house," suggesting both permanency and the development of larger aspirations for the Montreal consortium.[83]

For the next fifty years, the Hudson's Bay Company and rival trading concerns from the St. Lawrence River Valley would compete for furs in the upper Great Lakes. The efforts of Askin and his partners—Corry, Blondeau, McBeath, and Todd—and their vacillating associates, suppliers, and creditors showed the viability of working in concert for the pursuit of a complex venture. Other French and British merchants and traders followed their path: men such as James McGill, Benjamin Frobisher, Alexander Henry, and Simon McTavish. Many of these men helped found the North West Company in 1779, when sixteen shares of joint stock were divided between eight Montreal and Quebec partnerships who wished to avoid the destructive consequences of their economic ambitions.[84] Through aggressive competition, sometimes employing deliberate acts of violence, sabotage, theft, and destruction, the North West Company established a hardnosed monopoly over a large swatch of North America's interior, and, in the process, pushed the fur trade farther and farther north and west.

Despite Graham's worries, Askin never replaced Corry in the frozen north, and it is ultimately unclear why he abandoned direct involvement in such a lucrative and expansive fur trade. Unlike many of his former partners who would go on to play important roles establishing the North West Company, monopolizing on these earlier efforts, Askin remained relatively independent and unencumbered. His close ties with Quebec and Montreal merchants and his new contract with Phyn, Ellice, and Company certainly shaped his decision to remain below Lake Superior, and his marriage to a Frenchwoman at Detroit may have made the decision that much easier.

After leaving northern New York, Askin made his way to Detroit in the summer of 1772, where he married Marie Archange Barthe, the daughter of Charles Andre Barthe.[85] Born in Montreal in 1722, Barthe, the son of the king's armorer, relocated to Detroit in the 1740s, where he took up his father's mantle and worked as an armorer and silversmith.[86] In western posts like Detroit skilled craftsmen proved pivotal to the community's success, as their work helped secure positive relationships with surrounding Indians. Such an occupation served as a path toward economic success and greater social standing.[87] In 1747, Barthe married Marie Therese Campeau, the daughter of one of the earliest families to settle in the community following its founding; she would die during childbirth in 1765. Barthe and his family lived comfortably on a farm inherited from his wife's father. Over time, through his work as a silversmith, Barthe became increasingly involved in the lucrative fur trade, where silver ornaments, especially bracelets, medals, armbands, earrings, and gorgets, played an important role in establishing ties and conducting diplomacy.[88]

With Barthe's brother, Pierre, living among the Indians of the Wabash River valley, the family seemed poised to establish a very profitable trade like that of many of their Detroit kin and extended family.[89] However, much like Askin, Charles Andre Barthe suffered through the aftermath of the Seven Years' War and Pontiac's War, yet, unlike Askin, he never found a sure footing on which to rebuild his former trade. By 1771, his family floundered in considerable debt, even owing Askin a significant sum.[90] Barthe sold or auctioned off his properties around Detroit to stave off financial ruin, before finally having to mortgage his family's own farm.

Despite widespread Francophobia, marriages between British merchants and Frenchwomen—often multiethnic daughters of established French traders—were common and transformative. For example, James Sterling married Marie Angélique Cuillerier, the daughter of Antoine Cuillerier dit Beaubian, the last French commandant of Detroit and a wealthy scion of a long-established fur trade family.[91] Speaking French and several Indigenous languages, she offered her husband valuable insight into the fur trade and Indian communities of the lower Great Lakes.[92] In fact, in a letter to John Duncan, Sterling wrote a paean about his new wife, stressing throughout the letter all of her wonderful and beneficial assets:

> She is a very prudent Woman & a fine Scholar; has been used to trade from her infancy, & is generally allowed to be the best Interpreter of the different Indn. Languages at this place; her famy. is in great Esteem amongst ye Inds.

> so much that her father was suspected to have been chosen by the Indians to Command [at Detroit] . . . he is pretty rich, has given me with his Daughter to the Value of near a Thousand Pounds in Houses, Money, & Peltry. . . . We shall carry on Trade much better & with a great deal less expence than formerly, my wife serving as Interpreter & I myself as clerk.[93]

The marriage was a boon for Sterling, as it instantly transformed him from interloper to insider in the eyes of the French and Indian communities of the Great Lakes and even, through his wife's labor, enhanced his reputation among his British counterparts to the east.[94]

After Askin's marriage to Marie, Charles Andre Barthe remained in Detroit and would rely on the generosity and forbearance of his new son-in-law for the rest of his life. Several years after his marriage to Marie, Askin gave her father a sizable loan, writing that he "hop[ed] [Barthe] applied the money I gave him to the discharging of his debts at Detroit, it realy hurts me to think of him indebted to any person."[95] Throughout the 1770s, Barthe tried to reenter the fur trade, but his various investments failed to take root or grow profitable. Yet, in the years before his death in the spring of 1786, Barthe watched as his sons and daughters left Detroit and migrated north to Michilimackinac, where they became wealthy and ensconced in Askin's burgeoning trade in the upper Great Lakes.

Of Barthe's eleven children, only Marie Archange, Jean Baptiste, Therese, Bonaventure Antoine, Louis, and Marie Felicité survived past infancy, and all but Therese, who would stay in Detroit with her father, spent time in Askin's household or participated in his trade at Michilimackinac. The movement of the Barthe children to Michilimackinac was far from a unique experience in the Great Lakes. Historian Karen L. Marrero points out that "families were consistently launching and re-launching themselves with family members acting as anchors across time and space."[96] In fact, their labor, felicity with languages, deep and horizontal familial connections, and intimate understanding of the French and Indian world of their father made Marie's brothers invaluable to Askin's newest schemes and transformed the scope and extent of his trade.

Askin's experience as a sutler, commissary, and then as a successful merchant in the frozen north taught him valuable lessons that he would carry throughout the 1770s. He knew firsthand the difficulties presented by a growing fur trade. It was more than the exchange of merchandise for furs; the furs' movement over time and space through long-established supply lines and trade routes threatened to fray and snap under too much distance. By the late eighteenth century, the movement of goods across both ocean and land began to confront the basic realities and limitations of existing technology. With the establishment of his first trading depot at Grand Portage in 1767, Askin anticipated the need for better infrastructure and began a decade-long series of investments designed to facilitate the development of the upper Great Lakes British fur trade.

Moreover, his marriage to Marie and the arrival of the family Barthe at Michilimackinac allowed Askin to incorporate their labor and energy into the development of well-placed depots, private trading vessels, and lucrative contracts that he hoped would institute him as one of the most important middlemen and conduits of the northern trade throughout the 1770s.[97] Eschewing membership in formalized partnerships and lacking the desire and capital to compete against his former colleagues in the arctic, Askin aspired to conduct as much business as possible, unencumbered. Though Askin's financial success would grow exponentially over the next several years, how well he and his multiethnic family's network of exchange would weather the burgeoning revolution depended, in part, on the lessons Askin learned from past wars, as security in trade was put to the test.

CHAPTER FOUR

One Should Never Give Offence in Trade

Michilimackinac, the American Revolution, and John Askin's Network of Exchange, 1774–1779

SWELTERING UNDER THE BLAZING SUN, BACKS AND BROWS DRENCHED IN rivulets of sweat, John Askin's slaves hauled Askin and his litter through the growing "suburbs" outside Fort Michilimackinac.[1] The men trudged toward the King's Storehouse, where Askin once again served as the garrison's deputy commissary. Inside his litter, Askin considered the progress workers had made on his new home, "a tolerabl[y] good House," he reasoned, "two Storry high."[2] He certainly needed the space. To Sampson Fleming, the long-serving British commissary at Detroit, Askin wrote that his "family consist[ed] of about 20 persons always."[3]

Most of these inhabitants were Askin's children, the offspring of multiple multiethnic relationships stretching back to his first years in North America. The oldest of these progeny—Catherine, Madeleine, and John Jr.—were born between Albany and Michilimackinac in the early 1760s, and now found themselves on the cusp of adulthood and marriage. Askin sent an adolescent Catherine, his eldest daughter, to a Catholic nunnery in Montreal to be educated; she would return in 1778 to marry into Askin's network of trade.[4]

Likewise, leveraging his connections with Phyn, Ellice and Company, Askin sent John Jr. to Schenectady to live among the Ellice family, where he would serve as a novice clerk and learn the skills of his father's trade. On August 13, 1774, Robert Ellice drafted a letter promising the elder Askin that he may "depend that all manner of Care shall be taken of your Son, and put to one of the best Schools in Schenectady."[5]

However, by early January 1775 John Jr. would be with Isaac Todd in Montreal, where the young man would finish his training and schooling. The move, possibly prompted by the growing imperial and revolutionary turmoil caused by "our Neighbors the Yankies," had the consequence of introducing the young John Jr. to the powerful mercantile communities of New York and Quebec.[6] By 1778, as the workers continued making progress on the new family home, Askin wrote to his old friend James Sterling in Detroit, "I shall be very glad to see my Boy here."[7] He could be put to work.

At Michilimackinac, beginning in February 1774, Marie Archange gave birth to the first of her nine children with Askin, and soon the wails of newborns, the soft patter of feet, and peals of laughter from small children once again filled the Askin household. The first of these children born into the family was a daughter named Theresa. A year and a half later, in October 1775, Archange Meredith was born. Befitting the daughter of an important fur trade family in Michilimackinac, she was sponsored for baptism into the Catholic faith by prominent members of the French community, Hypolite Chaboillez and Felicity Barthe.[8]

Like Catherine and John Jr., Theresa and Archange Meredith would eventually find themselves connected to Askin's trade in the Great Lakes in ancillary ways. Theresa would eventually marry Captain Thomas McKee, the multiethnic son of Alexander McKee, in the spring of 1797. Thomas's father was one of the most influential British Indian agents in the Ohio Valley.[9] Later, in a postrevolutionary world where Great Britain and the United States vied for control and dominance of the interior, the McKees' strong standing among the Indian communities of the Ohio Valley, particularly among the Shawnee, would benefit Askin, who openly speculated in large tracts of land and worked to develop a profitable fur trade in the region. The marriages of Askin's children helped further tie his family into the larger fur trade society of the Great Lakes, and would burnish his reputation and develop his wealth.

As his family and household grew, Askin busied himself inventorying his estate during the early years of the American Revolution. Hunched over his desk, putting quill to paper, Askin itemized "Shiping," "Houses Lands," "Slaves," "Cattle," "Carriages & Harness," "Tools," "Necessaries," "Books and writing implements," "House Furniture & Utensils," and "Merchandize."[10] In December 1776, he valued his property at £7,213 NYC. Fur trade merchandise worth £3,841 NYC accounted for 53 percent of his assets, while real estate in houses, farms, shops, and warehouses represented 15 percent, at a value of £1,068 NYC.[11] Finally, two ships, the *Welcome* and the *De Peyster*, worth a total of £900 NYC, accounted for 12 percent of his estate. All told, Askin was worth £14,611 15s. 2.5d. NYC.[12] Two years later, in the winter of 1778, he repeated the process, and found his net value had shrunk to £12,882 17s. 1.75d. NYC, representing a 12 percent loss.[13] However, these numbers are deceptive; they hide the cost of developing his fur trade and the crises and consequences of a large-scale colonial rebellion.

For example, between 1776 and 1778 he relinquished his vessels to the British military, and the value of his shipping concerns dropped to just £82 NYC. However, the value of his houses, farms, shops, and depots grew an astounding 43 percent, reflecting major investments in the economic infrastructure of the Great Lakes. Spectacularly, the value of merchandise he had on hand grew by 128 percent, ballooning from £3,841 NYC to £8,763 NYC.[14] By investing in new ventures, carrying heavier debts, employing new engagés, and trafficking more merchandise, Askin leveraged his position, family, and connections to develop a hold on the Great Lakes. In fact, his aristocratic sedan chair, his new spacious house, and his slaves, both African and Indian, were outward manifestations of a long period of success and growing economic power that began in 1768 and intensified four years later with his marriage to Marie Archange Barthe and the relocation of her French family north from Detroit.

During the mid-1770s, Askin and his family took advantage of the complex

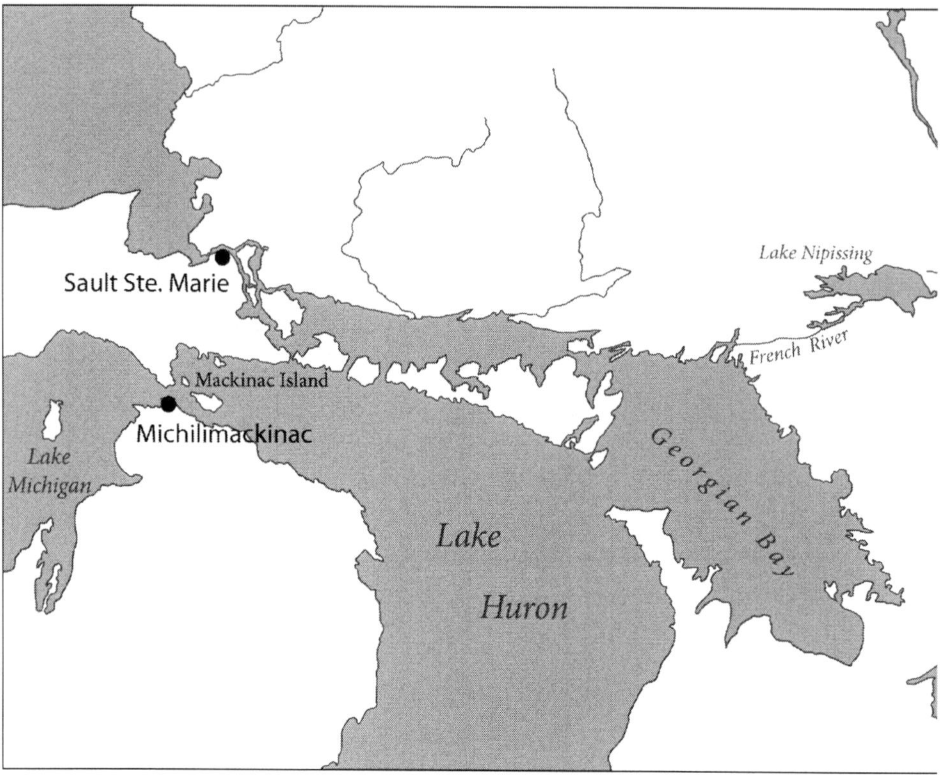

fur trade stretching further northwest as the competition between consortiums of French and British merchants and traders became increasingly acute, profitable, and dangerous. Such a trade required cooperation and coordination, and for Askin it meant intense reorganization and regional development. Askin's efforts proved expansive, and his family, his financers, and his relationship to the British military—particularly Captain Arent Schuyler de Peyster, the commandant of Michilimackinac—shielded his ambitious efforts from the developing war in the east. However, Askin's private labors coincided with the American Revolution, and warfare, especially along the St. Lawrence River and in the Ohio Valley, threatened the already delicate and volatile fur trade of the Great Lakes.[15] Nearly forty years old, Askin knew plenty about the disorder and

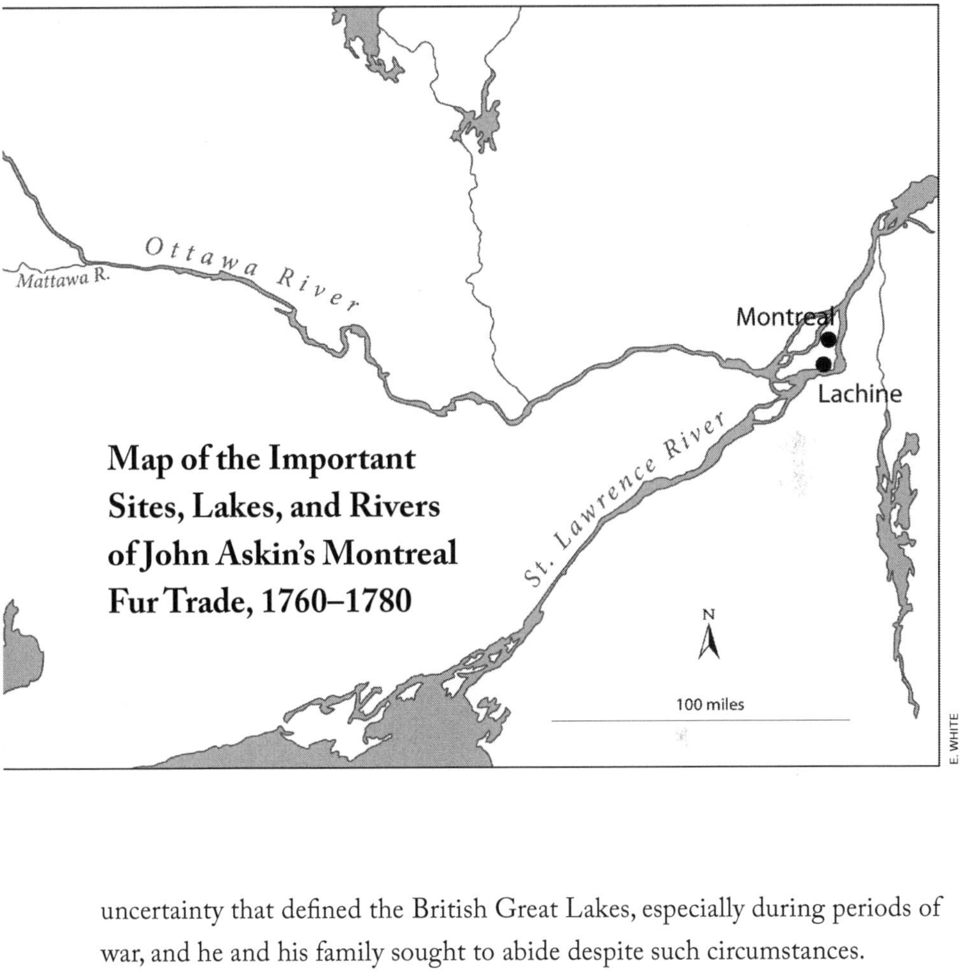

Map of the Important Sites, Lakes, and Rivers of John Askin's Montreal Fur Trade, 1760–1780

uncertainty that defined the British Great Lakes, especially during periods of war, and he and his family sought to abide despite such circumstances.

For a while, it proved easy. Inside Askin's new house, his wife, children, and many visitors gathered around a finely appointed table, and all seemed in order, even if the colonial rebellion seemed poised to disturb the British world. They dined with expensive pewter plates and fine china and took coffee from an ornate silver pot.[16] Their larder was well stocked with "Tea & loaf Sugar," "Chocolate," and "Coffe" alongside fresh milk, wheat, oats, barley, salt pork, beef, and eggs from Askin's farms.[17] They drank wine with dinner and brandy afterward. In the evening hours, Askin retired to a "fine large Arm Chair," where he read from his extensive library, perusing one of his volumes dedicated to accounting, French literature, or the words and deeds of famous Roman statesmen.[18] He owned treatises on navigation, Benjamin Franklin's *Observations on Lightning*, a dictionary, and the complete four-volume set of the Earl of Chesterfield's letters.[19] Eventually, he would grow restless, and walk to his well-crafted writing desk, where stacks of letters necessitated his continual attention. This work—the tedium of his trade—took up much of his time, especially as he centered a large fur trade on himself and his household.

From the parlor, Marie Archange, busily repairing one of Askin's fine waistcoats, occasionally grabbing her cloth brush to tease out dirt, called to her husband about the dress she wanted made. "Mrs. Askin begs," Askin later wrote to Isaac Todd and James McGill in Montreal, that they should "deliver [to Madam Perinault] the piece of Silk with the trimmings, that's coming or come from England" so that it might be turned into a fine, well-crafted dress.[20] He reassured his wife it had been ordered and would arrive by ship, if the war did not forestall it. She had her own desk and bookcase and a generous wardrobe, access to magazines and periodicals, and the economic means to engage in fashion trends in both Paris and London.

They went to bed above, changed into their night garb, and closed the curtains to their canopy and secured the darkness all around them. In the winter, the heavy fabric would have cut the draft of the frigid winds coming off the lake. As they drifted to sleep, their house slaves (much like the two "panis girls from 9 to 16 years of age" whom Askin had once inquired about in a letter) kept the fires stoked and woke up early to prepare the stoves for breakfast.[21] Charlotte and Clariss, "Paunisse Wench[es]" valued at £50 NYC and £40 NYC respectively, kept the Askin household clean and orderly.[22]

In spite of the war, the families of Michilimackinac continued the best they could. Writing to John Hay, a fur trader in Detroit, in April 1778, Askin claimed the community "passed out Winter as agreeably as the place would admit of [with] a dance every week."[23] Askin and Marie made particularly favorable impressions at these events, especially after they had borrowed a "Country Dance Book" from Sampson Fleming.[24] Askin also kept "2 fiddles" and "fiddle Strinks [strings]" handy.[25] During these events, Askin toasted some of the wealthiest French and British merchants and traders in the Great Lakes and welcomed into his parlor the aristocratic officers of Fort Michilimackinac, most notably Captain Arent Schuyler de Peyster and his wife, Rebecca.[26]

A member of a prominent and influential New York Dutch-Huguenot family and veteran of the Seven Years' War, de Peyster came west to Michilimackinac with the Eighth or King's Regiment in the summer of 1774. Like his predecessors, he threw himself into the vexing role of commandant, meeting with the numerous Indian communities surrounding his new post.[27] De Peyster encountered Askin, his commissary, early in his tenure, and the two men developed a strong rapport cemented in the shared struggle of supplying and protecting a distant and isolated garrison. Served by slaves, de Peyster and many others supped on Askin's finest fare. Dressed for the occasion, they danced to the fiddle, and as they paired off they might have been able to forget that rebellious colonials had ever captured Montreal, or that the entire British government was on a war footing with France, Britain's long-standing rival that had allied with the American cause.[28]

Askin's vast trade ensured the quality of life that he and his family enjoyed at Michilimackinac, and they took full advantage of the splendid material prosperity offered by the British Empire in the late eighteenth century.[29] In the eyes of outsiders, gold watches, stately carriages, and finely made bed curtains all marked Askin as a gentleman-merchant—a coveted status, not quite genteel, but one that allowed him to translate his economic success into growing social authority.[30] He brought his charm, authority, and experience to bear as he negotiated the rocky waters of competition and imperial violence. He contracted, supplied, and transported, never restricting his efforts to a singular concern. He had learned lessons from Pontiac's War.

Askin oversaw the details of his voluminous, multifaceted trade and directed a fleet of private ships carrying carefully chosen merchandise, listed in precisely drawn manifests and inventories, to family-operated depots or installations in Michilimackinac, Sault Ste. Marie, Cheboygan, Milwaukee, Fort Erie, and Grand Portage.[31] By 1778, he extended his holdings across the Great Lakes, establishing multiple productive farms, a blacksmith for repairs, and several warehouses to support his efforts and streamline the movement and transport of goods for his Montreal and Quebec suppliers.[32] Well positioned to take advantage of the chaos and confusion of war, as well as the preoccupation and occasional collusion of British officials, Askin sought, in his own words, to place the "Key of Canada in his Pocket."[33]

But, first, he had to survive the war. Askin was astute enough to know that distance alone would not keep the battles at bay, and while distance offered the opportunity to skirt restrictions, it also provided the prospect for so much worse. He knew better than most the ways imperial discord lurched awkwardly and crashed disastrously. Askin had already seen some troublesome signs. British officials, even those amenable and willing to close their eyes to the more unscrupulous behavior of the fur traders, worked to subordinate the fur trade to the interest of the British military as they struggled to wage successful campaigns against the rebellious Americans. Shortages arose, and even vital supplies like wheat and rum became scarce or closely guarded in the Great Lakes. Even Askin, who felt the sting of want less than most, had to admit to a colleague trying to sell him an African slave that his own family "want[s] Bread more than Cooks."[34] Still, three years into the war, Askin's centers mostly held, and he and his family encountered only minor setbacks as they expanded their efforts.

For example, in August 1776 a fur trader named Adhemar St. Martin wrote a desperate letter to Henry Hamilton, the lieutenant governor of Fort Detroit. A year earlier, a ship called the *Chippewa* had been caught in a gale and crashed into Presque Isle, a crooked finger of land jutting out into Lake Erie. Rather than allowing the ship's cargo to fall into the hands of the rebellious colonial army attacking Montreal, the captain had ordered everything destroyed. St. Martin was distraught over the loss of £400 of merchandise, and he wanted Britain to remunerate his misfortune.[35] That day, John Askin also lost a valuable cargo of rum. It was not a tremendous blow, such as the kind that crippled his trade so many years earlier, and for a while he weathered it well. By 1778, however, as the American rebellion intensified and spread deep into the Ohio Valley, he was complaining to Isaac Todd and James McGill, his suppliers in Montreal, that he had "no news about the Payment of [his] Rum," and he desperately wanted his goods back.[36]

The seeds of the American rebellion began in the aftermath of the Seven Years' War and wrought havoc beyond the scuttling of the *Chippewa*. After Pontiac's War—the pivotal event that convinced many imperial officials of the need for more efficient and effective colonial administration—Parliament began taking steps to rationalize its new territories, close loopholes while expanding its outdated trade laws, and reduce overall military costs. Largely, these efforts meant reigning in the more egregious behaviors of its North American colonials—that is, of men like John Askin who had illegally trafficked in rum in the Great Lakes or been involved in the shocking and widespread practice of clandestine trading with the French during the Seven Years' War. The Royal Proclamation of 1763, for example, forbade colonial settlement west of the Appalachians as a way of temporarily staunching Anglo-Indian violence, while the Sugar Act of 1764 raised taxes for the empire by forcing New England merchants trading with the West Indies to adhere to preexisting legislation. In 1765, Parliament passed the Stamp Act, which required North American legal documents, official licenses, newspapers, and even playing cards to be printed on stamped and taxed paper imported from Great Britain.[37]

Few parliamentarians expected a firestorm. In Boston, New York, Philadelphia, and Williamsburg, large segments of colonial society, from wealthy landowners, merchants, and lawyers to artisans, dockworkers, and freedmen, spoke against Parliament's usurpation of their rights as freeborn Englishmen.[38] Intense colonial backlashes, in the form of protests, petitions, organizing, vigilantism, and mob violence, met the passage of the Sugar, Stamp, and Quartering Acts, and debates over common law and constitutional authority became increasingly revolutionary.[39] A bewildered Parliament responded limply to the outcry with the Declaratory Act. It asserted that Parliament "had . . . full power and authority to make laws and statutes of sufficient force and validity to bind the colonies and people of America."[40] Consecutive ministries struggled with the need to generate revenue from a deeply resistant colonial population by passing the Townshend Duties in 1767 and the Tea Act in 1772. Boycotts and violence ensued. In 1770, a Boston mob attacked a squad of British soldiers, who fired into the crowd. Three years later, Bostonians, dressed as Mohawk Indians, dumped East India Company tea into the harbor.

For New York fur trade merchants in Albany and Schenectady, these colonial protests could not have come at a worse time.[41] The collapse of Sir William Johnson's and Gage's fur trade policies in 1768 and the subsequent politicization of transatlantic trade during the buildup to the American Revolution disrupted the New York fur trade to its core. The merchants had been relatively united behind Johnson's and Gage's efforts to restrict and control the fur trade to established posts, but when the British Parliament devolved authority over the trade back to its North American colonies, the community fractured. Albany merchants, many of them Anglo-Dutch, wanted a fur trade centered and focused on Niagara, while their Scottish counterparts, often at Schenectady, wanted to compete with the French and British at Quebec by directly engaging the upper Great Lakes fur trade. Johnson eventually supported the Schenectady traders and pushed for aggressive expansion, and partnerships like Phyn, Ellice, and Company leveraged their access to cheap New England rum and built relationships with men like John Askin at Michilimackinac to extend their reach and press their advantages in the lands beyond the Mohawk River Valley.

New York merchants could have weathered competition with Montreal and Quebec, but for the developing colonial protests against the Stamp Act and Townshend Duties, and the rise of transcolonial boycotts and nonimportation agreements. Pressured by protest groups like the Sons of Liberty, New York fur trade merchants found themselves cut off from their London factors and the merchandise they needed to conduct their trades. Merchants complained that such efforts would destroy the New York trade and place the fur trade into the hands of their Quebec counterparts, who were under no compulsion to limit their imports and could quickly step in to fill the vacuum. Phyn and Ellice noted in late August 1769, "Respecting Indian goods & almost every sort of dry goods there is hardly any to be gotten."[42] To John Porteous, they complained: "It's impossible to conceive how scarce goods are at NY not one article has been imported and no prospect before next Spring."[43] In the face of economic disaster,

Phyn, Ellice, and Company took a bold step and circumvented the boycott by ordering their British supplier to send their goods directly to Quebec and stationed an agent there to receive them.[44] In an era where mob violence could result from noncompliance, Phyn and Ellice put themselves in considerable personal danger, and justified their actions as helping to save a vital aspect of New York's economy.

The New York fur trade carried on, but the summer of 1774 proved pivotal and transformative. In northern New York, Sir William Johnson, a longtime advocate for an effective Indian policy and fur trade reform, suffered a stroke and passed away while conducting an Indian council at Johnson Hall.[45] In London, Parliament, fearing it "must risk something" or its authority over the colonies would be "all over," passed a series of laws designed to reprimand the insolent inhabitants of Boston, protect its imperial officials from malicious colonial prosecution, and restructure the government of Massachusetts and the western territories.[46] Strident and punitive, the laws became known throughout the colonies as the Intolerable Acts.

For John Askin at Michilimackinac, the Quebec Act, in particular, would have a profound effect on his trade and family over the next several years. Expanding on the provisions of the Treaty of Paris and the Royal Proclamation of 1763, the new law ceded the Great Lakes and the Ohio Valley to the newly established colony of Quebec and placed its control in the hands of a governor and his legislative council.[47] In light of the increasing colonial hostility along the Atlantic seaboard, Parliament hoped to bind the French population of Canada firmly to the Crown; the new act restored French civil law and allowed the free practice of Roman Catholicism. The act provoked outrage across British North America. Certain fur trade merchants feared that Crown authority might disrupt their trades, while the American colonials saw the act as further evidence of Parliament's desire to limit the rights of Englishmen.

New York fur trade merchants, in particular, viewed the Quebec Act with suspicion and apprehension. While it did not forbid them from pursuing their trades in the Great Lakes, New Yorkers found themselves operating in Quebec territory and under Quebec's policies. Moreover, Parliament passed a revenue law in 1774 that made the importation of New England rums into Quebec more costly; cheap rum had been Albany's and Schenectady's key advantage since Pontiac's War.[48] It was eventually repealed, but both acts, which came in quick succession, seemed to benefit Quebec traders. Phyn and Ellice complained bitterly: "this Cannada Law about Rum is so partial to the trading People of that Colony, as to take the trade intirely from [New York]."[49] They continued to refocus their attention on Quebec, establishing strong ties with Isaac Todd at Montreal, who served them as a forwarding agent for their merchandise coming in from Great Britain.[50]

At Michilimackinac, Askin found these developments had the consequence of drawing him away from New York and centering his supplies and supply lines along the Montreal corridor, shielding him from colonial disruptions in New York. In a letter to Todd, Phyn and Ellice wrote, "it will be a great disappointment to both us and Mr Askin should we not be able to fulfill the agreement between us."[51] It would prove a struggle, but one that would come to benefit Askin and his fellow Michilimackinac merchants; the struggles of the New York merchants and traders created a vacuum they could certainly profit from.

By the winter of 1774, a Continental Congress of the Atlantic colonies developed a new policy of nonimportation that would go into effect in September 1775, and many New York merchants, except Phyn, Ellice, and Company, chose to not purchase supplies for the next fur trade season. By the spring of 1775, the American Revolution had started, and Phyn, Ellice, and Company disbanded over the summer and moved to reform and reestablish itself in Montreal.[52] The New York fur trade—the trade where Askin had cut his teeth in the early 1760s—all but collapsed in the face of a colonial rebellion.

Meanwhile, as colonials debated the implications of the Quebec Act, Quebec's new governor, Guy Carleton, called for a series of new lieutenant governorships at Detroit, Vincennes, Kaskaskia, and Michilimackinac to assist in administering the new province.[53] These officials would oversee the administration of Indian policy and maintain domestic tranquility and rule of law, though in practice their position proved tremendously ambiguous, as their authority was largely undefined and they lacked the military control or required personnel to enforce their decisions.[54] In early April 1775, Carleton appointed an Irishman named Henry Hamilton to serve as the lieutenant governor and superintendent of Indian Affairs of Detroit.[55]

Born in 1734, Hamilton was a scion of a noble Scottish family who had migrated to Ireland in the seventeenth century, where they held sway in the counties and lands in which Askin and his family had dwelt. Young, well educated, and yearning for adventure, the twenty-one-year-old Hamilton joined the British army and served, like so many others of his generation, in the Seven Years' War. In 1758, Hamilton was wounded at the siege of Louisbourg, and a year later he fought alongside General James Wolfe at the Battle of Abraham Plains, outside of Quebec. After the war, he spent most of his military career along the St. Lawrence, where he rose to the rank of major and commandant of Crown Point. However, in 1775, desiring a life in politics, he sold his commission and took up his new post, even as rebel forces under the command of General Richard Montgomery began the invasion of Canada.[56] Upon arriving in Detroit in November, Hamilton worked to leverage his experience and authority into diplomatic efforts designed to keep the French and Indians loyal to the Crown.

North of Detroit, at Michilimackinac, Captain Arent Schuyler de Peyster, the commander of two companies of the King's Eighth Regiment of Foot, awaited the arrival of the post's new lieutenant governor.[57] He would wait three more years; in the meanwhile, the military and civilian authority of the post fell entirely into his hands. Born to a wealthy and politically connected New York City Dutch family in 1736, de Peyster grew up privileged, was educated in London, and joined the British army as an ensign at the age of nineteen. During the Seven Years' War he served in northern New York before being taken to France as a prisoner of war. Upon his parole he found himself in Germany, then Scotland, and finally, in 1768, he returned to North America, where he rose in rank and became the commandant of Michilimackinac in 1774. He and his Scottish wife, Rebecca, made quick acquaintance with the elite French and British merchants of the post, particularly with his commissary, John Askin, on whom de Peyster soon came to rely.[58]

During his first year as commandant, de Peyster worked diligently to build rapport among the Saginaw Ojibwa and the Odawa of Arbre Croche.[59] He demonstrated an open readiness to rely upon the expertise of French and British merchants and traders and, more importantly, men like Charles de Langlade, the nephew of the Odawa war chief, Nissowaquet, and Louis Chevalier, who married an influential fur trade matriarch among the Potawatomi of the St. Joseph River valley.[60] Such men were the British-facing avatars of a complex network of Indigenous kinship; they represented a complex array of overlapping and competing Indigenous economic, political, and diplomatic demands, which both empowered and limited their agency.[61] Astute British commanders valued such men, even as the British often misinterpreted the wellspring of their authority.[62] In fact, de Peyster's willingness to participate in the multiethnic landscape of the upper Great Lakes paid dividends in the spring of 1775, when he brokered a peace between the Sioux and the Ojibwa of Lake Superior.[63]

After the passage of the Intolerable Acts, tensions in the colonies reached a breaking point; American colonists began organizing militias and stockpiling weapons and ammunition. The British military, concentrated in Boston under the command of General Thomas Gage, heard rumors of aggressive action and marched to Lexington and Concord hoping to seize a cache of rebel supplies. Instead, on April 19, 1775, they found themselves confronted by colonial militia; shots were fired and nearly three hundred British regulars were killed, wounded, or disappeared during their long bloody retreat back to Boston. Decades of political debate exploded into outright hostility.[64]

Over the next several months, colonial militia surprised the British garrisons at forts Ticonderoga, St. Johns, and Crown Point, and the American Congress organized an invasion of Canada. In the first year of the war, success seemed to follow success with the capture of Montreal and the retreat of the British military, led by General Guy Carleton, to Quebec in late autumn. Caught in the tumult of the war, which had once seemed so distant, the French and British fur trade merchants of the Great Lakes sought neutrality and the continuation of their trades. The Americans occupied Montreal in November, and the articles of capitulation signed by John Porteous and James McGill asked "that trade. . . . shall be carried on freely as heretofore" and not "to take up arms against the Mother Country."[65] In the order of articles, trade came first.

However, beyond trade, the capture of Montreal and the collapse of the New York fur trade could have been disastrous for the British in the Great Lakes. The fur trade and Anglo-Indian diplomacy were intimately and inextricably connected; fur traders like Askin at Michilimackinac, for example, operated within the context of a complex and multifocal British Empire, and often found themselves supporting British officials and their visions of imperial policy. Likewise, diplomatic merchandise purchased from local traders helped affirm and establish alliances with the Indian communities of the Great Lakes. Moreover, Indigenous language of diplomacy was often used by French and British traders to initiate and open trade encounters. Without the fur trade and a steady supply of merchandise, British officials like de Peyster could not make peace between Indian peoples and their headmen, and, in the context of the colonial war, ties between the British and the Indians could not be refreshed. American control of Montreal threatened the entire alliance structure of the region, which could have crippled British control of the Great Lakes and the vital St. Lawrence River. As the war morphed from an internal struggle within the British Empire into a larger European affair, including colonial powers France and Spain, the importance of the fur trade and its link to diplomacy intensified.

Fortunately for the British, on December 31, the tide of American success crested and broke at the calamitous battle of Quebec, ushering in a new year of continual British military success. Quebec, Montreal, and the St. Lawrence River reverted to British hands; the sick and beleaguered Americans retreated south in the face of British reinforcements. Throughout 1776, as the British army retreated from Boston and the Continental Congress moved toward declaring independence, both Hamilton and de Peyster continued their efforts to rally the Indians of the Great Lakes and Ohio Valley to their cause and shore up their posts.[66] At Michilimackinac, de Peyster repaired the wooden palisades of his post, confiscated an armed vessel, and engaged influential multiethnic leaders, such as Charles de Langlade, to raise Indian warriors to bolster British control of the St. Lawrence River.[67]

East of the Appalachian Mountains, the Americans declared independence and the British military captured the port of New York City, chasing the dwindling American army led by a desperate George Washington, the commander-in-chief of the American forces, across New Jersey. The collapse of the rebellion seemed imminent in 1777.[68] General William Howe, the commander of the British army that captured New York, in August traveled south, where he defeated and outmaneuvered Washington and captured the rebel capital of Philadelphia. Meanwhile, another large British army supported by German mercenaries and Indians raised by de Peyster and Hamilton left Quebec in June. Its commander, General John Burgoyne, hoped to dash south through the woods of northern New York and capture Albany, splitting the colonies in half. For men like Askin, at the distant post of Michilimackinac, it seemed the war would be over before its flames could spread further west.

However, the first sparks drifted west in March 1777, when Guy Carleton, the governor of Quebec, received direct orders from London. The secretary of state, Lord George Germain, ordered Carleton to "direct Lieut. Governor Hamilton to assemble as many of the Indians of his District as he conveniently can . . . [and] employ them in making a Diversion and exciting an alarm upon the frontiers of Virginia and Pennsylvania."[69] During the early days of the war, the Crown had been apprehensive about using Indians against its rebellious subjects. However, the rebellion intensified and spread, leading British officials on both sides of the Atlantic to press more and more for their use. Hamilton began hearing American and Spanish overtures, and worked to keep "the Indians firm to the King's interest."[70]

In the middle of June 1777, Hamilton called a council of the Miami, Shawnee, Delaware, Ojibwa, Odawa, Potawatomi, and others at Detroit, and delivered presents. He spoke to the assembled: "I have the pleasure to inform you some of your younger brothers are desirous of having an axe delivered to them, to use against your enemies who have rebelled against the King—it is here ready for them."[71] During a two-year period, as Hamilton struggled with the intransigence of his commanders and his own desire for a more direct role in frontier campaigns, the continuous raids into Kentucky by the Mingo, Shawnee, Delaware, and Miami deprived the American settlers of the chance "to sow grain." According to Daniel Boone, an influential Kentucky backcountry man held captive by the Shawnee, the region had become impoverished and vulnerable and expected little "relief from the [Continental] Congress."[72] Desperate refugees fled the frontier and took the Wilderness Road east to Virginia, hoping to find security and safety. In October 1777, a young man named George Rogers Clark traveled with them; he carried a plan, and hoped the Virginia governor would listen.

Born in 1752, Clark began his career as a surveyor laboring to chart the newly opened treaty lands of Fort Stanwix.[73] With a new boundary line that followed the sluggish Ohio River southwest deep into Indian Country, British settlers gained access to the long-coveted soils of Kentucky, while the Shawnee, Mingo, Delaware, and Cherokee found their hunting grounds invaded. Clark, in his early twenties, inhabited a landscape devolving into bloodshed and cruelty. In the fall of 1772, for example, a war party fell upon a group of settlers heading west, and a few months later, in early spring, a party of Mingo was ambushed in retaliation. By May 1774, the governor of Virginia, Lord Dunmore, and the Virginian House of Burgesses declared war on the Shawnee and their allies. Soon after, Clark joined the Virginian militia, and the war ended with an indecisive battle that cowed the Indians of the Ohio Valley until the onset of the American rebellion. For the next several decades, the Ohio Valley would remain, to quote Cherokee war chief Dragging Canoe "a dark and bloody ground."[74] In 1776, the governor of Virginia, Patrick Henry, made Clark a major in the newly created militia of Kentucky County. In the aftermath of Hamilton's endeavors, and with the frontier mired in violence, Clark presented a plan to Henry with the intent of "seiz[ing] upon the British post & stores at Kaskasquia [Kaskaskia] in the Illinois Country."[75] By early May 1778, after months of recruitment, training, shipbuilding, and gathering supplies, Clark and his men traveled west where, at the falls of the Ohio River, they would invade Illinois Country.

Meanwhile at Michilimackinac in June 1778, Askin began to read more and more complaints. Then he inked his quill and scrawled a terse letter to Jean Baptiste Barthe, Marie's brother and a major partner at Sault Ste. Marie. "I am mortified," Askin complained, "that you did not send Mr. [Forrest] Oakes's share of merchandise." He feared breaking a lucrative contract. More importantly, however, he relied upon his brother-in-law to control and organize a significant portion of the family's fortune, and bad practices could jeopardize their trades. Scarcity or not, he warned Barthe that "one should never give offence in trade," and, no doubt thinking about his experience after Pontiac's War, "To go the other extreme, I mean to please everybody."[76]

Askin's efforts "to please everybody" began when he built his first warehouse at Grand Portage. Such warehouses expedited the voluminous movement of furs and merchandise across the Great Lakes region, and Askin saw a tremendous profit from his. In 1775, he expanded his efforts to Sault Ste. Marie with Jean Baptiste Barthe and his son-in-law Samuel Robertson, a well-known ship captain who married Askin's daughter, Catherine.[77] They further partnered with John Baptiste Cadot, an influential Frenchman and British Indian agent at Sault Ste. Marie.[78] Their new post consisted of a wooden palisade surrounding a storehouse and trader's cabin. For example, befitting its role as a forwarding station, the Sault Ste. Marie depot employed the labor for or provided merchandise to around fifty engagés, traders, and fellow merchants. In fact, Barthe and Robertson took account of their partnership at Sault Ste. Marie in 1779, and estimated the value of its stock, credits, and debts at 133,592 livres 18 sous. They owed Askin two sums: 66,329 livres 13 sous, and 1,892 livres 18 sous. Together, they shared a profit of 64,436 livres 15 sous.[79]

In the summer of 1778, Askin ordered Robertson to sail north from Michilimackinac "to examine the coast along the French River [at Georgian Bay]" and discover a suitable location on which to establish a new trading depot.[80] This route, long used by British and French merchants and traders, connected Montreal to the Great Lakes via the Ottawa River, Lake Nipissing, the French River, and the Georgian Bay. He hoped to circumvent the disruptions caused by the American rebellion and the collapse of the New York fur trade, and, as he wrote to Barthe, he hoped his new investment would "facilitate the transport of my goods from Montreal by the Grand River."[81] Luring in Benjamin Lyon, an established fur trader at Michilimackinac, as a new investor in the scheme, Askin hoped to further streamline the fur trade and exploit quicker turnarounds.[82]

Askin supported his operations at Michilimackinac and Sault Ste. Marie with several smaller but integral undertakings for the fur trade and the British military. For example, he extracted timber and hay from the mouth of the Cheboygan River; these materials went to houses, ships, coopers, and blacksmiths, keeping Askin's saw pit and carpenters busy.[83] Likewise, he owned a bake house and produced bread for British soldiers and British and French traders. He owned a press to pack furs.[84] His farms and close proximity to the Odawa village of Arbre Croche kept him well supplied with wheat and Indian corn.

Corn, in particular, ensured the success and vitality of the Great Lakes fur trade by supplying sustenance to wintering traders and traveling canoe men. Askin's ship, the *Welcome*, regularly visited the Saginaw River and Milwaukee Bay collecting large quantities of corn.[85] In a letter to Isaac Todd and James McGill, Askin boasted that he would send "A Young Brother-in-law of mine to [go to] Millwakee as much on acct. of the Corn to be got there as the Peltry."[86] At Michilimackinac, he owned all of the implements to transform corn into a transportable product: "stages for drying Corn," "2 Large Kittles in a furnace," and "A New London Corn Mill." In December 1776 he carried "138 Bushels of Detroit Corn" and "11 Bushels of Abra Croche Corn."[87] Two years later he had "285 Bags Corn at Chaboyagan." Food and edibles accounted for roughly 14 percent of the total value of Askin's merchandise in 1778.[88]

However, even as Askin diversified, he continued to traffic in rum and spirits. In 1775 Askin received a license to bring two bateaux full of rum and brandy, ten barrels and 160 kegs, to Michilimackinac.[89] The following year, after Phyn, Ellice, and Company temporarily shuttered their enterprise and relocated to Montreal, Askin received no license, reflecting a period of readjustment and delay caused by the American Revolution. However, on April 20, 1777, Askin imported 5,000 gallons of rum and brandy, secured by James McGill at Montreal, into Michilimackinac.[90] A total of forty-six merchants and traders received licenses that year, and together they imported 12,132 gallons of spirits to Michilimackinac.[91] Askin alone accounted for 41.2 percent. Only to the south, in Detroit, did other merchants, like Alexander Macomb and Simon McTavish, rival Askin's intensity in the spirits trade. By 1778, Askin imported an additional 3,000 gallons of rum and brandy. His partner and brother-in-law, Jean Baptiste Barthe, transported another 1,040 gallons.[92] Again, their spirits accounted for 40 percent of the 10,092 gallons brought to the northern Great Lakes.

Askin's inventories of his estates for 1776 and 1778 offer finer grade detail of the kinds of liquors he and his family trafficked. In 1776, he had "2 Gall: of Cherry Brandy"; two gallons of shrub, a brandy or rum sweetened by sugar or citrus fruit; port wine; Malaga wine; red wine; British and French brandy; and two different kinds of rum, from the West Indies and New York.[93] Two years later, the variety diminished, possibly reflecting growing scarcity and disruptions caused by the war. Regardless, by 1778 alcohol represented roughly 42 percent of the value of Askin's fur trade merchandise.[94]

Beyond rum and brandy, Askin's inventories broadly reflect the demands Indigenous peoples in the Great Lakes placed on merchants in regard to their furs. Notably, Askin paid close attention to the Indian cloth trade and the material bounty of Great Britain's consumer revolution: breeches, mittens, multiple styles of blankets, shirts, trousers, strouds, calico, flannels, beads, dye, paint, gartering, ribbon, a variety of jackets, bolts of fabric, needles, thimbles, and thread.[95] These items, chosen to conform to exacting Indigenous specifications, especially in regards to color, size, and utility, would be exchanged for furs, and then, once in Indian hands, they were reworked and refashioned.[96] Indians modified blankets into skirts, robes, and even loincloths; they preferred large shirts worn past the waist and cinched; and they incorporated ribbons and paint into warrior attire. These materials would account for roughly 7 percent of the total value of Askin's fur trade merchandise in 1778.

Further, Askin and his family began investing heavily in Great Lakes shipping, a development precipitated, in part, by a fortuitous marriage and the tremendous volume of merchandise Askin now managed. In 1774, Marie's sister, Therese, the daughter who stayed behind in Detroit to care for their ailing father, married Commodore Alexander Grant, a former soldier during the Seven Years' War who now served as the navy superintendent of the Great Lakes.[97] He held a position of considerable power and authority. Beyond maintaining the readiness of the British fleet and overseeing the construction and repair of new and old ships, Grant controlled access to their cargo holds.[98] In other words, he supervised whose merchandise left port, and whose did not. By 1768, Grant had effectively monopolized shipping in the Great Lakes and even used his power to curtail the development of rival shipping concerns.

For example, in the early 1770s Phyn, Ellice, and Company constructed several ships and a new depot at Fort Erie with the intent of offering a mercantile challenge to Grant's imperial dominance.[99] The partnership built the *Angelica*, a forty-five-ton trading vessel, and used it to ship their merchandise across Lake Erie to Detroit. Grant retaliated aggressively; he stalled their goods and stymied them in port, gave preferential shipping rates to Phyn, Ellice, and Company's competitors, and lost his own money undercutting the prices of their merchandise in the upper Great Lakes. The partnership caved and sold their ship to Grant. With the advent of the American rebellion, his hold over the trade only grew tighter.

Under Grant's auspices, Askin and his family built their own cargo ship at Detroit in 1774, and christened her the *Archange*.[100] Named after Askin's wife, the vessel transported goods across Lake Erie from Fort Niagara to Detroit. Over the next two years, investments in the *Welcome*, *Mackinac*, and *De Peyster* followed.[101] Supported by a contingent of bateaux and canoes, Askin's fleet carried a tremendous volume of freight across the Great Lakes, moving the heavy bulk supplies or packs of fur to one of his many depots.

Writing to his brother-in-law, "We must never disappoint people in the matter of shipping goods," Askin relied on his family and his slaves to pilot these vessels to fulfill the contracts he made.[102] Askin's African slaves, Pompey and Jupiter, showed how slavery fit into his numerous shipping enterprises.[103] In a diary he kept during this period, Askin noted that "Pomp Entered on Board the Sloop Archange," seemingly to preform trade-related work, and during the American rebellion, while piloting the *Felicity*, Robertson noted that "negros with [a] little vessel" passed Arbre Croche while sailing to Michilimackinac.[104] Likewise, Askin sold an Indian slave for being "too stupid to make a sailor or to be any good whatever."[105]

Beholden labor, whether in the form of family or slaves, ensured control over a sprawling enterprise that required extreme coordination during the best of times. Later, in 1781, for example, toward the end of the American rebellion and after years of disruptions, a group of French and British merchants wrote to General Frederick Haldimand, the governor of Quebec, about Askin and his family. "[Jean Baptiste] Barthe," they complained, "has the advantage of all other Merchants trading at the posts of Ma[c]kina[c] and Detroit by forwarding his goods to the earliest markets and demanding an exorbitant price for the freight of Merchandise belonging to others."[106]

Much of the cargo Askin and his family carried through the Great Lakes came from a shifting and vacillating series of Montreal-based partnerships. Elite French and British merchants such as Benjamin and Joseph Frobisher, James McGill, Isaac Todd, Charles Chaboillez, Simon McTavish, and numerous others began coordinating and consolidating their fur trade efforts in the upper Great Lakes, sidestepping the potentially destructive consequences of competing against each other for a market share.[107] By the mid-1770s, they became known as the North West Company, and over the next several decades they solidified their membership into a joint-stock system and began to aggressively, violently, and even illegally absorb or shutdown rival partnerships in the Great Lakes.[108] In the late 1780s, for example, men from the North West Company shot and killed John Ross, a onetime partner in the company, who had allied himself with the new insurgent rival, Gregory, McLeod, and Company.[109] By the turn of the century, their efforts largely succeeded.

Following in the wake of Askin's earlier partnership, the North West Company used Grand Portage as its staging area, ignoring the Hudson's Bay Company's monopoly on the far north, and their intense rivalry pushed the fur trade deeper into the North American interior. Like Phyn, Ellice, and Company in upper New York, the North West merchants relied upon intermediaries and wintering traders to conduct their business.[110] While never a partner or investor,

Askin enjoyed a lucrative and beneficial relationship with the company, many of whose members he counted as close colleagues or former partners.

Askin's letter book for 1778 shows how much of his attention went to ensuring the swift and smooth transfer of North West Company merchandise and provisions throughout the Great Lakes on his ships and through his depots, and to the ensuing profits he reaped. Writing to Isaac Todd and James McGill, his major suppliers at Montreal, Askin called the North West Company "the most respectable both as proprietors & amount."[111] He forwarded vessels laden with "Rum, Corn & what's Most necessary" to Grand Portage, where North West Company partners, like Forrest Oakes and Charles Chaboillez, supervised the exchange of those goods for peltry. Canoes of "corn, Sugar, Gum, Bark, & Watap" followed.[112] Askin's importance to the company should not be discounted.

In June 1778, for example, he wrote to Joseph Frobisher and James McGill, who "transact[ed] the business of the N. W. Co," to assert his independence and desire to profit widely. To Askin, though the North West Company had "the Preference" of his ships, depots, and efforts, he intended "to serve others" as well.[113] He wrote to James Sterling in Detroit that he had "positive contracts for above thousand [pounds]" of flour.[114] He carried on a brisk trade in high-quality alcohol for the aristocratic British officers and wealthy merchants of the upper Great Lakes. He ordered the "best Madeira" for an officer and set aside a "barrel of good port wine and two barrels of whiskey" for his brother-in-law's personal enjoyment.[115] Success followed success, and in 1780, Captain Samuel Robertson estimated that their trading house at Sault Saint Marie alone was worth around £7,000.[116]

Moreover, Askin was not opposed to organization or collusion if it helped him, his fellow merchants, or the British Crown. For example, in the spring and summer of 1779, Askin, along with twenty-five other Michilimackinac merchants and traders, including David McCrae, Ezekiel Solomons, Henry Bostwick, Benjamin Lyon, and Louis Chevalier, established a general store. De Peyster gave them the idea, stating that it "would be very useful in a time as critical as the present" to "out all their merchandise in a general Store for trading with the savages." As a way of restricting competition and overcoming potential merchandise shortages, the general store would centralize their merchandise, fix prices for their goods, refrain from private, individual trade with the Indians, and prevent "harm[ing] the interests of the Company, under penalty of losing all their goods, without any return." Its leadership would be a rough democracy of shareholders. A committee of members, chosen by a majority vote, would adjudicate disputes; appoint clerks, interpreters, and engagés to trade with the Indians; and supply de Peyster, and his eventual replacement, Captain Patrick Sinclair, when the supplies they received from the British Crown arrived late, or proved too sparse.[117] They chartered the general store until July 31, 1780, and they found some success.

Interestingly, Askin worked to have himself excluded from the clause of the store's charter that concerned private trade with the Indians. In fact, he was the only merchant with a special dispensation. Article 15 stated: "As Mr. Askin wishes to avoid every dispute or blame for the future, he warns all the subscribers that he has interests at Sault St. Marie; therefore the 6th Article shall not be put in execution against him."[118] Working together was well and good, but not, Askin thought, if it threatened what he had already built.

Askin would be a member until the store dissolved with some acrimony and discontent in late summer 1780. Over the preceding year, the Indians asked why they should "take their goods from one particular store at an advanced price when their Former Traders desired only to have their goods in their possession."[119] The traders and merchants also found cooperation hurtful to their bottom lines, and when they found access to bountiful goods, they preferred to trade alone. By then, though, Askin had different troubles and manifold worries, and the collapse of the store was the least of his concerns.

Since the summer of 1778, the consequences of the American rebellion began to compound, and Askin and his family experienced the effects of the empire's efforts to maintain an effective war footing. In early May, for instance, Major Arent Schuyler de Peyster confiscated and armed the *Welcome* to protect Michilimackinac.[120] Meanwhile in Detroit, the lieutenant governor, Henry Hamilton, occupied with sponsoring Indian raids in the backcountry and struggling with "extravagant price[s] of Grain & Flour" at his own post, began to restrict the movement of goods northward.[121]

Since 1776, General Guy Carleton, the governor of Quebec, began restricting and controlling private shipping on the Great Lakes to stymie the spread of colonial discord. By and large, this put private vessels into the Crown's hands, and, in general, ensured the movement of military supplies to vital posts across the region. For merchants and traders like Askin and his colleagues, Carleton's efforts meant their goods became second-class cargo as the British military mobilized its resources for war. In late May 1777, Carleton wrote a letter to Hamilton in Detroit and explained the contours of his new policy: "The traders may be accommodated with a passage on Board of these Vessels, provided the same can be done without the least inconvenience to the King's Service."[122] However, British imperial control over shipping, especially regarding the far-flung fur trade, meant supply crunches, scarcity, and disruptions.

"I do declare," Askin wrote to Todd and McGill, "as things now go on, I don't know what to order, of all I write for nothing Arrives."[123] By the end of May he had to apologize to Charles Chaboillez at Grand Portage about sending whiskey instead of his requested rum. "We are told," Askin explained, "Governor Hamilton will not allow either liquor or provisions to leave [Detroit]."[124] With shortages of vital goods becoming more acute, and disappointments more common, he resorted to an ad hoc system of proportional supplying. He ordered his son-in-law "to divide [his] merchandise equally between . . . two vessels in manner so that . . . [the] trader[s] would receive some goods," rather than nothing at all.[125] After apologizing, he began to complain. Finally, he issued a dire warning to Sterling: if ships failed to carry a large supply of flour and corn north, "Some persons in [the] back country will perish & the trade will be hurt."[126]

Finding it increasingly difficult to "please everybody" and to "never give offence" in matters of trade, Askin appealed directly to the imperial and familial authority of de Peyster and Grant to get his merchandise moving again. In late April 1778, he asked Grant to "acquaint the Governor [of Detroit]" with the shortages of vital supplies, arguing that he, at least, "ought to be a judge of the

Provision necessary to carry on the trade of [Michilimackinac]."[127] Pointing to his own position as deputy commissar and his tremendous success as a fur trade merchant in the upper Great Lakes, Askin readily positioned himself as an arbiter of empire and trade with the experiential and economic authority to question the wisdom of British officials like Hamilton. Likewise, he bolstered his position by appealing to de Peyster to "make known to Governor Hamilton the bad consiquences of laying an Imbargo on Provisions & ct. without which it's impossible that trade be Supported."[128] In fact, de Peyster and Askin's growing relationship allowed Askin to draw much-needed supplies directly from the king's stores at Michilimackinac, even though he often found the flour "so bad."[129] In early June, de Peyster even allowed him to send a ship directly to Detroit for his merchandise with "such Vouchers as [he] hop[ed] [would] convince the Governor of the necessity of its coming."[130] His efforts seemed to have paid off. By the end of June, he wrote to Chaboillez that his "vessel from Detroit arrived."[131]

Askin and his family went to work as soon as the ship docked. On June 30, 1778, he sent the bill of lading of the *Archange* to Jean Baptiste at Sault Ste. Marie, and ordered him to "Mark 38 barrels of rum N W for the North West Company, and the remaining 10 barrels mark C CH for Mr. Charles Chaboillez."[132] However, after inventorying the ship, Askin found that "instead of being loaded for [him] Solely, She was obliged to bring the Kings Store & even other things, so that [he] only got in her some Rum & Flour."[133] Despite de Peyster's letter, which Askin "imagine[d] . . . explained fully . . . [the] reasons for letting [his] Vessell go to Detroit," Hamilton's decision to use Askin's ship for military ends represented, in Askin's mind, a failure to appreciate the significance and true value of the trade.[134] This proved disappointing and economically disturbing, obstructing the kind of regional and infrastructural development in which Askin and his family excelled. "All my attempts are vain," he wrote in a letter to members of the North West Company, "my own Vessell is treated in the same manner as if she was paid by the Crown, if this continues rather than have the anxiety I have had this Summer I will not contract with any person."[135] Surveying the situation from Michilimackinac, Askin came to a decision. For the first time since 1768, he refused to take on new contracts, explaining, "There is too much risk, besides the blame one incurs."[136]

By late summer 1778, the exigencies of war took their toll on Askin's patience and trade. Despite the disruptive effects of Hamilton's embargos, Askin remained mostly unscathed and well placed to pursue his efforts once the rebellion collapsed and the Crown reestablished its authority in North America. In fact, he felt secure enough to continue developing his new depot with Benjamin Lyon, who had himself "Suffer[ed] much by his goods not comeing," and ordered goods from Isaac Todd and James McGill for their "trade at the entrance of the french River."[137] For most of the war, Askin had used his family's skills and labor, his working relationship with imperial officials like de Peyster and Grant, and his own intimate and hard-won understanding of the intricacies of the Great Lakes fur trade to minimize and overcome risk, while preparing for the future. For him, this meant not to repeat the past.

In late June, he wrote to Alexander Henry, his longtime colleague at Michilimackinac and fellow survivor of Pontiac's War, reflecting on "these troublesome times" and how they cause "many disputes in which a man often gets involved, notwithstanding his great desire to the contrary."[138] Once, as a younger man, he had traveled to Detroit to pursue his trade with disastrous consequences. Now, nearly forty years old, Askin "did not go to Detroit . . . as [he] intended," but resolved to avoid the violence and turmoil of the rebellion, and remain at Michilimackinac where, he wrote to Henry, "I'm sure to live in peace."[139]

"Our news," John Askin wrote to Sampson Fleming in Detroit, "is that Genl Clintons Army defeated Genl Gates below Albany & killed him with 7000 of his people, which prevented any attempt against Canada last Winter."[140] At a distant and isolated post like Michilimackinac, rumor and conjecture came ashore in fits and starts with the arrival of every new eastern canoe, and then swirled and rippled around the community. For the British war effort, the destruction of a large American army would have seemed to spell the end of the rebellion, and for Askin and so many others who had heard nothing but accounts of British military success since early 1776 the rumor seemed plausible.

However, events began to clarify themselves quickly, and just two weeks after the letter to Fleming, Askin wrote in a short note to Richard Dobie, a Montreal merchant, "The affair of General Burgoyne makes us anxious for our friends."[141]

Burgoyne and his nearly 7,100 British and Hessian soldiers pushed into the wilderness of northern New York in the summer of 1777. Despite a slow and laborious pace, the British invasion saw early victories, capturing Fort Ticonderoga, a former French fort that had helped its defenders decimate a large British army during the Seven Years' War. The Americans retreated, burning bridges, chopping down trees to block roads, and destroying whatever supplies they could find, while Burgoyne gave chase, losing soldiers along the way to garrison duty, skirmishes, and work detail. Moving slowly through a hostile countryside, and stretching their supply lines daily, Burgoyne and his lieutenants sent out raids to forage for foods, draft animals, and horses, but the resulting theft, destruction, and death, especially at the hands of Burgoyne's Indian allies, infuriated loyalists and rebels alike.

By the middle of August, American forces defeated and captured a large contingent of Hessian soldiers, and a new commander—a former British officer named Horatio Gates—took command of the rapidly growing American army at the mouth of the Mohawk River. Moving ever south, seven thousand British and German soldiers faced off against nine thousand Americans, and on September 19, a few miles west of the Hudson River near the village of Stillwater, the two armies met.[142] The British kept the field, but lost twice the number of men; still more Americans came to fight, while Burgoyne watched many of his soldiers run away and clung to the hope that a British army from New York City would save him and those who remained.

For several weeks, the British and American forces waited, and for Burgoyne no help came. Running low on food and refusing to retreat, on October 7 he and his bloodied army attacked the Americans. In the days of fighting, they lost nearly one thousand men. Ten days later, he surrendered his sword. The British had lost an entire army in northern New York. Across the Atlantic, the kingdom of France, which had long provided the American rebels with money and supplies, began negotiating an alliance with the Continental Congress in

December, and by March 1778 France officially declared war on Great Britain. The Spanish and the Dutch quickly followed suit, and what had once been a civil war devolved into a worldwide struggle of empire.[143]

Across Indian Country, pro-American agents began trumpeting the new alliance, hoping to rekindle the belief that the French father would return to his children.[144] By the end of the summer, Major Arent Schuyler de Peyster at Michilimackinac fired off a letter to Haldimand and reported a rumor spreading that "the french are soon to take possession of that country as there are no troops to prevent the Virginians from going there."[145] Two weeks later, de Peyster learned the truth of the situation, and relayed in a short letter that "the rebels are in possession of all of the Illinois."[146] Lieutenant Governor Henry Hamilton, in Detroit, got the news even quicker, and he began to prepare an expedition to oust the Americans by early September, and the peace that Askin desired became less certain.

George Rogers Clark and his Virginians caught the British unaware. On June 24, 1778, a force of nearly two hundred Americans left the falls of the Ohio River and cut through forest and prairie, traveling over one hundred miles to arrive, half starved, outside of Kaskaskia. In the early morning of July 5, Clark and his men captured Fort Gage without exchanging gunfire. Writing to Haldimand at Quebec, de Peyster revealed that the commandant of the post and several other inhabitants were put "in Irons for having refused the oaths of Allegiance to the King of Spain, the French King and the Congress."[147] With Kaskaskia as a base of operations, Clark's forces, bolstered by the region's pro-American French inhabitants, fanned out across Illinois Country, capturing the important communities and administering loyalty oaths. Hamilton predicted to Carleton that the Americans would "probably send to St. Vincennes for the purpose" and by early August 1778, Clark, the twenty-six-year-old Virginian, had conquered a large swatch of British North America.[148]

De Peyster understood the implications of Clark's occupation: "I fear," he wrote to Haldimand, "that if [the Americans] are not routed by some means that the whole Mississippi Trade is knocked up."[149] Meanwhile in Detroit, in mid-September Hamilton promised the governor of Quebec that "the preparative[s] for our little enterprize are forwarding with alacrity," detailing the baking of bread, the raising of militia, and the repairing of boats.[150] By October, as the leaves began to change and the frigid cold descended across the land, Hamilton planned to march south and throw the Americans out of Illinois Country for good.

At the garrison's commissary in Michilimackinac, Askin heard about the military expedition preparing to head south and believed Hamilton and his men would oust the rebels come spring. At the King's Storehouse, Askin kept track of the garrison's supplies; over the frozen winter, cut off from Detroit by ice, careful accounting became vital to survival. In the northern Great Lakes, the day darkened early. Askin lit extra candles and worked his way around the room, taking careful account of the garrison's flour—the same variety that helped save his reputation and trade over the summer's shortages. As he set out to prepare for another frigid Great Lakes winter, his family and trade in relative accord, he reflected on how his carefully nurtured relationships with imperial officials such as Captain Arent Schuyler de Peyster and Alexander Grant, the talents and labor of his network of French kin, and his own insight into trade and access to British goods had all proved elastic enough to weather the potential injury of outside adversity. Yet it was not the trials of war and revolution, but the tribulations of merchant and empire in conflict, that would irrevocably fracture the peace and prosperity Askin had worked years to sustain.

CHAPTER FIVE

The Key of Canada in His Pocket

Michilimackinac, the British Empire, and John Askin's Banishment, 1779–1781

In September 1779, John Askin and several influential merchants of Michilimackinac commissioned an ornate silver punch bowl, etched with an immense symbolic turtle. They presented the dish to Major Arent Schuyler de Peyster in celebration of his promotion to Detroit and to commemorate his tenure at Michilimackinac.[1] Such generosity touched him. "The approbation of my conduct," de Peyster wrote, "during a long command, in the critical situation of affairs, cannot be otherwise than flattering to me." He had made it his "study to promote the trade of this Post and its Dependencies,"[2] and these efforts had endeared him to many merchants, especially Askin.

Effective Michilimackinac commandants negotiated the demands of the British military and government and the expectations of its Indian allies, and ensured the vitality of the fur trade. Being able to manage contradictory impulses, directives, or exigencies proved, in many ways, to be the central command challenge of Michilimackinac once the British took possession of it in the early 1760s. It is fair to say that when de Peyster left Michilimackinac in 1779, he took with him more than a bowl of finely etched silver. He carried with him a vast store of knowledge and the tangled web of relationships that made his tenure as commandant workable and effective. And while Detroit gained an able officer, de Peyster's absence created a vacuum at Michilimackinac that put Askin and his family at tremendous risk. De Peyster's replacement, Captain Patrick Sinclair, tasked to ferret out those "unbecoming the Fidelity & Allegiance they owe their Sovereign," during the height of the American Revolution, struggled with the extent of his authority and mistrusted the individuals and relationships that undergirded his command; in essence, he undermined the vital ties and relationships that tethered the British Empire, its Great Lakes fur trade, and its Indian allies together.[3]

Unlike other British commanders whose arrogance or Francophobia often blinded them to "the social complexities" of the upper Great Lakes, de Peyster worked tirelessly to build, maintain, and shore up relationships with the French and Indian communities that surrounded him.[4] Early in his tenure, for example, de Peyster organized a council with the Ojibwa and Sioux to the west, helping to establish peace between both communities as Great Britain and its Atlantic colonies warred.[5] His skillful negotiations ensured their continued allegiance to Great Britain. Likewise, by generating reciprocal relationships with multiethnic men like Louis Chevalier and Charles de Langlade, who were tied into the wider French and Indian world of the Great Lakes through kinship and marriage, de Peyster organized Indian war parties for the military.[6] Through de Peyster's influence, de Langlade and his warriors helped recapture Montreal and served in the British invasion of upstate New York.

Likewise, the Indian communities of the upper Great Lakes felt the loss of de Peyster just as acutely as Michilimackinac's merchants and traders. During a council meeting shortly before de Peyster traveled to Detroit, the old Odawa chief Jinquis Tawanong declaimed:

> Father,—I rise to bid you farewell in the name of the Ottawa nation. I am, likewise, to speak for the many strangers assembled at this council-fire—our old men, our wives and children, have hired me to speak for them likewise. It is with my tongue they bid you farewell, but it is with their own eyes they will

> weep your loss. They will stand upon the lakeside and strain their eyes until they can see your bark no more.[7]

To seal his words, he gestured to several of his men, and together they presented and placed in front of de Peyster presents of 150 bags of Indian corn, and packs of skins and furs. Then Jinquis Tawanong sat down, and Quieouigoushkam, another chief, stood up and took his place. "Farewell, father!," Quieouigoushkam spoke to de Peyster, "We lose you; but the vile Kitchikomokamans [Americans] shall pay for it. They shall carry water at this fort of Michilimackinac."[8] Solemnized by gifts and the promise to turn Great Britain's enemies into slaves, the two speeches, alongside the commemorative gift given by Michilimackinac's merchants and traders, offer a window that reveals more than the tremendous esteem and respect held by many for de Peyster: it demonstrates the central relationships that propelled the British administration within Indian country.

In terms of trade and empire, de Peyster knew better than most that the strength of the British Empire in the Great Lakes rested on establishing strong ties and relationships with the region's Indian communities. Pontiac's War and the troubled years that followed confirmed the need of post commanders like Captain William Howard and Major Robert Rogers to occasionally avoid imperial policy and the cost-saving demands of an intensely budget-minded Whitehall to achieve diplomatic ends. For example, council meetings required gifts; Indians gave British leaders smaller, more symbolic presents, while de Peyster and his fellow commandants provided copious quantities of necessary items: cloth, strouds, shirts, flour, tools, knives, needles, gunpowder, and some liquor. In the hands of chiefs and headmen, these goods were distributed to community members, and soft chains of obligation emanated outward from Michilimackinac to vital Indian communities like the Odawa village of Arbre Croche. Peaceful relationships kept costs down for the British government and, more importantly, kept the Great Lakes fur trade free of turbulence. Alienating Indians through imperial parsimony, or allowing untrammeled warfare to develop between different communities across the Great Lakes, would have meant disaster for French and British merchants and traders from

Michilimackinac to London. War disrupted seasonal hunting and trapping and the growing of corn; there would be no furs, no sustenance, and the goods from Europe would go unsold or unredeemed. When government supplies arrived too late in the season or proved too few to meet the demands and expectations of His Majesty's Indian allies, post commanders like de Peyster could count on merchants like Askin to step in and provide necessary merchandise and goods. At times, de Peyster relied upon French and British merchants and traders to help bolster his efforts, while they relied upon de Peyster to create peace and stability for their own economic endeavors.

As a middleman at Michilimackinac, Askin had prospered under de Peyster's command, building an expansive, multiethnic network of exchange that encompassed a large swatch of the western Great Lakes. Upon hearing news of de Peyster's promotion, the middle-aged merchant reflected on the "various acts of kindness" his commandant had shown him, even as he worried over the uncertainties that a new commandant might inspire when taking charge of the important post.[9] At forty, Askin was still, in the words of a former trading partner, "pretty much of a schemer," attempting to prosper in a climate characterized by destructive warfare.[10] For example, he sent Samuel Robertson, Askin's son-in-law, "to examine the coast along the French River [at the Georgian Bay]" for a suitable place "to build a [trading] house."[11] A man like Askin understood that a rapidly burgeoning and increasingly expansive fur trade required effective means of storing, transporting, and facilitating the movement of merchandise and furs.[12] This new French River depot would "facilitate the transport of [Askin's] goods from Montreal by the Grand River" and circumvent the long, dangerous, and costly trek from the St. Lawrence River to Michilimackinac and the upper Great Lakes.[13] It would further reduce shipping and labor costs for his Montreal suppliers; their goods would require less markup, and Askin could leverage their cheaper cost into more furs and higher profit margins. Collaborating with Benjamin Lyon, a Jewish trader whose early life in North America mirrored Askin's own, the two men saw it as an important investment in an imperially contested region.[14] Little did Askin know that the arrival of the new commandant would cause his plans to go horribly askew.

In Quebec, Captain Patrick Sinclair, de Peyster's replacement, quarreled with General Frederick Haldimand, the Switzerland-born royal governor of Quebec.[15] It was late August 1779. For nearly four years, Sinclair had struggled across the Atlantic Ocean toward the western Great Lakes, but the turmoil of the American rebellion thwarted his aspirations.[16] When he finally arrived at Quebec, poised to take up his long-coveted post at Michilimackinac, Sinclair learned that his command seemed only to invite others to undermine his authority and offer the "annihilat[ion] [of] his military rank."[17] Haldimand and Sinclair wrangled over the aftermath of American George Rogers Clark's successful invasion of the Ohio Valley and Illinois Country.[18] In the frantic months after Clark's invasion in 1778, Henry Hamilton, the lieutenant governor of Detroit, organized a small force of British soldiers, French militia, and Indian warriors.[19] Setting out in October, they began the arduous three-hundred-mile trek south, trying to rally Indian support against Clark and the Americans along the way.[20] Two months later, Hamilton's men recaptured Vincennes. Confident that the Americans were too far away to counterattack, Hamilton allowed his Indian and French forces to disperse for the winter, leaving only a skeleton crew of British soldiers to hold the post. However, nearly two hundred miles away at Kaskaskia, Clark immediately organized a party of American soldiers and set off across the flooded Illinois landscape. In the cold of February, Clark laid siege to the British soldiers within the fort. Hamilton held his position overnight, before surrendering in the morning. Clark clapped Hamilton, his soldiers, and the post's traders in chains and sent them to Virginia.

Hamilton's capture resulted in a reshuffling of the British command in the Great Lakes, and sparked efforts to rethink the nature of Sinclair's command at Michilimackinac. In his orders to Sinclair, Haldimand explained that his new post would "re-unite as much as possible the Civil and Military Powers in the same Hands," but would ultimately remain a civilian position. At Michilimackinac, Sinclair would, of course, "receive the Honors usually paid to the Commanding officer" and wield the powers "necessary for the Security of the Post and its immediate Defense," but only in the absence of a senior military officer. For the most part, the posting required him "to pay great attention to the Indians" and "study the Humours and Dispositions of the several Persons attached to [the] post, the Traders thereto and Interpreters . . . should any of them behave in a manner unbecoming the Fidelity & Allegiance they owe their Sovereign."[21] For his part, Sinclair brooded over his orders and begged Haldimand to reconsider. He grew disturbed when the general replied that he could not "invest him with fuller powers." Finally, Sinclair sat down and, in a terse and disingenuous reply, petulantly reminded Haldimand that he had never solicited his appointment to Michilimackinac, nor did he wish to embarrass the British Crown as Hamilton had. He asked for immediate "leave to return to England."[22]

Patrick Sinclair, born in Lybster, Scotland, in 1736, joined the British army at the height of the Seven Years' War. At eighteen, he joined the Highlander Forty-Second Foot as an ensign, the most junior rank of commissioned officers. He saw his first significant military action in 1759 during the British conquest of Guadeloupe, an important French sugar island. Soon after, he found himself in northern New York, where, like Askin, he served under the command of General Jeffrey Amherst during the campaign against the French along the St. Lawrence River. He took command of a French vessel, sparking an interest in the waterways of North America. Rising in rank, he became a lieutenant, and in the fall of 1761, he transferred from the Forty-Second Foot to the Fifteenth Foot, where he patrolled the waters of Lakes Ontario and Huron as a marine. He saw service during Pontiac's War in 1763, and a year later he played an important role in reestablishing British authority at Michilimackinac. Between 1763 and 1767, Sinclair built relationships with the local Ojibwa communities and the traders and merchants in Detroit, and oversaw the navigation of Lake Huron; he provisioned ships and helped vessels in distress, protected traders from Indian attacks or raids, conducted exploration and mapping expeditions, and supported and helped supply the disparate garrisons of the Great Lakes. However, when Sir William Johnson's Indian policy and fur trade reforms failed, the British Crown cut the military's budget and mustered Sinclair out of active service. The merchants of Detroit presented him a silver bowl as a "public testimony of their gratitude" for "the encouragement experienced upon all occasions by the merchants in the Indian countries." Likewise, in the summer of 1768, Sinclair received a title for land on the Huron River from the Ojibwa and Odawa communities of Detroit. The land was given as an example of "the love and regard [the Ojibwa and Odawa] bear for our friend Lieut. Patrick Sinclair and . . . for the many charitable acts he has done us, our wives and children."[23] He returned to his family home in Scotland in 1769, received a promotion to captain, and spent six long years semiretired working as a military recruiter, all the while petitioning the British Crown for a new commission in North America. To his fortune, the Quebec Act, which reorganized the governance and territories of the Great Lakes and St. Lawrence River Valley, offered a chance for him to return as one of the new lieutenant governors of the western posts.[24] He had long waited to reenter the Great Lakes region, and, once at Michilimackinac, he planned to use his previous experiences to make a substantial mark on the fur trade community.

Back in North America, the heat and histrionics of August caused Haldimand to boil over; he refused to placate Sinclair's tantrum any further, and ordered the angry Scotsman directly to Michilimackinac, posthaste.[25] Taut with frustration, Sinclair arrived at Michilimackinac in early October 1779. He passed through the post's sea-gates and made his way to the commandant's quarters, where he encountered Major Arent Schuyler de Peyster. According to Sinclair, de Peyster's "unwearied attention . . . left [nothing] unessayed to attach the Indians to the Government" and left the "place in a state which does him great credit."[26] It is here that Askin made his appearance; he took the initiative to meet the new commandant, or perhaps, as deputy commissar, de Peyster called for him. However, what is known is that Askin failed to make a good first impression. According to Sinclair, Askin, elated by his newest investment at French River, "vaunted before Major de Peyster of having the Key of Canada in his Pocket." Such boasting spoke to Askin's economic hold and reach in the Great Lakes fur trade, but its stridency incensed Sinclair, who looked upon the actions of the merchant with considerable suspicion and mistrust. "The King's Provision store," Sinclair lamented, "required not only my strict Attention, but my vigilance, being in the charge of a man who has a contract with the North

West Traders." Not content with simple surveillance of Askin, he promised action "to put every key in this part of the Country in [Haldimand's] Hands."[27]

Surveillance and security became the watchwords of Sinclair's new administration. After taking leave of de Peyster and Askin, Sinclair ordered the French and British traders who wintered among the Indians to swear an oath of allegiance to the British Crown. From there, he then surveyed Michilimackinac and its environs. Sinclair wrote to Lieutenant Dietrich Brehm, the aide-de-camp of General Haldimand, protesting that the fort, with its windswept wooden palisades, was "[incapable] of being secured against any annoyance but small arms, of giving any protection to vessels, and Traders, or any collection of Fuel, Forage, or other Articles necessary . . . for the Garrison." In fact, Sinclair already had a tangible alternative in mind. He had spent several hours surveying a small island within eyesight of the current fort that seemed to offer a good natural harbor, productive farmlands, and, more importantly, military protection from direct attacks. Sinclair argued to his superiors that Mackinac Island "would be our place of greatest safety."[28] Soon after his arrival, with prior approval from Haldimand, he began the arduous process of transferring the entire community of Michilimackinac—its military and trading establishment—across the straits. He ignored the protests of the elite French and British merchants who bore the costs of transporting their own houses, merchandise, and families, and appointed Captain Samuel Robertson, Askin's son-in-law, to oversee the construction taking place on the island.

"With [the] aid of a Mr. Robertson," Sinclair was able "to erect a Block House" and expand the new wharf out "150 feet" into "two fathoms of water." Impressed by Robertson's work and efforts, Sinclair praised him as "an able artificer and sensible man," and they made significant progress toward the commandant's ultimate goal of protecting Michilimackinac from hostile agents, both abroad and at home.[29] This was an important development, especially as the new year of 1780 brought Sinclair his first call to arms. However, the campaign that he and others would engineer against the Spanish who held Louisiana and the Americans in the Illinois Country would serve as an important backdrop for his conflicts with Askin and Askin's family.[30] In fact, during the campaign and its aftermath, Sinclair would take action against several other key figures in the Great Lakes (most notably, the Chevalier family at St. Joseph), revealing the degree to which the exigencies of war empowered him to undermine behaviors and relationships that he found threatening and disruptive to the British Crown.

With Great Britain at war with the Spanish forces west of the Mississippi River, Sinclair tapped Jean Baptiste Cadot at Sault Ste. Marie in February 1780 to recruit a party of Ojibwa and join up with Wabasha and a Sioux war party.[31] In a dispatch to Haldimand, Sinclair vouched for Cadot: "the Indians are under the absolute authority of Mr. Cadot, who is a very honest man."[32] Warriors were raised among the Objiwe, Sioux, Menominee, Ho-Chunk, Sac, Fox, Odawa, Potawatomi, and Kickapoo. By recruiting "Canadians in the Upper Country" and "sen[ding] away as many as I can of the Indians," Sinclair hoped to "attack the Spanish Settlements as low down [the Mississippi River] as they possibly can."[33] By May 1780, Sinclair had raised "Seven hundred fifty men including Traders, servants and Indians" under the leadership of trader and former soldier Emanuel Hesse, and secured Charles de Langlade, "with a chosen Band of Indians and Canadians" to station themselves at Chicago as a secondary force; together they would wage "an attack on the Spanish & [the Americans]."[34] However, news of their efforts soon reached the Spanish, who quickly fortified St. Louis.[35] In late May, the British force attacked, but instead of surprising an unsuspecting community, they faced entrenched Spanish soldiers and fiery spouts of cannon fire; the Indians and their French allies fled from obvious danger, and the British campaign in the Illinois Country ended in retreat and failure.[36]

In early July 1780, Sinclair wrote to Haldimand and complained that "The . . . Indian nations would have stormed the Spanish Lines if the Sacks [Sacs] and Outagamies [Meskwaki] under the treacherous leader Mons'r Calvé had not fallen back so early, as to give them but too well grounded suspicions that they were between two Fires." Other French traders, like Jean Marie Du Charme, "who traded in the country of the Sacks kept pace with Mon'r Calvé in his perfidy." Sinclair pointed to self-interest as the cause of their misconduct: "They have long shared the Profits arising from the Lead Mines & from the commerce with the Illinois." He further reported that Du Charme "permitted two profligate French who were in his charge as Prisoners, to go to the Illinois [Country]."[37] The two Frenchmen were from St. Joseph and lived among the Potawatomi. The men were also connected to Louis Chevalier, a French fur trader there who had married the important Potawatomi fur trade matriarch, Marie Madeleine.[38] Sinclair had found a scapegoat.

Louis Chevalier had a complicated reputation among the British in the Great Lakes. In 1776, Henry Hamilton, then at Detroit, "attributed [to Chevalier] the assassination of several traders at St. Joseph."[39] However, in June 1777, de Peyster, more perceptive, expressed surprise at the St. Joseph Potawatomi: "their behavior [at Michilimackinac] has been Remarkably good." They had come to Michilimackinac "under the conduct of Monsr. Le Chevallier a man spoken very ill of at Detroit," and de Peyster had expected worse. Despite his reservations, de Peyster understood a deeper truth about Chevalier, one that spoke to Chevalier's value as an intermediary between the British and their Indian allies: "I . . . perceive by the great attachment those Indians have to him that he had better be caressed at present than otherwise."[40] Trust and forbearance paid dividends. A year later, in 1778, Chevalier warned de Peyster about Potawatomi warriors traveling to negotiate with the Americans in Illinois and then helped thwart their efforts.[41] Chevalier continued to be a source of intelligence for the British until the end of the war. However, Sinclair viewed him, like Askin, with suspicion. He wrote to Haldimand in May 1780: "Mr. Chevalier will certainly endeavour to introduce a French or Rebel party at St. Joseph's if our movements do not take place before Autumn."[42] Citing concerns over potential French disloyalty, he moved to oust the Chevalier family from the St. Joseph River valley.[43] He sent Joseph-Louis Ainsse, a Michilimackinac trader, interpreter, and Chevalier's nephew, with six canoes full of merchandise to oversee their removal.[44] Some forty-eight French and Indian men, women, and children were eventually relocated.

To Sinclair, the St. Joseph French were a "lawless strange class of People . . . [who] for many years settled for the sole purposes of overawing Commerce & making themselves usefull to whoever did most for their services . . . [and were] ever more ready for doing bad than good."[45] Though Sinclair removed what he saw as a potential French threat, as historian Susan Sleeper-Smith pointed out, he "left the community firmly in the control of Marie Madeleine's [multiethnic] kin network."[46] In other words, he failed to appreciate how durable were French and Indian ties of kinship, and he underestimated how the Potawatomi might react to the loss of their traders and kin. Sinclair, even if his suspicions were justified, failed to appreciate the larger context of the situations he engineered.

At Michilimackinac, Sinclair confined both Chevalier and Ainsse to the fort shortly after they arrived in late summer of 1780. He criticized Ainsse for meeting with Indians without his express permission. Sinclair complained that Ainsse had "interpreted for one of the Ottawa Chiefs who desired that Mr. Chevalier and Mr. Ainse should return to St. Joseph's."[47] Next, Sinclair confiscated Chevalier's private papers, "which were all the letters of the Commandants & their orders, and [Sinclair] promised to return them which he has not done." According to Chevalier, "After this treatment, which was as hard as unexpected, the petitioner asked for permission to go down to [Quebec]" to plead his case to Haldimand.[48] Ainsse demanded the same, but before he allowed them to leave, Sinclair forced them to pay a bond; they hired canoes and left the commandant of Michilimackinac behind.

By early July, de Peyster at Detroit noted that "the Pottawatimies . . . demand of me the reason why all their Traders are forced from them without leaving even their Smith." He worked to quell their alarm, promising them "that their Father at Michilimackinac will not withhold Traders from them." Still, de Peyster, like the Potawatomi, wondered why they would be deprived "at a time when they most heartily entered into the cause of their Father the King of Great Britain."[49] A few months later, in September 1780, Sinclair received a letter from de Peyster, who warned that "unless the Potawatomi have Traders among them they will in time become quite estranged or else become a great Burthen to Government at [Detroit.]"[50] Traders were sent, but the damage had already been done. Only months later, in February 1781, Louison Chevalier, the son of Louis and Marie Madeleine, served as a guide and translator for an invading Spanish force, bolstered by an even larger contingent of alienated Potawatomi warriors.

Back in February 1780, as the British ramped up their campaign against St. Louis and the Illinois Country, Sinclair returned his attention to Askin and his family and found a way to rein in the upstart merchant and deputy commissar of Michilimackinac. Sinclair worried that elaborately built fur trade depots would alert French, Spanish, and American agents to the important and strategic waterways of the upper Great Lakes. Also, if captured, the depot's walls offered defensive protection. At Sault Ste. Marie, Askin, Askin's brother-in-law, Jean Baptiste Barthe, and Robertson built their depot at their own considerable expense, and Sinclair ordered it dismantled. He wrote to Cadot "to remove part of a square of 120 feet per side fortified [depot built] by Messr. Askin &c. &c."[51]

Just a month later, on March 15, 1780, Sinclair crossed over to Mackinac Island to survey Samuel Robertson's work. While there, Sinclair asked Askin's son-in-law for the use of one of his ships stationed at Sault Ste. Marie, and, late in the evening, they left the island on friendly terms. However, soon after departing, Robertson intercepted a letter written by Sinclair, and had Louis Barthe, another of Askin's brothers-in-law, translate it. Sinclair later explained that his recruitment of the Sault Ste. Marie French "militated against [Robertson's] Private Views" and would be disruptive as "Canadians managed Mr. Robertsons Vessels & Trade."[52] Worried, Askin's son-in-law and brother-in-law "had the rashness to gain an Indian to deliver a Letter . . . [which they] broke open and cut out the words in it which offended." A day later, a patrol of British soldiers found the body of a young cabin boy named John Taylor lying sprawled in a snowdrift, frozen to death. Tucked in the youth's pocket lay the letter written by Sinclair containing detailed instructions for the recruitment of "Canadian Volunteers" to fight against the Spanish and Americans in the Illinois Country.[53]

Writing to Haldimand, Sinclair conceded that his case was circumstantial, but even so, he placed Robertson and Barthe under arrest. Like Chevalier and Ainsse, Sinclair took this opportunity to uproot members of another influential and well-connected fur trade family without considering the larger ramifications of his actions. In the short term, the incarceration proved disastrous for Robertson, who had left supplies on Mackinac Island—liquor, furniture, and flour—which, unguarded, were ransacked and stolen.[54] After letting Robertson spend nearly forty days imprisoned in Michilimackinac's guardhouse, Sinclair accepted a bond offered by Montreal-based merchants Joseph Frobisher and William Grant for his release.[55] Robertson promised to leave Michilimackinac and travel east to Quebec to appear before Haldimand. After just six months, the once-beneficial working relationship between Sinclair and Robertson had collapsed, and the consequences began to ripple outward.

Soon after, in mid-April 1780, Sinclair received clear instructions from Haldimand asking him to curtail expenses related to Indian diplomacy. Brehm, Haldimand's aide, wrote to Sinclair:

> Major De Peyster from his established character & from every report during his command at Michilimackinac has been zealous, active & attentive to his Duty—but from the very enormous sum that has been expended at that Post in the course of the last 18 months (for which nothing appears, to have been done) very far exceeding that at Niagara for the whole six nations, including the Pay of their officers (not contained in the Michilimackinac accounts) it appears impossible but that some very great abuses have been made by those employed in the Indian Department, many of whom are very improperly concerned in Trade—whose Interest it becomes to excite the Indians to everlasting Requisitions from the commanding officer—who taught to believe that they must be indispensably complied with, thinks himself obliged to submit.[56]

With the Americans, French, and Spanish incapable of supplying the Indian communities of the upper Great Lakes, Haldimand argued that Sinclair was in a position to hold the loyalty of the region's Indians with fewer goods; they were "absolutely dependent on you, for every necessary which it will be in your power to Extend or withhold according to their merits."[57] Haldimand's advice echoed General Jeffery Amherst's Indian policy after the Seven Years'

War—controlling diplomatic costs by rewarding good Indian service—which had not been well received.

The letter alarmed Sinclair. Haldimand had praised his performance, which was certainly good, but Sinclair had just organized an extensive campaign in the Illinois Country, and the costs associated with supporting so many warriors proved staggering. Likewise, Sinclair knew that the presents supplied by Great Britain to Michilimackinac often failed to meet diplomatic demands; he often needed, like de Peyster and the others before him, to buy from local merchants to supplement his supply. It was well and good, Sinclair mused, to say that he should reward the good behavior of His Majesty's Indian allies, but denying desperate Odawa or Ojibwa men and women much-needed supplies would have been a disastrous diplomatic blunder. Still, Sinclair knew that he needed to make an effort to improve the economy of Michilimackinac, and, in light of Robertson's recent impertinence, he turned his full attention to Askin, his deputy commissar.

In May 1780, Sinclair ordered Askin to inventory the King's Storehouse, and when he learned of the final tally, he felt vindicated.[58] Official records told Sinclair the storehouse contained 830 gallons of rum. However, Askin's count revealed that the commissariat was short by 27 gallons. Sinclair thought he had 115,420 pounds of flour to feed the garrison. He had only 98,000. Sinclair expected to find 53,220 pounds of salt pork, but Askin delivered him 49,220. The commandant immediately "place[d] a sentry on the Provisions stores," relieved Askin of his duties, and gave "the charge of [the storehouse]" to David Mitchell, the post's regimental surgeon.[59] Handing over the keys and accounts to Mitchell, Askin paid a £4,000 bond to Sinclair, and waited anxiously for permission to travel south to Detroit to deal with the repercussions of his removal.[60] After nearly sixteen years at Michilimackinac, Askin was made vulnerable by recalcitrant officials and the vagaries of North American warfare. Askin could explain the discrepancies, and de Peyster would vouch for his activities and character, but that could take weeks. With Robertson in jail and de Peyster in Detroit, Askin lacked close allies. Only Jean Baptiste Barthe, the other major partner in Askin's network, remained free to look after their operations.

Like Askin, Sinclair's attention also moved north to Sault Ste. Marie, where he ordered the trading post's "Clerk, Merchandise & every [employee of Askin's] to come to Michilimackinac."[61] Once they arrived, he seized and vaulted the goods without providing receipt, and effectively destroyed one of the Askin family's most extensive investments in the Great Lakes. Meanwhile, traveling north from Detroit, Jean Baptiste Barthe carried with him a letter written by de Peyster that "promised him [de Peyster's] protection, as a Person proper to be instructed with the Execution of the Commanding officers orders at St. Mary's," marking Barthe as Cadot's temporary replacement while Cadot was away from Sault Ste. Marie recruiting Indians.[62] However, upon reaching Michilimackinac, Barthe immediately encountered Sinclair, who refused to allow the Frenchman to travel further north. Instead, Sinclair "ordered [Barthe to] immediately . . . settle his Business & Return to Detroit," contravening de Peyster's instructions and dashing Askin's hopes. With no one left to travel to Sault Ste. Marie to oversee their trade, "Everything there became lost, even Debts Due . . . by Traders." According to the jailed Robertson, Sinclair's actions placed "the whole of [their] Property [roughly] 6 & 7000 Pounds N.Y.C. . . . into the possessions of others."[63] Shortly after, Sinclair also gave the order to "[remove] the Houses at the entrance of the French River," Askin's and Lyon's trading venture, and accomplished his boast "to put every key in this part of the Country in [Haldimand's] Hands."[64]

Upon hearing of Askin's malfeasance, Haldimand declaimed: "I am sorry that a man capable of Dishonesty has been so long entrusted with a charge of such consequence as the King's Provision Store," and applauded Sinclair's diligence.[65] "They are capable of telling many Falsehoods," Sinclair commiserated, "I know so little of [Askin and Robertson] . . . excepting their Demerit."[66] It was true: Askin, Barthe, and Robertson took liberties with their responsibilities; their depots straddled strategic river openings in the Great Lakes; and they used and protected their multiethnic ties to French and Indian labor to expand their trades. Askin's removal was both a personal triumph and an expression of Sinclair's authority; it was a step toward asserting the prerogatives of the British military over the competing and fractious needs of its merchants and traders during a period of imperial crisis. But, as with the Chevalier family on the St. Joseph River, Sinclair failed to locate Askin and his efforts within the context of the wider Great Lakes world, which had lasting repercussions on his effectiveness as a commander.

In July 1780, Major Arent Schuyler de Peyster used every spare moment he came across to pore over the stacks of missives that continually accumulated on his wooden desk. He opened letter after letter, until he encountered something curious: a petition drafted by two companies of British soldiers at Fort Michilimackinac. For almost an entire year, he had commanded Fort Detroit and worked to secure it against American attacks. It was a daunting task. He broke the wax-sealed petition and read. By the time he finished, de Peyster, familiar with the internal politics of the British army, understood the origins of the soldiers' complaints. More importantly, he glimpsed Sinclair's larger intent. The soldiers complained that they had not been paid for nearly eleven months and seldom "received more than one Gill of Rum per day & some days but a chew of Tobacco apiece." In fact, before petitioning, some of the more intrepid soldiers took their complaints directly to Sinclair, but "his answers always [were] *damn you for a pack of Villains & Scoundrels, none of your Majors or Mr. Askin's ways with me—it* won't *do.*" The soldiers claimed that their "poor usage [was] principally give[n] to provoke us to do something that may bring a Scandal on the Regiment."[67]

Not content with dismantling John Askin's network of trade or removing the Chevalier family from the St. Joseph River valley over questions of loyalty, Sinclair sought to discredit the intermingling of trade and empire that helped foster Askin's and Chevalier's malignant motivations, and to do so he subtly connected their perfidy and the soldiers' discipline to de Peyster's tenure as commandant. According to Sinclair, the disloyalty and greed of Michilimackinac's merchants and traders, as characterized by Askin, resulted from lax imperial administration coupled with ambiguous and overlapping borders between the needs of empire and the wants of trade. But in Sinclair's opinion, if not stopped, men like Askin would take advantage and ultimately hurt the British cause. For Sinclair, a commandant who privileged the primacy of empire and his own authority, such relationships simply "[wouldn't] do."[68]

De Peyster, however, wasted no time defending Askin and himself from Sinclair's insinuations. "A little Patience will bring everything to light," de Peyster promised the soldiers, claiming that "he never gave any occasion for Captain Sinclair to mention his name in a Slighting Tone or any way's with disrespect."[69] He fired off a letter to Haldimand in Quebec, assuring the general that he "ever found Mr. Askin & his family most usefull & faithful Servants to Government, & as such was always ready to do him any Civility in my power." Reminding Haldimand of the destructive and uncertain consequences war had on military and private supply lines, de Peyster described the ways in which he worked to minimize its effect. He explained, "Mr. Askin hearing that his Flour to a considerable amount was put into the King's Store at Detroit—Represented to me the distress his numerous family must be in unless I suffered him to borrow some Flour out of the Store." With more than two years' worth of flour at Michilimackinac, de Peyster agreed to let Askin borrow "a few Barrels," and if more were taken it was, certainly, without his permission. Given the complex realities of late eighteenth-century supply lines and the nature of spoilage and damage, de Peyster could not "be persuaded that [Askin] was actuated by dishonest principles." He then shifted the tone of the letter. "If Mr. Sinclair thinks he was," de Peyster continued pointedly, "he certainly pays me a very bad complement."[70] A war of words had begun.

Into this fire, de Peyster deployed John Mompesson, a captain in the King's Eighth Regiment, and a company of soldiers to Michilimackinac to relieve the men stationed there.[71] Mompesson carried with him a copy of the soldiers' petition. Sinclair was apoplectic. In a letter to Haldimand, Mompesson declared he was "a Senior officer to [Sinclair] in Rank," and therefore he had the right to command the post's soldiers.[72] Just as Sinclair feared, the ambiguity of his command allowed challenges to his authority. Mompesson's arrival exacerbated the fractious politicking that began with Askin's dismissal. Sinclair complained that the upstart officer "conveyed amongst the Troops . . . that they are to obey him as Commanding Officer."[73] As the two men squabbled, the petition carried by Mompesson resulted in an inquest of Lieutenant George Clowes, the gentleman who served as the soldiers' commanding officer during the controversy.[74] Proclaiming the entire situation of "the strangest nature" in a letter to Haldimand's aide, Sinclair expressed confusion over the insulting language of the soldiers' petition, and argued: "The Arts practiced against the Services of the Post, whether meant against me or not, have been many."[75] De Peyster later commented to another commander, "No doubt . . . [Sinclair] will explain away some passages in his Letter, which appear to me to be rudely couched."[76]

As the conflict spiraled out of control, Sinclair sent an epistle directly to de Peyster, imploring: "It remains with you to put a stop to every unsettled demand set up against me." Sinclair expressed shock that he "became the object of [de Peyster's] Enmity," despite having implicated the commandant in Askin's fraud.[77] In his response, de Peyster retorted, "I surely have accounts enough to settle at Detroit without interfering with those of Michilimackinac," continuing on to say he bore "no enmity."[78] Yet, in a series of letters, de Peyster had skillfully framed Sinclair as irrational. He explained to Haldimand that his "disputes with Capt. Sinclair [were] all chimerical, the mere produce of his own brain for as God is my Judge."[79] However, both men struggled to get past their clash without damaging their reputations or hindering their effectiveness as commanders.

Meanwhile, in Quebec, by the end of the summer of 1780, Haldimand encountered a flock of Michilimackinac exiles replete with their own complaints and recriminations against Sinclair: Joseph Ainsse, Louis Chevalier, and Samuel Robertson. He met each of them in turn, but he soon discovered that he lacked evidence and testimony to proceed against them; instead, Haldimand let them go, and even paid out drafts they carried.[80] Haldimand then turned his wearied attention to another of Sinclair's quarrels, which involved Captain Alexander Harrow of the *Welcome* in early August 1780, whom Sinclair had arrested over Harrow contravening his orders for another ship, the *Felicity*.[81] Now privy to the voluminous and combative exchanges between Sinclair and de Peyster, Haldimand glimpsed the danger of having two antagonistic commanders jockeying for support and allies in the Great Lakes. Having urged both men to make amends, when they reached a détente, Haldimand commented that the experience had been "very disagreeable," and expressed happiness in "being spared the pain of investigating them."[82]

As the war of words trickled to an end, and having spent the summer and fall of 1780 confined to Michilimackinac with his trade and family in shambles, Askin desperately sought a resolution. "My situation is the most disagreeable I ever was in, added to my being out of business and living at great expense."[83] Askin appreciated de Peyster's letter—it was a vote of support from a man he truly respected—but it came too late to effectively change the circumstances on the ground at Michilimackinac; Sinclair destroyed Askin's depots, disrupted his network of exchange, allowed his debts to go uncollected, and caused his merchandise to be stolen. What took years to build, took Sinclair only a Great Lakes spring to destroy.

In the heat of late July, Askin and his wife, Marie, were standing at Michilimackinac's wharf.[84] His slaves and servants carried his household's possessions and loaded the items onto a small sailing vessel bound for Detroit. His wife and family embarked, with a promising wind and sturdy sails propelling them gradually southward. Askin would shortly follow. After sixteen years of assembling a family, as well as a dominant and expansive trade, he would leave Michilimackinac just as he had first entered it: nearly bankrupt.

A year later, in the summer of 1781, Haldimand wrote to a fellow general that he had "long but in vain attempted to restrain within moderate limits the expences incurred at the several Posts in the Upper Country in the Indian Department."[85] In late June, writing to de Peyster at Detroit, he explained, "I have determined in future, to supply the wants of the Indians, as mentioned to you in a former Letter, from England or this place, and to Transport the Goods at the King's expence." In other words, British commandants across the Great Lakes would have to rely upon the largesse of the Crown, and would no longer be allowed to buy merchandise from British and French merchants and traders to supply the Great Lakes Indians.[86] Without reform, Haldimand, like Amherst, Gage, and Johnson before him, worried that such tremendous costs could not "fail of attracting the serious observation of the King's Ministers and ought to command the most unremitting attention of every officer."[87]

With the Americans holding the Illinois Country and the Spanish operating along the Mississippi River, Sinclair knew, perhaps more than most, just how tentative Great Britain's hold on its Indian allies really was. Haldimand's decree took away an important avenue of shoring up Indigenous support when times were desperate. For Sinclair, the fact remained: paltry gifts or no gifts at all would be seen as insults, and, thereby, were dangerous. In early June 1781, sizable Ojibwa, Odawa, Sac, Fox, Ho-Chunk, Sioux, and Menominee delegations came to Michilimackinac, when Indian presents were already low.[88] The cost of maintaining their allegiance, whether Haldimand liked it or not, had to be paid, as the vitality of the British Empire and its fur trade in the Great Lakes depended on it. Sinclair made a fateful decision:

> I have the honor to advise Your Excellency of my having drawn in favour of Mr. Macnamara & Coy; for the Amount of Forty nine Thousand, five Hundred and three Pounds, twelve shillings & four pence N. Y. Currency, a charge against the Indian Department. The late arrival of the Indian Presents by the King's Canoes, with the unusual number of Indians at the Post have swelled the Accounts very much. The Provisions from Europe have been Spared by the quantity of Corn & Grease which has been purchased, still the Indians are more expensive when inactive.[89]

He sent the drafts east to Quebec, and by the end of September 1781, as the autumnal leaves began to fall, he would draw upon the stores of local merchants for a total of £89,000 NYC.[90]

Hoping to dull the sting of such expenses, Sinclair wrote to Haldimand, "It is necessary to remark to your Excellency that the great part of the Expenses for the Indian Department has arisen from the charges made by the Traders unauthorized to do so in their Wintering Grounds."[91] He tried to explain away these charges by revealing that "the scanty supply sent by the Kings Canoes, and always too late for the Post, will be scarce sufficient to stop that Practice." He supplied the Indians "their usual quantity of Rum" out of fear of causing "much discontent." He ended his letter: "I shall only add that I make no purchases from Traders, when the necessary articles are in Store."[92] He overspent the year before, and the cost of building his new fort on Mackinac Island was ballooning. He had defied Haldimand's orders.

Far away, George Washington, the Virginian commander-in-chief of a ragtag American army, marched south from his entrenched position outside of New York City to lay siege to a small Virginian community called Yorktown. Coordinating his march with a large French fleet sailing north from the Caribbean, Washington and his allies surrounded and forced the surrender of a large contingent of British troops under the command of General Charles Cornwallis. All told, on October 19, 1781, over seven thousand British and Hessian soldiers surrendered, and, two years later, American and British delegates signed the Treaty of Paris, officially ending the American Revolution.[93]

At Michilimackinac, Captain Patrick Sinclair's tenure proved fraught with controversy, and he placed some of the burden on Askin. "Quarrelling with one Commissary," Sinclair wrote in a letter, "has procured me many Enemy's, I am afraid that some may be practiced below & get to His Excellency's Ears."[94] Attempting to make amends, he wrote to de Peyster, "Sir—As I before assured you, it is my desire and wish to be on good terms with you & to satisfy all in my power those who I have had unfortunate dispute with."[95] Sinclair even went as far as ordering the bonds he took from Askin and Benjamin Lyon returned, claiming, "The matter which brought them on will be, I hope, forgotten."[96]

In December 1780, Sinclair invited Lyon to his quarters at Michilimackinac. In a letter, Lyon reported that Sinclair "received me kindly, and told me he was very sorry that he ever had any falling out with my Friend Askin." Sinclair begged Lyon to inform Askin that "he could never be easy till he should have it in his power to serve [him] and Captain Robertson."[97] At Detroit, Askin must have found the news bittersweet. The damage had been done, and there was little Sinclair's apology could do to revive his crippled trade. Askin and Sinclair encountered one another during a pivotal moment in the history of the British Empire in North America, and while they were peripheral players to the larger course of the American Revolution, their relationship reveals the complicated and fraught nature of empire and trade in the Great Lakes. Askin's trade survived decades of violence and scarcity only to be undone by vague orders and an imperious official.

After the American Revolution, the context that confronted Askin should have been familiar, but unlike previous iterations, it introduced a different cast of characters who relied upon new authorities and centers of power.[98] He could no longer trust his connections to British officials to clear hurdles or sanction his motives. Yet, still determined, Askin worked to match the schemes of his younger days, only to find that each endeavor went awry. In 1786, with Isaac Todd and James McGill as his Montreal-based suppliers, Askin helped form the Miami Company, a fur trade consortium that focused its efforts on the Maumee-Wabash River valley in the Illinois Country.[99] As soon as the consortium began, it encountered difficulties. The ongoing conflict between the United States and the Western Confederacy of Indians caused havoc and ruin throughout the region, and few Indians continued to devote time to the fur trade.[100] Frenchman Louis Lorimier, a minor company agent, complained, "The persistent menace of an influx of Americans . . . induces me to think of going elsewhere, and thus avoid the pillage they threaten to all engaged in the Indian trade."[101] Later, he would cross the Mississippi River into the Spanish Empire, just as the Miami Company collapsed. By the early 1790s, Askin's debt hovered around £20,000. "If therefore you have for us . . . regard & friendship which I never doubted," McGill begged Askin to repay his debts in order to "prevent us from being the greatest Sufferers that can probably be instanced in Trade to your part of the world."[102] Askin would survive on the forbearance and the kindness of his close friends.

Around the same time, Askin invested in Great Lakes, Ohio Valley, and Upper Canadian real estate. He spent most of the 1780s and early 1790s buying up old French titles and pressuring Indian communities to sell land to him and his partners, ensuring Indian communities that they would benefit more from selling to the British than acquiescing to the invading Americans.[103] After the Battle of Fallen Timbers in 1794, Askin, and others like his old friend Alexander Henry, schemed to buy a large swatch of northern Ohio from the Indians. A year later, John Askin Jr., Askin's son, traveled with "Several Indian Chiefs of the Chippewa and Ottawa Nation" to serve as their translator.[104] Askin saw this as an opportunity to validate their land claims and force the Americans to recognize their titles, advising his son to "use [his] Utmost Influence, not only with the Indians but also with all others . . . to Endeavors [*sic*] that the first article of the Treaty . . . Should be that [the Indians] are sole Masters of their Lands."[105] Instead, General Anthony Wayne intercepted a dispatch from Askin and arrested his son, claiming he "looked upon [him] as a Spy & that [he] deserved death."[106] Askin Jr. languished in prison, while the Indians signed the Treaty of Greenville in 1795, effectively ensuring American sovereignty over the interior. Fallen Timbers, Greenville, as well as Jay's Treaty, which called for the British to abandon its posts in the Great Lakes and Ohio Valley, all ended Askin's grandiose speculative schemes in lands claimed by the United States.

Sinclair remained at Michilimackinac to carry out his duty. His command incurred incredible expenditures trying to keep the Indians of the Great Lakes and the Ohio Valley loyal to the British Empire. Unlike de Peyster, who was promoted to lieutenant colonel and left the region widely respected and admired, Sinclair never received approbation for his service. Instead, Haldimand and the British military refused to pay out Sinclair's large drafts and loans, and, in 1782, subjected him to an official audit and full investigation into his conduct as commandant.[107] The enormous expenses prompted an irritated Haldimand to send a delegation "to apply for such temporary remedies to the different abuses that might appear as were most expedient."[108] The delegation's criticisms fell on Sinclair's shoulders: the fort he built was shoddy and the garrison was too small; bad management of the King's Storehouse meant spoiled meats and inexact accounting; they saw wasteful wages and too many employees on the payroll; and they could not believe the staggering costs of feeding and placating Indians.[109]

Like so many years ago, fury once again guided Sinclair's hand and he asked to be relieved of his command at Michilimackinac and be allowed to travel to Quebec to defend himself against malicious charges. However, this time, Haldimand—polite as ever—agreed: "Your Attendance at Quebec will be indispensably necessary," he wrote to Sinclair.[110] Ironically, the official who criticized Askin for the mismanagement of the king's stores would spend the remaining years of his life trying to settle and come to terms with his accounts at Michilimackinac. He returned to Great Britain, whereupon his creditors jailed him. Upon his release, he sued Haldimand without success. Sinclair died in 1820, relatively poor.

It is hard to tell what would have happened had Sinclair built the kind of relationship with Askin and his cohorts as de Peyster had. Surely, their cooperation would not have secured a significantly different end to the American Revolution, but each man was ambitious; Askin certainly had vision, Sinclair without doubt had dedication. Both men, successful and strong, would have been an imperial asset in the Great Lakes, especially as Great Britain and the United States contested for the region into the early nineteenth century. Instead, they spent the rest of their lives negotiating the consequences of their conflict at Michilimackinac, where the thread between trade and empire frayed, then tore, and both men received only misfortune and financial ruin.

EPILOGUE

A Drink Generally Closes the Scene

Alexander Henry's Lament and John Askin's Death

Montreal's streets clamored with the hustle and bustle of carts and horses, and the shouts and gruff words of industrious men and women. The carts and horses carried Great Lakes fur and merchandise. From his home, Alexander Henry could hear it all. In May 1809, Henry, now seventy years old and one of the richest and most respectable men living in the community, sat down at his desk to write a letter to his old friend and longtime colleague, John Askin.

"Montreal is much changed since your time," Henry wrote Askin, who now lived on a sizable farm east of the Detroit River, at a place near Sandwich. "I meet twenty young men in the Street in a day that I do not know." And in the never-ending contest between the young and old, Henry complained to Askin that "all the new North westards are a parcel of Boys and upstarts, who where [*sic*] not born in our time, and supposes they know more of the Indian trade than any before them."[1] For nearly a half-century, since the tail end of the Seven Years' War, Askin and Henry had been principal players in the Great Lakes trade, and now, as old men, they watched others take their place.

West of Montreal, a seventy-year-old Askin read Henry's letter with a mixture of joy and sadness, pausing at the line: "My dear friend I do not expect to live long."[2] Neither man could have guessed Henry would live for an additional fifteen years, but Askin understood Henry's sentiment. They were both long-lived and still in good health, but that could quickly change. He folded the letter, and put it away, went back to his diary, and began writing about his farm, a lifelong habit he still dutifully maintained.

Askin and his family left Detroit in 1796; he followed the British military across the Detroit River and remained, forever, a British subject.[3] Over the next couple of decades, Askin lived the life of a gentleman farmer, and enjoyed his position as a prominent and respectable member of Canadian society. He served as justice of the peace for the Western District of Upper Canada and served as a lieutenant colonel of the local militia. His debts were forgiven by Isaac Todd and James McGill, or they accepted lands for repayment and never deprived him of hearth or home.[4] In 1805, Askin had written to Arent Schuyler de Peyster, now commanding a regiment in Dumfries, Scotland, and described his life:

> For my own part though I do not see 20 or thirty people at my Table as formerly, my Spirrits have not decreased in the smallest degree or why should they. To those who call I can give a Glass of Wine, my Health thank God is very good, all my Children thank [God] continue to behave as I could wish And I think Mrs. [Marie Archange] Askin and I have lived so long at peace with each other that I do not dread any rupture will take place in future. I dislike no Man on Earth, though perhaps some deserve it & I know no House where the Door would be shut against me.[5]

And for his budding military career, Askin joked: "On[c]e a Year I put on my best Cloths & . . . make [the militia] Fire in Honor to the best of Kings. If we dont all Fire at once that's no matter. A Drink generally closes the Scene."[6]

His children, sons and daughters alike, left his home and married influential British and sometimes American spouses—military men, fur trade women, or eminent local officials—becoming important figures in Canadian society. John

Jr. became a fur trader, Indian leader, and minor British official, and during the War of 1812 he would participate in the capture of Mackinac Island from the American garrison.[7] Likewise, Madeleine married Robert Richardson, a surgeon for the Queen's Rangers at Fort George. She gave birth to John Richardson in 1796; he became an author of international fame, writing *Wacousta*, a novel of historical fiction.[8] Charles, Askin's oldest son with Marie Archange, led soldiers during the War of 1812, took part in General Isaac Brock's campaign against Detroit, and, when his father's health declined, took control over his business interests and estate.[9]

During the War of 1812, as the American Republic, British Empire, and their Indian allies contested for the Great Lakes, Askin and his family found themselves in the middle of the conflict as campaigning armies crisscrossed the Detroit borderland.[10] For example, in August 1812, Tecumseh, leader of a confederacy of Great Lakes and Ohio Valley Indians, and the British General Isaac Brock forced the surrender of a sizable American garrison at Detroit, but, almost a year later, in September 1813, the American commodore Oliver Hazard Perry decisively defeated the British Royal Navy at the Battle of Lake Erie.[11] The defeat forced the British and their Indian allies to retreat from Detroit a month later, marching close to Askin's estate, only to suffer a defeat at the Battle of the Thames, where Tecumseh fell.[12] Luckily for Askin, his family, estate, and trade made it through the war mostly unscathed.

Three months after the war's indecisive end in May 1815, Henry, still at Montreal, picked up his pen once again. "I must say that I experience every day the want of Old acquaintance," he lamented to Askin. "They are all dead." Isaac Todd was in England, "at Bath taking the Mineral Waters, and says if his leg gets better he will return to this Country, as he has no friends in any other." James McGill died suddenly, deprived "of doing more good to those who wanted it." Towards the end of the letter, Henry asked Askin directly: "My dear friend are we never to meet in this World"?[13] The two friends never would. A few months later, John Askin passed away. He was seventy-six years old.

In November 1815, as a testament to the close-knit nature of his family, Madeleine, his daughter from a relationship with an Indian slave woman, wrote to Marie Archange to offer condolences. "Yes, dearest, afflicted Mother, no one can appreciate the weight of your sorrow more than we. You have lost the most beloved of husbands and we the tenderest of fathers. Our tears will not bring him back to us, and we must then submit to the will of Almighty God."[14] The loss was felt intensely.

Soon after, the family opened Askin's will. He made his wife, Marie Archange, "sole executrix" of his estate, and put all properties "for her use and at her entire disposal." Upon her death, the estate would then be "equally divided between the whole of [his] children without exception." They buried their father according to his final wishes, "avoiding all unnecessary expenses and vain pomp," and, after a lifetime of success and failure, innovation and disruption, Askin was laid to rest.[15]

The merchant John Askin and the British Empire at Michilimackinac in the eighteenth century were mired in competing and contradictory impulses. He arrived in the Great Lakes as the British Empire struggled to assert its authority over the complex and multiethnic region, and his rich and varied existence therein created an equally rich historical archive that provides an intimate and revealing glimpse into a now lost eighteenth-century world. Askin was front and center in many pivotal moments of British Great Lakes history. He survived the Seven Years' War and Pontiac's War; he served as a sutler and commissar to the British military; he pushed the fur trade into the upper Great Lakes and competed with the Hudson's Bay Company; and he helped set the course for the North West Company in the nineteenth century.

During his life, Askin weathered the collapse of his trade, bankruptcy, and threats of jail, and he built with British officials relationships that eventually snapped, stretched, or recoiled against him as conditions shifted. He invested heavily in the infrastructure of the Great Lakes fur trade; he built depots, ships, warehouses, sawmills, bakeries, blacksmiths, and fur presses, and watched them get destroyed, confiscated, or repurposed. With periods of success and failure, moments of collapse and recovery, Askin's life illustrates the unique possibilities, creative constellations, and tremendous risks the Great Lakes, the British Empire, and the fur trade offered those who participated in that world.

In the end, it is impossible to tell how Askin wished or even hoped to be remembered; his humble funeral suggests a degree of restraint and modesty. But within the history of the interwar period of the British Empire in North America lies a narrative of thirty years in a man's life, and Askin must be remembered as part of a larger story about the nature of empire and those moments when individuals in distant places shape and influence its contours and margins. To remember Askin's life is to appreciate how he twisted, tied, and bound competing and contradictory impulses of trade and empire into a workable understanding of what it meant to be a successful British subject and merchant in the Great Lakes.

Notes

Prologue. I Was Born at Aughnacloy in the North of Ireland in 1739: A Ubiquitous Man, the Great Lakes Fur Trade, and the British Empire

1. John Askin to John Erskine, July 1, 1793, *The John Askin Papers*, vol. 1, ed. Milo M. Quaife, 2 vols. (Detroit: Detroit Library Commission, 1931), 1:477–478 (hereafter cited as: *Askin Papers*). For outlines of Askin's life, see: Milo M. Quaife, "Introduction," *Askin Papers*, 1:1–21; David R. Farrell, "John Askin," in *Dictionary of Canadian Biography*, vol. 5 (Toronto: University of Toronto Press, 1983); John Gram, "John Askin at Michilimackinac," an unpublished manuscript, June 1995, Mackinac State Historic Parks Library, Mackinac City, Michigan; John Askin to John Erskine, July 1, 1793, *Askin Papers*, 1:478.
2. For extended accounts of the British Empire in the North American Midwest during the late eighteenth century, see Jack M. Sosin, *Whitehall and the Wilderness: The Middle West in British Colonial Policy, 1760–1775* (Lincoln: University of Nebraska Press, 1961); Nelson Vance Russell, *The British Regime in Michigan and the Old Northwest, 1760–1796* (Philadelphia: Porcupine Press, 1978); Richard White, *The Middle Ground: Indians, Empires, and Republics in the Great Lakes Region, 1650–1815* (Cambridge: Cambridge University Press, 1991); Michael N. McConnell, *A Country*

Between: The Upper Ohio Valley and Its Peoples, 1724–1774 (Lincoln: University of Nebraska Press, 1992); Eric Hinderaker, *Elusive Empires: Constructing Colonialism in the Ohio Valley, 1673–1800* (Cambridge: Cambridge University Press, 1997).

3. For an excellent example, see David A. Armour and Keith R. Widder, *At the Crossroads: Michilimackinac during the American Revolution* (Mackinac Island, MI: Mackinac Island State Park Commission, 1978). Armour and Widder offer an excellent and extremely detailed account of Michilimackinac during the American Revolution, and Askin appears as an important, albeit minor, actor; even at the center of events, he is still somewhat peripheral. In fact, few books, especially those set during the interwar or revolutionary period of British North American history, use Askin's life as effectively or widely; he is there for two or three paragraphs as an example.
4. See Susan Sleeper-Smith, *Indian Women and French Men: Rethinking Cultural Encounter in the Western Great Lakes* (Amherst: University of Massachusetts Press, 2001).
5. Sleeper-Smith, *Indian Women and French Men*, 63–64. Her rendering of Askin's sexual relationships and marriage partners is standard across most historical accounts of his private life; this portrait stems from a single historical source.
6. See Quaife, "Introduction," *Askin Papers*, 1:12–13.
7. Quaife writes, "It is a matter of record that John Askin Jr. was born at L'Arbre Croche, probably about the year 1762. L'Arbre Croche was an Ottawa town, and this fact would favor the presumption that Askin's consort was a member of this tribe. On September 9, 1766, Askin manumitted, at Detroit, Manette (or Monette), a slave woman whom he had purchased from M. Bourassa at Mackinac. We have no further record of this woman, but the act of manumission, taken in connection with the chronological relation between the act and the births of Askin's children, suggests that she may have been their mother." Quaife, *Askin Papers*, 1:12–13. Historian John Gram argues that Askin's consort was not an Odawa woman, but an Indian slave, or Panise; it would have been unlikely for Askin to keep an Odawa woman as a captive that close to the principal village of the Odawa people. I was able to find some confirmation of Askin's relationship with an Indian slave woman in a letter, which mentioned Askin's son-in-law, and claimed that his wife was "the Daughter of a Pawaneese slave taken in war, by a respectable Merchant [named Askin] near Detroit who has since married a white woman." As quoted in Ruth B. Philips, *Patterns of Power: The Jasper Grant Collection and Great Lakes Indian Art of the Early Nineteenth Century* (Kleinburg, Ontario: McMichael Canadian Collection,

1984), 16. Askin's relationship and personal history is more complicated than previously stated.

8. See Justin M. Carroll, "John Askin's Many Beneficial Binds: Family, Trade, and Empire in the Great Lakes" (doctoral diss., Michigan State University, 2011). Whenever possible, I reference and refer to the printed versions of the primary sources I cite; I wanted to include the most accessible and legible references. I want the reader to be able to follow and check my references as easily as possible. When I could not find a printed version, I reference the original manuscript and where it is housed.
9. For excellent recent works employing Askin's life after Michilimackinac, during the years between 1780 and 1815, see John Clarke, *Land, Power, and Economics on the Frontier of Upper Canada* (Montreal: McGill-Queen's University Press, 2002); Catherine Cangany, *Frontier Seaport: Detroit's Transformation into an Atlantic Entrepot* (Chicago: University of Chicago Press, 2014).
10. See Quaife, "Introduction," *Askin Papers*, 1:12–13. One of the fundamental difficulties of writing a history of Askin's early years at Michilimackinac is the paucity of sources. His written record does not become truly robust until 1778, and before that, Askin exists in the fragments of his trade, such as vague receipts, or references by other historical actors. When direct sources about Askin's life are lacking, I have tried to fill in or contextualize the blanks through other sources; for example, in trying to discern aspects of Askin's fur trade in Detroit after the Seven Years' War, I used material from the letters and writings of James Sterling, a contemporary, to offer a composite sketch. This approach has limitations, but Askin, new to the trade, seemed to have followed paths similar to those taken by Sterling, John Porteous, and Alexander Henry, and some similarities can be assumed.
11. For the David Armour manuscript, see David Armour, "Untitled" (unpublished manuscript, Mackinac State Historic Parks, Library, Mackinac City, Michigan). For the John Gram manuscript, see John Gram, "John Askin at Michilimackinac" (unpublished manuscript, Mackinac State Historic Parks Library, Mackinac City, Michigan, June 1995).
12. White, *The Middle Ground*, xi. In the twenty-five years since the publication of White's work, the specific concept of the middle ground has outgrown its original confines of the Great Lakes and, much to the consternation and bemusement of White, has come to define any region of cross-cultural negotiation and mediation. See Susan Sleeper-Smith, "Forum Introduction: The Middle Ground Revisited," *William and Mary Quarterly* 63, no. 1 (January 2006): 3–8; Richard White, "Creative

Misunderstandings and New Understandings," *William and Mary Quarterly* 63, no. 1 (January 2006): 9–14.

13. White, *The Middle Ground*, x. See also Kathleen Wilson, "Introduction: Histories, Empires, Modernities," in *A New Imperial History: Culture, Identity and Modernity in Britain and the Empire, 1660–1840* (Cambridge: University of Cambridge Press, 2004), 11–13. Wilson notes: "The legacies and specificities of power and its failures need to be analyzed, not assumed: there is no universal colonial condition or imperial experience, but discrete practices of power and ways of imagining it in specific historical periods." (11).
14. See John Darwin, "Imperialism and the Victorians: The Dynamics of Territorial Expansion," *English Historical Review* 112 (June 1997): 614–642. Although Darwin focuses on Victorian, or late nineteenth-century Great Britain and its empire, his work includes useful comments. Darwin's focus on "the chaotic pluralism of private and sub-imperial interests: religious, commercial, strategic, humanitarian, scientific, speculative and migrational" as drivers of British expansion warrants application and exploration (641). He continues: "The role of government was sometimes to facilitate, sometimes to regulate, this multiple expansive momentum. Government had its own purposes: containing its financial and military commitments; avoiding diplomatic embarrassment or worse. . . . But it could rarely afford to obstruct powerful expansionist groups or identity itself too closely or for too long with any one of them" (641).
15. Michael A. McDonnell, *Masters of Empire: Great Lakes Indians and the Making of America* (New York: Hill and Wang, 2015), 3–58. For a similar study, one that highlights the degree to which Europeans had to capitulate to the aims, expectations, and ambivalences of an equally complex, opaque, multifocal, and contradictory Indian world, see Michael J. Witgen, *An Infinity of Nations: How the Native New World Shaped Early North America* (Philadelphia: University of Pennsylvania Press, 2012).
16. See Heidi Bohaker, "Nindoodemag: The Significance of Algonquian Kinship Networks in the Eastern Great Lakes, 1600–1701," *Williams and Mary Quarterly* 63, no. 1 (January 2006): 23–56.
17. McDonnell, *Masters of Empire*, 14.
18. See Gregory Evans Dowd, *War under Heaven: Pontiac, the Indian Nations, and the British Empire* (Baltimore: Johns Hopkins University Press, 2004).
19. For the "fatal victory" of the Seven Years' War, and the negotiation and fragility of the British Empire in the eighteenth century, see H. V. Bowen, "British Conceptions of Global Empire, 1756–83," *Journal of Imperial and Commonwealth History* 26 (1998):

1–27; Fred Anderson, *Crucible of War: The Seven Years' War and the Fate of Empire in British North America, 1754–1766* (New York: Vintage, 2001), 453–556; Elizabeth Mancke, "Negotiating an Empire: Britain and Its Overseas Peripheries, 1550–1780," in *Negotiated Empires: Centers and Peripheries in the Americas, 1500–1820*, ed. Christine Daniels and Michael V. Kennedy (New York: Routledge, 2002), 235–265; Bernard Bailyn, "The First British Empire: From Cambridge to Oxford," *William and Mary Quarterly* 57, no. 3 (July 2000): 647–660.

20. The work of sociologist Zygmunt Bauman, even though his work focuses on postmodernity, offers an important explanatory lens into a Great Lakes world in the eighteenth century defined by violence, disaster, disruptions, and uncertainty. With officials, agents, traders, and merchants unable or unwilling to conform to preexisting behaviors and processes of behavior, the British Empire's control over the region was contested, ephemeral, and occasionally nonexistent. Social structures that once "limit[ed] individual choices" slowly unraveled, and individuals, "abandoned by the state," confronted "quandaries generated by vexingly volatile and constantly changing circumstances." In such a world, "Past successes do not necessarily increase the probability of future victories," and yesterday's strategies become "downright counterproductive" tomorrow. Where "there are no authoritatively endorsed recipes" for success, individuals are left to create such for themselves. Zygmunt Bauman, *Liquid Times: Living in an Age of Uncertainty* (Cambridge: Polity, 2007), 1–3.
21. Captain Patrick Sinclair to General Frederick Haldimand, July–August 1780, *Michigan Pioneer and Historical Collections*, 2nd ed. (Lansing: Michigan Pioneer and Historical Society, 1908–), 9:564 (hereafter cited as *MPHC*).
22. For the centrality of the Indigenous experience in the processes of empire, see also James Merrill, *The Indians' New World: Catawbas and Their Neighbors from European Contact through the Era of Removal* (Chapel Hill: University of North Carolina Press, 1989); White, *The Middle Ground*; Daniel Usner Jr., *Indians, Settlers, and Slaves in a Frontier Exchange Economy: The Lower Mississippi Valley before 1783* (Chapel Hill: University of North Carolina Press, 1992); Kathleen Duval, *The Native Ground: Indians and Colonists in the Heart of the Continent* (Philadelphia: University of Pennsylvania Press, 2006); Juliana Barr, *Peace Came in the Form of a Woman: Indians and Spaniards in the Texas Borderlands* (Chapel Hill: University of North Carolina Press, 2007).
23. John Askin to Sampson Fleming, May 10, 1778, *Askin Papers*, 1:86.
24. Natalie Zemon Davis, *The Return of Martin Guerre* (Cambridge: Cambridge University Press, 1983), 1. While not technically a microhistory, many microhistorical

techniques—the use of biographical and literary techniques to explore how one man's life can exemplify larger historical trends or processes—were used in the construction of this book. The following works, in their own subtle ways, influenced this project: Carlo Ginzburg, *The Cheese and the Worms: The Cosmos of a Sixteenth-Century Miller* (Baltimore: Johns Hopkins University Press, 1976); Laurel Ulrich, *A Midwife's Tale: The Life of Martha Ballard, Based on Her Diary, 1785–1812* (New York: Vintage Books, 1991); Jill Lepore, "Historians Who Love Too Much: Reflections on Microhistory and Biography," *Journal of American History* 88, no. 1 (June 2001): 129–144.

Chapter One. Pretty Much of a Schemer: Albany, Pontiac's War, and John Askin's Bankruptcy, 1758–1764

1. For an account of James Gordon's life and Askin's scheming in the early 1760s, see James Gordon, "The Reminiscences of James Gordon," ed. Josephine Mayer, *Quarterly Journal of the New York State Historical Association* 17 (1936): 430.
2. Gordon, "Reminiscences of James Gordon," 430. Smuggling developed as a consequence of state power and government efforts to regulate trade, collect taxes, and police borders and economies. According to historian Alan L. Karras, in effect, smuggling represents "a negotiation between state and subject," and played an important role establishing the extent and limits of individual initiative. Likewise, Karras argues, "In many cases, corrupt officials facilitated smuggling," which was "especially true in colonies that were located far from metropolitan legal centers that were determined to enforce the letter of the law." Alan L. Karras, *Smuggling: Contraband and Corruption in World History* (New York: Rowman & Littlefield, 2010), 50, 57.
3. For overviews of the post–Seven Years' War transatlantic fur trade, see Walter S. Dunn Jr., *The New Imperial Economy: The British Army and the American Frontier, 1764–1768* (Westport, CT: Praeger, 2001), 4–6, 9–24, 29–39; Howard A. Innis, *The Fur Trade in Canada: An Introduction to Canadian Economic History* (Toronto: University of Toronto Press, 1967), 166–175; Thomas Elliot Norton, *The Fur Trade in Colonial New York, 1686–1776* (Madison: University of Wisconsin Press, 1974); Paul Chrisler Phillips, *The Fur Trade*, vol. 1 (Norman: University of Oklahoma, 1961).
4. Gordon, "Reminiscences of James Gordon," 327.
5. For discussions of the Seven Years' War and its global theaters, see Fred Anderson, *Crucible of War: The Seven Years' War and the Fate of Empire in British North America, 1754–1766* (New York: Vintage Books, 2001); Daniel Baugh, *The Global Seven Years*

War, 1754–1763 (New York: Pearson Press, 2011).

6. For an overview of the New York fur trade, see Norton, *Fur Trade*.
7. For an overview of the material culture and movement of goods across North America and the Atlantic Ocean, see Dean L. Anderson, "The Flow of European Trade Goods into the Western Great Lakes Region, 1715–1760," in *The Fur Trade Revisited: Selected Papers of the Sixth North American Fur Trade Conference, Mackinac Island, Michigan, 1991*, ed. Jennifer S. H. Brown, W. J. Eccles, and D. P. Heldman (East Lansing: Michigan State University Press, 1994), 93–115; Carolyn Gilman, ed., *Where Two Worlds Meet: The Great Lakes Fur Trade* (St. Paul: Minnesota Historical Society, 1982); Robert C. Wheeler, *A Toast to the Fur Trade: A Picture Essay on its Material Culture* (St. Paul, MN: Wheeler Press, 1985); Eugene T. Petersen, *Gentlemen on the Frontier: A Pictorial Record of the Culture of Michilimackinac* (Mackinac Island, MI: Mackinac Island State Park Commission, 1964).
8. Gordon, "Reminiscences of James Gordon," 429.
9. For extended discussions of the British fur trade at Albany and Schenectady and its importance within the context of the British Empire and its contest for North America, see Arthur H. Buffington, "The Policy of Albany and English Westward Expansion," *Mississippi Valley Historical Review* 8 (1922): 327–366; Timothy J. Shannon, *Iroquois Diplomacy on the Early American Frontier* (New York: Penguin, 2008), 56–58; Norton, *Fur Trade*; R. H. Fleming, "Phyn, Ellice and Company of Schenectady," *Contributions to Canadian Economics* 4 (1932): 7–41; Dunn, *The New Imperial Economy*, 140–142.
10. For a rendering of Albany as Askin would have first encountered it, see "A Plan of Albany, as It Was in the Year 1758," Library of Congress, https://lccn.loc.gov/gm71000691.
11. Norton, *Fur Trade*, 101. For the role the Iroquois Confederacy played in shaping the contour of empire in North America, see Richard White, *The Middle Ground: Indians, Empires, and Republics in the Great Lakes Region, 1650–1815* (Cambridge: Cambridge Press, 1991), 1–10; Daniel K. Richter, "War and Culture: The Iroquois Experience," *William and Mary Quarterly* 40, 3rd ser., no. 4 (October 1983): 537–544; Timothy J. Shannon, *Iroquois Diplomacy on the Early American Frontier* (New York: Penguin, 2008).
12. For a discussion of the French fur trade in North America, see W. J. Eccles, *The Canadian Frontier, 1534–1760* (New York: Holt, 1969), 103–131; White, *The Middle Ground*, 94–141; Innis, *Fur Trade in Canada*, 9–83.
13. For Indians as consumers of European wares, see Bruce M. White, "Encounters

with Spirits: Ojibwa and Dakota Theories about the French and Their Merchandise," *Ethnohistory* 41 (1994): 369–405; Arthur J. Ray, "Indians as Consumers in the Eighteenth Century," in *Old Trails and New Directions: Papers of the Third North American Fur Trade Conference*, ed. Carol M. Judd and Arthur J. Ray (Toronto: University of Toronto Press, 1980), 255–271.

14. For a detailed discussion of colonial imports, especially in regard to British fur trade merchandise, see Dunn, *The New Imperial Economy*, 95–112.
15. For a discussion of French and British smuggling, see Innis, *Fur Trade in Canada*, 77–81; Norton, *Fur Trade*, 121–151.
16. In the eighteenth century, British business practices from London spread to the peripheral centers of the empire; for a discussion of an increasingly transatlantic economy, see David Hancock, *Citizens of the World: London Merchants and the Integration of the British Atlantic Community, 1735–1785* (Cambridge: Cambridge University Press, 1995), 25–39, 85–114.
17. For a discussion of the Seven Years' War and French and British campaigns in the St. Lawrence River borderland, see Ian K. Steele, *Warpaths: Invasions of North America* (New York: Oxford University Press, 1994), 188–196, 199–220; Fred Anderson, *Crucible of War: The Seven Years' War and the Fate of Empire in British North America, 1754–1766* (New York: Vintage Books, 2001).
18. Gordon, "Reminiscences of James Gordon," 333; Josephine Jane Mayer, "Major Robert Rogers, Trader," *Quarterly Journal of the New York State Historical Association* 15 (1934): 392; Milo M. Quaife, ed., "Detroit Biographies: Alexander Macomb," *Burton Historical Collections Leaflet* 10 (1931): 3. Spelling was rough and ready in the time and place (e.g., "Lisle" for "Lyle"). I have reproduced, rather than corrected, the spellings in the quoted documents, without comment except where misunderstanding seems likely.
19. Gordon, "Reminiscences of James Gordon," 426. For a short biography of Robert Rogers, see C. P. Stacey, "Rogers, Robert," in *Dictionary of Canadian Biography*, vol. 4 (Toronto: University of Toronto Press, 1979).
20. A Permit Provided by General Jeffery Amherst to Supply Rogers, Papers Concerning Robert Rogers and Rogers' Ranger Manuscript, New York Public Library: Archives & Manuscripts, New York City, New York (hereafter cited as Rogers Manuscripts).
21. For Robert Rogers's life in the Great Lakes and early relationship with John Askin, see John F. Ross, *War on the Run: The Epic Story of Robert Rogers and the Conquest of America's First Frontier* (New York: Bantam Books, 2011), 311–312; Mayer, "Major Robert Rogers, Trader," 390; Gordon, "Reminiscences of James Gordon," 429. Sutlers

were civilian merchants or traders who followed an army into the field and supplied it with goods and merchandise. For a discussion of sutlers, see H. C. B. Rogers, *The British Army of the Eighteenth Century* (London: George Allen & Unwin, 1977), 85–87.

22. Gordon, "Reminiscences of James Gordon," 428.
23. For an overview of Rogers' role in the capitulation of the French posts of the western Great Lakes, see Brian Leigh Dunnigan, *Frontier Metropolis: Picturing Early Detroit, 1701–1838* (Detroit: Wayne State University Press, 2001), 48–51; Keith Widder, *Beyond Pontiac's Shadow: Michilimackinac and the Anglo-Indian War of 1763* (East Lansing: Michigan State University Press, 2013), 55–66; Ross, *War on the Run*, 296–316.
24. Paul Burbeen to Abraham Douw, September 22, 1760, Rogers Manuscripts.
25. Ross, *War on the Run*, 274–276, 311–313.
26. Ibid., 296–297. Also see Edward Cole's rendering of the State of the Accounts of Sundry Merchandise Shipped at Niagara for Detroit, October 1760, Rogers Manuscripts.
27. Edward Cole's rendering of the State of the Accounts of Sundry Merchandise Shipped at Niagara for Detroit, October 1760, Rogers Manuscripts.
28. Sir William Johnson to General Jeffery Amherst, February 12, 1761, *The Papers of Sir William Johnson*, 14 vols. (Albany: University of the State of New York, 1921–1965), 3:331 (hereafter cited as *Sir William Johnson Papers*).
29. For overviews of the post–Seven Years' War reforms to Indian and fur trade policy in the Great Lakes, see Jack M. Sosin, *Whitehall and the Wilderness: The Middle West in British Colonial Policy, 1760–1775* (Lincoln: University of Nebraska Press, 1961), 27–51; Widder, *Beyond Pontiac's Shadow*, 95–122; White, *The Middle Ground*, 256–268. For a biography of General Jeffery Amherst, see Lawrence Shaw Mayo, *Jeffery Amherst: A Biography* (London: Longmans, Green, 1916). For a biography of General Thomas Gage, see John Richard Alden, *General Gage in America* (Baton Rouge: Louisiana State University Press, 1948). For a biography of Sir William Johnson, see Fintan O'Toole, *White Savage: William Johnson and the Invention of America* (London: Faber and Faber, 2005).
30. See General Jeffrey Amherst to Colonel Henry Bouquet, June 7, 1762, *MPHC*, 19:128, 148–149.
31. See General Jeffrey Amherst to Sir William Johnson, February 22, 1761, *Sir William Johnson Papers*, 3:343–347.
32. Copy of the Conference sent by Capt. Campble at a Council held at the Wiandot Town near Fort Detroit 3d. July 1761 by the Deputy's of the six Nations with the

Ottawa, Wiandots, Chipeweights, & Powtewatamis, *Sir William Johnson Papers*, 3:473–474; Instructions to the Officers, September 16, 1761, *Sir William Johnson Papers*, 3:527–528.

33. General Jeffery Amherst to Sir William Johnson, August 9, 1761, *Sir William Johnson Papers*, 3:343–347, 515.
34. Donald Campbell to Bouquet June 1, 1761, *The Papers of Colonel Henry Bouquet for 1761*, ed. Sylvester K. Stevens and Donald H. Kent (Harrisburg: Pennsylvania Historical Commission, 1941), 183–184.
35. Sir William Johnson to General Jeffery Amherst, June 12, 1761, *Sir William Johnson Papers*, 10:286–287; General Jeffery Amherst to Sir William Johnson, December 26, 1761, *Sir William Johnson Papers*, 10:348.
36. Gordon, "Reminiscences of James Gordon," 429.
37. Captain Robert Rogers' Power of Attorney to John Askin, March 17, 1761, Rogers Manuscripts.
38. Gordon, "Reminiscences of James Gordon," 429.
39. See Drafts Notes Recepts & Bonds Paid Commencing February the 11th 1761 and Ending July 17th 1762, Box 21, John Askin Manuscripts, Burton Historical Collection, Detroit Public Library, Detroit, Michigan (hereafter cited as Askin's Receipt Book).
40. John Macomb Receipt, June 1, 1761, Askin's Receipt Book.
41. John Macomb Receipt, December 14, 1761, Askin's Receipt Book.
42. See Abraham Douw Receipts, May 25, May 26, June 22, 1761, Askin's Receipt Book. The Great Lakes fur trade was an elaborate transatlantic exchange economy that was precarious, risky, and fraught. For a conversation about British capital, debt, and credit, see Harry W. Duckworth, "British Capital in the Fur Trade: John Strettell and John Fraser," in Brown, Eccles, and Heldman, *The Fur Trade Revisited.*
43. Edward Cole Receipt, February 10, 1761, Askin's Receipt Book.
44. Packs consisting of roughly 50–70 furs were stacked fur to fur, then pelt to pelt, and placed into a press. The best furs, such as higher quality beaver, were placed in the middle, while the less valuable skins, like deer skins, were placed on the outside. Tied in the press, each pack weighed roughly 90 pounds and each pack was worth roughly £30 to £50. For Askin's relationship with Cesar Cormick, see Cormick Receipts, April 2, 1761; June 1, 1761; August 24, 1761; December 3, 1761; and January 4, 1761, Askin's Receipt Book.
45. John Fletcher Receipt, April 3, 1762, Askin's Receipt Book.
46. For an overview of transatlantic shipping and the role London merchants played in

managing it, see Hancock, *Citizens of the World*, 115–142; Dunn, *The New Imperial Economy*, 29–50.

47. For a discussion of what constitutes an "outfit," see Dean L. Anderson, "The Flow of European Trade Goods into the Western Great Lakes Region, 1715–1760," in Brown, Eccles, and Heldman, *The Fur Trade Revisited*, 97.
48. A Receipt for John Askin, June 26, 1762, Askin's Receipt Book.
49. For a detailed discussion of the fur trade transportation route between New York and the Great Lakes, see Dunn, *The New Imperial Economy*, 155–159.
50. For a discussion of the carrying place of Niagara, see Daniel Ingram, "A Year at Niagara: Violence, Diplomacy, and Coexistence in the Eastern Great Lakes, 1763–1764," in *Indians and British Outposts in Eighteenth-Century America* (Gainesville: University Press of Florida, 2012), 121–155.
51. For a history of Detroit under the French Empire, see Dunnigan, *Frontier Metropolis*, 6–47; White, *The Middle Ground*, 146–149.
52. For a discussion of the intertribal conflicts that arose around Detroit, see White, *The Middle Ground*, 82–90, 193–196; Michael Witgen, *An Infinity of Nations: How the Native New World Shaped Early North America* (Philadelphia: University of Pennsylvania Press, 2012), 283–297; Dunnigan, *Frontier Metropolis*, 19–21.
53. Edward Cole Receipt, June 9, 1762, Askin's Receipt Book.
54. For the important role French fur trade intermediaries played in the British fur trade, see Keith R. Widder, "The French Connection: The Interior French and Their Role in French-British Relations in the Western Great Lakes Region, 1760–1775," in *The Sixty Years' War for the Great Lakes, 1754–1814*, ed. David Curtis Skaggs and Larry L. Nelson (East Lansing: Michigan State University Press, 2001), 125–143.
55. See Dunn, *The New Imperial Economy*, 155–158.
56. For a detailed discussion of the French and Indian world of the Great Lakes, see White, *The Middle Ground*, 1–93.
57. See White, *The Middle Ground*, 28, 58, 65; Susan Sleeper-Smith, *Indian Women and French Men: Rethinking Cultural Encounter in the Western Great Lakes* (Amherst: University of Massachusetts Press, 2001), 18, 42; Charles E. Cleland, *Rites of Conquest: The History and Culture of Michigan's Native Americans* (Ann Arbor: University of Michigan Press, 1995), 107.
58. Sleeper-Smith, *Indian Women*, 18, 42–43.
59. For the role Indian women, cross-cultural relationships, and multiethnic children played in the social, economic, and cultural patterns of the Great Lakes, see Sylvia Van Kirk, *Many Tender Ties: Women in Fur-Trade Society, 1670–1870* (Norman:

University of Oklahoma Press, 1983); Jennifer S. H. Brown, *Strangers in Blood: Fur Trade Company Families in Indian Country* (Norman: University of Oklahoma Press, 1980); Jacqueline Peterson and Jennifer S. H. Brown, eds., *The New Peoples: Being and Becoming Métis in North America* (Winnipeg: University of Manitoba Press, 1985); Clara Sue Kidwell, "Indian Women as Cultural Negotiators," *Ethnohistory* 39 (1992): 97–107; Susan Sleeper-Smith, "Women, Kin, and Catholicism: New Perspectives on the Fur Trade," *Ethnohistory* 47 (2000): 423–452; Sleeper-Smith, *Indian Women*.

60. For a biography of James Sterling, see Burton Historical Collection Staff, "Sterling, James," in *Dictionary of Canadian Biography*, vol. 4. See James Sterling Letter Book, William L. Clements Library, University of Michigan, Ann Arbor, Michigan (hereafter cited as James Sterling Letter Book). For an overview of the British fur trade at Detroit, see Dunn, *The New Imperial Economy*, 136–138.
61. James Sterling to Walter Rutherford, October 1761, James Sterling Letter Book.
62. Ibid.
63. James Sterling to John Duncan, January 10, 1762, James Sterling Letter Book.
64. Sleeper-Smith, *Indian Women*, 4–5, 54–66, 61–67.
65. James Sterling to James Syme, June 8, 1762, James Sterling Letter Book.
66. Askin Receipts for July 16, 1762, Askin's Receipt Book.
67. Edward Cole Receipt, June 9, 1762, Askin's Receipt Book. See also Gordon, "Reminiscences of James Gordon," 429.
68. Edward Cole's rendering of the State of the Accounts of Sundry Merchandise shipped at Niagara for Detroit, October 1760, Rogers Manuscripts.
69. James Sterling to John Duncan, January 10, 1762, James Sterling Letter Book.
70. James Sterling to Captain George Etherington, May 31, 1762, James Sterling Letter Book.
71. James Sterling to John Duncan, January 10, 1762, James Sterling Letter Book; General Jeffrey Amherst to Sir William Johnson, *Sir William Johnson Papers*, January 16, 1762, 10:354.
72. General Jeffery Amherst to Sir William Johnson, December 30, 1761, *Sir William Johnson Papers*, 3:597–598.
73. Captain Donald Campbell to Colonel Henry Bouquet, May 21, 1761, *MPHC*, 19:68.
74. Major William Walters to Sir William Johnson, April 27, 1762, *Sir William Johnson Papers*, 3:721.
75. Ibid., 722.
76. Bruce M. White, "'Give Us a Little Milk': The Social and Cultural Meanings of Gift Giving in the Lake Superior Fur Trade," *Minnesota History* 48 (Summer 1982): 66–67.

77. For a detailed discussion of the liquor trade and the role it played in the British fur trade, see Peter C. Mancall, *Deadly Medicine: Indians and Alcohol in Early America* (Ithaca, NY: Cornell University Press, 1995), 29–61, 155–167.
78. General Jeffrey Amherst to Sir William Johnson, November 22, 1761, *Sir William Johnson Papers*, 3:570–571.
79. White, *The Middle Ground*, 342.
80. James Sterling to James Syme, June 8, 1762, James Sterling Letter Book.
81. Captain Donald Campbell to Sir William Johnson, July 8, 1761, *Sir William Johnson Papers*, 3:450.
82. General Jeffrey Amherst to Sir William Johnson, August 22, 1762, *Sir William Johnson Papers*, 10:489.
83. James Sterling to James Syme, June 17, 1762, James Sterling Letter Book.
84. James Sterling to Ensign Robert Holmes, July 6, 1762, James Sterling Letter Book.
85. Letter written by James Sterling, September 4, 1762, James Sterling Letter Book.
86. James Sterling to John Duncan, October 25, 1762, James Sterling Letter Book.
87. Peter Van Brugh Livingston and Walter Rutherford, January 25, 1763, James Sterling Letter Book.
88. The Earl of Egremont to General Jeffery Amherst, December 12, 1761, *Sir William Johnson Papers*, 3:588.
89. Ross, *War on the Run*, 333.
90. Gordon, "Reminiscences of James Gordon," 430.
91. Captain Donald Campbell to William Walters, June 17, 1761, *Sir William Johnson Papers*, 3:405.
92. Copy of the Conference sent by Capt. Campble at a Council held at the Wiandot Town near Fort Detroit 3d. July 1761 by the Deputy's of the six Nations with the Ottawa, Wiandots, Chipeweights, & Powtewatamis, *Sir William Johnson Papers*, 3:451.
93. Sir William Johnson to General Jeffery Amherst, June 12, 1761, *Sir William Johnson Papers*, 10:286.
94. Edmond Moran to Joseph Spear and Company, May 16, 1763, *Sir William Johnson Papers*, 10:669.
95. Henry Gladwin to General Jeffery Amherst, April 4, 1762, *Sir William Johnson Papers*, 10:421.
96. As quoted in Albert Miller, "An Incident in the Capture of Mackinaw," *MPHC*, 13:501. Michael A. McDonnell, "Charles-Michel Mouet de Langlade: Warrior, Soldier, and Intercultural 'Window' on the Sixty Years' War for the Great Lakes," in Skaggs and Nelson, *Sixty Years' War*.

97. For detailed discussions on the importance of gifting in the Great Lakes, see White, *The Middle Ground*, 94–99; Cleland, *Rites of Conquest*, 54–58; Cary Miller, *Ogimaag: Anishinaabeg Leadership, 1760–1845* (Lincoln: University of Nebraska Press, 2010), 32–33. For a classic account of gifting within archaic societies, see Marcel Mauss, *The Gift: The Form and Reason for Exchange in Archaic Societies*, trans. W. D. Halls (New York: Norton, 2000).
98. For accounts of Pontiac's War, see Francis Parkman, *The Conspiracy of Pontiac and the Indian War after the Conquest of Canada*, vol. 1, 10th ed., vol. 2, 9th ed. (rpt. Lincoln: University of Nebraska Press, 1994); Howard Peckham, *Pontiac and the Indian Uprising* (Detroit: Wayne State University Press, 1994); Gregory Evans Dowd, *War under Heaven: Pontiac, the Indian Nations and the British Empire* (Baltimore: Johns Hopkins University Press, 2004); David Dixon, *Never Come to Peace Again: Pontiac's Uprising and the Fate of the British Empire in North America* (Norman: University of Oklahoma Press, 2005).
99. For Pontiac's War as a spiritual struggle, see Gregory Evans Dowd, *A Spirited Resistance: The North American Indian Struggle for Unity, 1745–1815* (Baltimore: Johns Hopkins University Press, 1993).
100. For Pontiac's War as a struggle over British imperialism and Indigenous sovereignty, see Dowd, *War under Heaven*.
101. General Jeffery Amherst to Sir William Johnson, May 29, 1763, *Sir William Johnson Papers*, 10:689.
102. Edward Jenkins to Henry Gladwin, June 1, 1763, *Sir William Johnson Papers*, 10:691.
103. For a more detailed discussion of the attack, see Widder, *Beyond Pontiac's Shadow*, 141–153.
104. Alexander Henry, *Alexander Henry's Travels and Adventures in the Years 1760–1776*, ed. Milo M.Quaife (Chicago: R. R. Donnelley & Sons, 1921), 79.
105. "Panis," or "panise," refers generically to Indian slaves in the French and then British Great Lakes. For a discussion of the term and how it evolved in North America in the seventeenth and eighteenth centuries, see Brett Rushforth, *Bonds of Alliance: Indigenous and Atlantic Slaveries in New France* (Chapel Hill: University of North Carolina Press, 2014), 165–173.
106. Henry, *Henry's Narrative*, 98.
107. For a narrative of Dalyell's and Rogers's efforts at Detroit, see Ross, *War on the Run*, 342–349; Widder, *Beyond Pontiac's Shadow*, 175–178.
108. For an overview of Henry Bouquet and his battlefield efforts, see Charles E. Brodine, "Henry Bouquet and British Infantry Tactics on the Ohio Frontier, 1758–1764," in

Skaggs and Nelson, *Sixty Years' War*, 43–61.

109. For the events and context of Niagara, see Ingram, "A Year at Niagara," 121–155.
110. Gordon, "Reminiscences of James Gordon," 430.
111. Ibid., 430–431.
112. For a discussion of Rogers's activity in Great Britain, see Ross, *War on the Run*, 351–367.
113. For a list of Askin's creditors, especially those whom he owed substantial sums, see John Askin Discharged from His Creditors, 24 December 1771, in *Askin Papers*, 1:43–45; Drafts Notes Recepts & Bonds Paid Commencing February the 11th 1761 and Ending July 17th 1762, Askin's Receipt Book.
114. See John Askin's Memorandum Book, 1766, National Archives of Ontario, Toronto, microfilmed by the Toronto Public Library. Copy on file at the Colonial Michilimackinac Archives, Petersen Center, Library, Mackinaw City, Michigan.

Chapter Two. There Have Been Many Who Complain Much against You: Michilimackinac, Fur Trade Reforms, and John Askin's Commissaryship, 1764–1767

1. For a detailed overview of Great Britain's reoccupation of Fort Michilimackinac after Pontiac's War, see Keith Widder, *Beyond Pontiac's Shadow: Michilimackinac and the Anglo-Indian War of 1763* (East Lansing: Michigan State University Press, 2013), 203–221. For a discussion of the British garrisons at Michilimackinac, see Brian Leigh Dunnigan, *The Necessity of Regularity in Quartering Soldiers: The Organization, Material Culture and Quartering of the British Soldier at Michilimackinac* (Mackinac Island, MI: Mackinac State Historic Parks, 1999), 12–16.
2. James Sterling to Captain William Howard, May 29, 1765, James Sterling Letter Book. This is one of the first references to Askin's role as commissary; Sterling writes, "Paddy Askin your [commissary] general."
3. Captain William Howard to Colonel John Bradstreet, October 15, 1764, Thomas Gage Papers, American Series, vol. 28, William Clements Library, University of Michigan, Ann Arbor, Michigan (hereafter cited as Gage Papers). For a discussion of the French community of Michilimackinac and the Great Lakes, see Widder, *Beyond Pontiac's Shadow*, 39–54. See also Widder, "The French Connection: The Interior French and Their Role in French-British Relations in the Western Great Lakes Region, 1760–1775," in *The Sixty Years' War for the Great Lakes, 1754–1814*, ed. David Curtis Skaggs and Larry L. Nelson (East Lansing: Michigan State University Press, 2001), 125–143.

4. Captain William Howard to Colonel John Bradstreet, October 15, 1764, Gage Papers, vol. 28.
5. Ibid. For Henry's account of his captivity among the Ojibwa during Pontiac's War, see Alexander Henry, *Alexander Henry's Travels and Adventures in the Years 1760–1776*, ed. Milo M. Quaife (Chicago: R. R. Donnelley & Sons, 1921), 101–173.
6. Captain William Howard to Colonel John Bradstreet, October 15, 1764, Gage Papers, vol. 28. For a discussion of French prosperity at frontier communities like Michilimackinac, see Jay Gitlin, *The Bourgeois Frontier: French Towns, French Traders and American Expansion* (New Haven: Yale University Press, 2010), 9–12. Gitlin describes French merchant families as "bourgeois to the core" and their communities in the Great Lakes as "cosmopolitan."
7. Karen L. Marrero, *Founding Families: Power and Authority of Mixed French and Native Lineages in Eighteenth-Century Detroit* (New Haven: Yale University Press, 2011), 181.
8. Captain Beamsley Glazier to General Thomas Gage, June 10, 1769, *Old Fort Michilimackinac* (Ann Arbor: University of Michigan Press, 1938), 11.
9. Captain William Howard to Colonel John Bradstreet, October 15, 1764, Gage Papers, vol. 28.
10. For a rendering of Michilimackinac as Askin would have first encountered it, see Lieutenant Perkins Magra's "Sketch of the Fort at Michilimackinac, 1765," in the gallery.
11. For a biography of General Thomas Gage, see S. F. Wise, "Gage, Thomas," in *Dictionary of Canadian Biography*, vol. 4 (Toronto: University of Toronto Press, 1979); John R. Alden, *General Gage in America* (Baton Rouge: Louisiana State University, 1948). For a discussion of Johnson's and Gage's view of Indian policy after Pontiac's War, see Richard White, *The Middle Ground: Indians, Empires, and Republics in the Great Lakes, Region, 1650–1815* (Cambridge: Cambridge University Press, 1991), 309–322.
12. General Thomas Gage to Colonel John Bradstreet, April 2, 1764, Gage Papers, vol. 16. For a discussion of Gage's campaign against the Indians of the Great Lakes and Ohio Valley, see White, *The Middle Ground*, 289–299; Widder, *Beyond Pontiac's Shadow*, 201–202. See also Gregory Evans Dowd, *War under Heaven: Pontiac, the Indians, and the British Empire* (Baltimore: Johns Hopkins University Press, 2002), 149–168.
13. General Thomas Gage to Colonel John Bradstreet, April 2, 1764, Gage Papers, vol. 16.
14. For an overview of Johnson's activities at the Niagara conferences, see Fintan

O'Toole, *White Savage: William Johnson and the Invention of America* (London: Faber and Faber, 2005), 250–262; White, *The Middle Ground*, 289–291; Widder, *Beyond Pontiac's Shadow*, 197–201.

15. Sir William Johnson's Conference with Indians at Niagara, July 9–14, 1764, *Sir William Johnson Papers*, 11:265.
16. Sir William Johnson's Indian Congress, July 17–August 4, 1764, *Sir William Johnson Papers*, 11:278.
17. Sir Thomas Gage to Sir William Johnson, August 15, 1764, *Sir William Johnson Papers*, 4:509.
18. Sir William Johnson to General Thomas Gage, August 5, 1764, *Sir William Johnson Papers*, 11:326.
19. Ibid., 325–326.
20. General Thomas Gage to Sir William Johnson, August 16, 1764, *Sir William Johnson Papers*, 11:333–334.
21. General Thomas Gage to Sir William Johnson, September 2, 1764, *Sir William Johnson Papers*, 11:343.
22. Sir William Johnson to the Lords of Trade, December 26, 1764, *Documents Relative to the Colonial History of the State of New York*, vol. 7 (Albany: Weed, Parsons and Company, 1856), 686 (hereafter cited as *Documents Colonial History New York*).
23. General Thomas Gage to Colonel John Bradstreet, October 15, 1764, Gage Papers, vol. 25.
24. John Montresor, "The Montresor Journals," in *Collections of the New York Historical Society*, vol. 14 (New York City: Printed for the Society, 1881), 283. For Captain Thomas Morris's account of his journey, see Captain Thomas Morris, "Journal of Captain Thomas Morris of his Majesty's XVII Regiment of Infantry," *Early Western Journals, 1748–1765*, ed. Reuben Gold Thwaites (Lewisburg, PA: Wennawoods Publishing, 1998).
25. Morris, "Journal of Captain Thomas Morris," 314.
26. For a discussion of Captain Thomas Morris's mission into the Illinois Country, and the continued hostility of the Illinois Indian communities, see White, *The Middle Ground*, 295–305; Morris, "Journal of Captain Thomas Morris," 305–307.
27. Montresor, "The Montresor Journals," 285.
28. Montresor, "The Montresor Journals," 286–288.
29. Ibid., 288–289.
30. Sir William Johnson to the Lords of Trade, October 30, 1764, *Documents Colonial*

History New York, 674.

31. Sir William Johnson to General Thomas Gage, December 6, 1764, *Sir William Johnson Papers*, 11:491–496.
32. For a broad discussion of the Indigenous communities of the Great Lakes, see Charles E. Cleland, *Rites of Conquest: The History and Culture of Michigan's Native Americans* (Ann Arbor: University of Michigan Press, 1995). For a detailed discussion of the Indigenous communities around Michilimackinac, see Widder, *Beyond Pontiac's Shadow*, 31–39. For a detailed discussion of Indigenous leadership and spiritual power, see Cary Miller, *Ogimaag: Anishinaabeg Leadership, 1760–1845* (Lincoln: University of Nebraska Press, 2010). For a classic anthropological study of the Indigenous people of the Great Lakes, see W. Vernon Kinietz, *The Indians of the Western Great Lakes, 1615–1760* (Ann Arbor: University of Michigan Press, 1989). For specific histories of the Ojibwa, Odawa, and Potawatomi, see R. David Edmunds, *The Potawatomis: Keepers of the Fire* (Norman: University of Oklahoma Press, 1978); James M. McClurken, *Our People, Our Journey: The Little River Band of Ottawa Indians* (East Lansing: Michigan State University Press, 2009); Andrew Blackbird, *History of the Ottawa and Chippewa Indians of Michigan* (Ypsilanti, MI: Ypsilantian Job Printing House, 1887); William W. Warren, *History of the Ojibway People*, ed. Theresa Schenck (St. Paul: Minnesota Historical Society, 2009).
33. For a detailed cartographic analysis of Great Lakes Indigenous history, see *Atlas of Great Lakes Indian History*, ed. Helen Hornbeck Tanner (Norman: University of Oklahoma Press, 1987), 48–67. See also McClurken, *Our People, Our Journey*, 1–9; Blackbird, *History of Ottawa and Chippewa*, 7–14; Cleland, *Rites of Conquest*, 45–46.
34. See Tanner, *Atlas*, 48–67; See also Blackbird, *History of Ottawa and Chippewa*, 7–14; Cleland, *Rites of Conquest*, 45–46.
35. For a discussion of the importance of the village in the Great Lakes and Ohio Valley, see White, *The Middle Ground*, 14–20; Cleland, *Rites of Conquest*, 45–46; Miller, *Ogimaag*, 40–46.
36. For a discussion of the seasonal food and movement patterns of Indigenous life in the Great Lakes, see Cleland, *Rites of Conquest*, 45–61; Miller, *Ogimaag*, 48–50, 92–94.
37. For detailed discussions on the importance of gifting in the Great Lakes, see White, *The Middle Ground*, 94–99; Cleland, *Rites of Conquest*, 54–58; Miller, *Ogimaag*, 32–33. For a classic account of gifting within archaic societies, see Marcel Mauss, *The Gift: The Form and Reason for Exchange in Archaic Societies*, trans. W. D. Halls (New York: Norton, 2000).
38. For the gender roles of Indigenous societies in the Great Lakes, see White, *The*

Middle Ground, 60–75; Cleland, *Rites of Conquest*, 44–49.

39. For a discussion of the French and Indian fur trade, see White, *The Middle Ground*, 94–141.
40. For discussions of intermarriage and the creation of multiethnic fur-trade communities in the Great Lakes, see Sylvia Van Kirk, *Many Tender Ties: Women in Fur-Trade Society, 1670–1870* (Norman: University of Oklahoma Press, 1983), 4; Jennifer S. H. Brown, *Strangers in Blood: Fur Trade Company Families in Indian Country* (Norman: University of Oklahoma Press, 1980); Jacqueline Peterson and Jennifer S. H. Brown, eds., *The New Peoples: Being and Becoming Métis in North America* (Winnipeg: University of Manitoba Press, 1985).
41. Henry, *Alexander Henry's Travels*, 41.
42. For a discussion of de Langlade as a cross-cultural mediator, see Michael A. McDonnell, "Charles-Michel Mouet de Langlade," in Skaggs and Nelson, *Sixty Years' War*, 79–103.
43. For biographical accounts of René Bourassa, see David Armour, "Bourassa, René," in *Dictionary of Canadian Biography*, vol. 4; Brett Rushforth, *Bonds of Alliance: Indigenous and Atlantic Slaveries in New France*. (Chapel Hill: University of North Carolina Press, 2012), 231–235; Joseph Lafitau, *Rare or Unpublished Documents, or the Aulneau Collection, 1734–1745*, ed. Arthur E. Jones (Montreal: Archives of St. Mary's College, 1893), 2:93–94.
44. For the records of these marriages, baptisms, and interrelationships, see "The Mackinac Register," in *Wisconsin Historical Collections*, vol. 19 (Madison: Wisconsin History Society, 1855–1911), 1–160; Christian Denissen, *The Genealogy of the French Families of the Detroit River Region, 1701–1936*, 2 vols. (Detroit: Detroit Society for Genealogical Research, 1987); "The St. Joseph Baptismal Register," ed. George Pare and Milo M. Quiafe, *The Mississippi Valley Historical Review* 13, no. 2 (September 1926): 201–239.
45. General Thomas Gage to Colonel John Bradstreet, April 2, 1764, Gage Papers, vol. 16.
46. Lieutenant Colonel John Campbell to Colonel John Bradstreet, November 10, 1764, Gage Papers, vol. 26.
47. Captain William Howard to Colonel John Bradstreet, October 15, 1764, Gage Papers, vol. 28.
48. Ibid.
49. Ibid.
50. For a detailed description of the attack on Fort Michilimackinac, see Widder, *Beyond Pontiac's Shadow*, 141–167. For a short biography, see David A. Armour,

"Nissowaquet," in *Dictionary of Canadian Biography*, vol. 4.

51. Widder, *Beyond Pontiac's Shadow*, 141–167.
52. Sir William Johnson's Indian Conference, August 9–11, 1763, *Sir William Johnson Papers*, 10:780.
53. Captain William Howard to Colonel John Bradstreet, October 15, 1764, Gage Papers, vol. 28.
54. Jack M. Sosin, *Whitehall and the Wilderness: The Middle West in British Colonial Policy, 1760–1775* (Lincoln: University of Nebraska Press, 1961), 82.
55. For a biography of John Stuart, see John Alden, *John Stuart and the Southern Colonial Frontier: A Study of Indian Relations, War, Trade, and Land Problems in the Southern Wilderness, 1755–1775* (Ann Arbor: University of Michigan Press, 1944).
56. Sir William Johnson to the Lords of Trade, November 13, 1763, *Documents Colonial History New York*, 574, 576, 578.
57. Sir William Johnson to the Lords of Trade, October 1764, *Documents Colonial History New York*, 664.
58. Sosin, *Whitehall and the Wilderness*, 75–78.
59. Sir William Johnson to the Lords of Trade, October 1764, *Documents Colonial History New York*, 664.
60. See Sir William Johnson's Indian Congress, July 17–August 4, 1764, *Sir William Johnson Papers*, 11:278; General Thomas Gage to Sir William Johnson, August 18, 1765, *Sir William Johnson Papers*, 11:903.
61. Ibid. For a discussion of violence and the fur trade, see White, *The Middle Ground*, 75–82.
62. Sosin, *Whitehall and the Wilderness*, 76, 82–83.
63. Ibid., 86–88, 94–95.
64. Sir William Johnson's Indian Congress, July 17–August 4, 1764, *Sir William Johnson Papers*, 11:276.
65. General Thomas Gage to Sir William Johnson, December 16, 1764, *Sir William Johnson Papers*, 4:618.
66. George Croghan to Sir William Johnson, July 12, 1765, *Sir William Johnson Papers*, 11:838. Croghan writes, "A Cheeff of the Cheapways from Misilamackinac Calld. Grand Sota [Minweweh] are Very Much Disafected and Treaten to Renew ye. Warr, & that they have been Now att ye. Illinioes & there Received privet presents from the french & Treatens to attack the fort att Misilamackinac." For a short biography, see David A. Armour, "Minweweh," in *Dictionary of Canadian Biography*, vol. 3 (Toronto: University of Toronto Press, 1974).

67. See George Croghan, "Croghan's Journal, May 15–September 26, 1765," in Thwaites, *Early Western Journals*, 126–166.
68. Captain William Howard to Sir William Johnson, June 24, 1765, *Sir William Johnson Papers*, 11:805. For a biography of Jean-Baptiste Cadot and a discussion of his importance in the upper Great Lakes, see David A. Armour, "Cadot, Jean-Baptiste," in *Dictionary of Canadian Biography*, vol. 5 (Toronto: University of Toronto Press, 1983); Theresa M. Schenck, "The Cadottes: Five Generations of Fur Traders on Lake Superior," in *The Fur Trade Revisited: Selected Papers of the Sixth North American Fur Trade Conference, Mackinac Island, Michigan, 1991*, ed. Jennifer S. H. Brown, W. J. Eccles, and Donald P. Heldman (East Lansing: Michigan State University Press, 1994).
69. Captain William Howard to Sir William Johnson, June 24, 1765, *Sir William Johnson Papers*, 11:806, 808.
70. Petition from the Traders at Michilimackinac to William Howard, July 5, 1765, *Sir William Johnson Papers*, 11:826.
71. Ibid., 827.
72. Ibid., 828.
73. Sir William Johnson's Response to the Traders of Michilimackinac, July 2, 1765, *Sir William Johnson Papers*, 11:816.
74. General Thomas Gage to Sir William Johnson, August 18, 1765, *Sir William Johnson Papers*, 11:903.
75. Sir William Johnson to General Thomas Gage, August 9, 1765, *Sir William Johnson Papers*, 11:880.
76. Captain William Howard to Ralph Burton, September 24, 1765, Gage Papers, vol. 43.
77. Lawrence Ermantinger to Sir William Johnson, September 17, 1765, *Sir William Johnson Papers*, 11:942–943.
78. Sir William Johnson to General Thomas Gage, November 14, 1765, *Sir William Johnson Papers*, 11:966. In another letter, Johnson further comments: "The Nature of the [Charges] against Capt. Howard are as You described them, and I believe may arise chiefly from the Jealousy of some of the Traders, who were desireous of the same indulgence with those he permitted to go among the Indians, they do not appear to amount to any positive accusation of private Interest." See Sir William Johnson to General Thomas Gage, December 21, 1765, *Sir William Johnson Papers*, 11:981.
79. General Thomas Gage to Sir William Johnson, August 18, 1765, *Sir William Johnson Papers*, 11:903.

80. Lieutenant Colonel John Campbell to General Thomas Gage, October 31, 1765, Gage Papers, vol. 45.
81. Captain William Howard to Colonel John Bradstreet, October 15, 1764, Gage Papers, vol. 28.
82. Lieutenant John Campbell to General Thomas Gage, May 31, 1765, Gage Papers, vol. 37.
83. Lieutenant John Campbell to General Thomas Gage, October 31, 1765, Gage Papers, vol. 45.
84. Ibid.
85. For the difficulty of supplying the British military in the Great Lakes, see Michael N. McConnell, *Army and Empire: British Soldiers on the American Frontier, 1758–1775* (Lincoln: University of Nebraska Press, 2004), 100–101.
86. See Diary of John Askin at Mackinac, 1774, *Askin Papers*, 1:50–58.
87. For the role of the deputy commissary in the British military, see Alan J. Guy, *Economy and Discipline: Officership and Administration in the British Army, 1714–1763* (Manchester: Manchester University Press, 1985), 27–28.
88. For a detailed discussion of the British Empire's effort to garrison and supply Fort Michilimackinac, see Dunnigan, *Necessity of Regularity*, 17–21.
89. Ibid., 17–18.
90. For the concept of the British soldiers' mess, see ibid., 21–23.
91. For a discussion of the difficulties facing outsiders at distant posts like Michilimackinac, see Daniel Morison, *The Doctor's Secret Journal*, ed. George S. May (Mackinaw City, MI: Mackinac Island State Park Commission, 1960). Morison found himself systematically harassed by soldiers and traders alike, many of whom Askin quickly befriended or worked with in the fur trade.
92. See Receipt for April 5, 1762, signed by Mary Patten, Drafts Notes Recepts & Bonds Paid Commencing February the 11th 1761 and ending July 17th 1762, John Askin Manuscripts, Burton Historical Collections, Detroit Public Library, Detroit, Michigan.
93. "John Askin's Memorandum Book, 1766," National Archives of Ontario, Toronto, microfilmed by Toronto Public Libraries, copy on file at the Colonial Michilimackinac Archives, Petersen Center Library, Mackinaw City, Michigan (hereafter cited as Askin's Memorandum Book).
94. Observer quoted in Ruth B. Philips, *Patterns of Power: The Jasper Grant Collection and Great Lakes Indian Art of the Early Nineteenth Century* (Kleinburg, Ontario: McMichael Canadian Collection, 1984), 16.

95. For an account of Askin's visit to Detroit as commissary, see John Porteous' Diary of Trip, Schenectady, Detroit, Mackinac, L'Arbre Croche, St. Marys, Channel Island, St. Ignace, Mackinac, March 15, 1765–May 23, 1766, John Porteous Manuscript, Burton Historical Collection, Detroit Public Library, Detroit, Michigan (hereafter cited as John Porteous Diary).
96. John Porteous Diary.
97. Ibid.
98. For a discussion of Sterling's and Porteous's activities within the context of Phyn, Ellice and Company, see R. H. Fleming, "Phyn, Ellice and Company of Schenectady," *Contributions to Canadian Economics* 4 (1932): 7–41.
99. James Sterling to John Duncan, November 12, 1764, James Sterling Letter book.
100. James Sterling to Lieutenant Magill Wallace, February 9, 1765, James Sterling Letter Book.
101. For a discussion of how the New York fur trade establishment responded to these reforms, see Thomas Elliot Norton, *The Fur Trade in Colonial New York, 1686–1776* (Madison: University of Wisconsin Press, 1974), 198–215.
102. James Sterling to John Askin, April 13, 1765, James Sterling Letter Book.
103. James Sterling to John Porteous, September 29, 1765, James Sterling Letter Book.
104. Ibid.
105. Askin's Memorandum Book.
106. For a discussion of French Jesuits and the village of Arbre Croche, see H. Bedford-Jones, *L'Arbre Croche Mission* (Santa Barbara: Self-printed, 1917); John C. Wright, *Stories of the Crooked Tree* (Harbor Springs, MI: Lakeside Press, 1915). In the 1760s, Jonathan Carver, a British explorer, described the landscape surrounding Michilimackinac as "sandy, dry, barren . . . troops and the traders [there] can scarsly find sufficient for gardens to raise greens on." See Jonathan Carver, *The Journals of Jonathan Carver and Related Documents, 1766–1770*, ed. John Parker (St. Paul: Minnesota Historical Society Press, 1976), 71.
107. Henry, *Alexander Henry's Travels*, 47.
108. For references of John Askin's ownership of the farm at Arbre Croche, see John Porteous Diary; Carver, *Journals of Jonathan Carver*, 17. Carver placed "Askin's Farm" on a map that accompanied his travel narratives. See also Donald P. Heldman, *Archaeological Investigations at French Farm Lake in North Michigan, 1981–1982: A British Colonial Farm Site* (Mackinac Island, MI: Mackinac Island State Park Commission, 1983), 8–10.
109. See Heldman, *Archaeological Investigations*, 9; Carver, *Journals of Jonathan Carver*, 17.

110. McConnell, *Army and Empire*, 103. McConnell notes that the "quantities of food were intended to meet the soldier's basic ration." For the various ways soldiers, merchants, and others improved and enhanced garrison diets in the Great Lakes, see McConnell, *Army and Empire*, 104–108; Dunnigan, *Necessity of Regularity*, 17–21.
111. For the kinds of foodstuffs that Askin farmed during his tenure at Michilimackinac, see Diary of John Askin at Mackinac, 1774, *Askin Papers*, 1:50–58.
112. For a discussion of fur trade agriculture, see D. W. Moodie, "Agriculture and the Fur Trade," in *Old Trails and New Directions: Papers of the Third North American Fur Trade Conference*, ed. Carol M. Judd and Arthur J. Ray (Toronto: University of Toronto Press, 1980), 272–290.
113. General Thomas Gage to Sir William Johnson, January 13, 1766, *Sir William Johnson Papers*, 13:380.
114. Sir William Johnson to Thomas Moncfieffe, January 30, 1766, *Sir William Johnson Papers*, 12:11.
115. For Major Robert Rogers's life and his career after the collapse of his trading partnership with Askin, see John F. Ross, *War on the Run: The Epic Story of Robert Rogers and the Conquest of America's First Frontier* (New York: Bantam Books, 2011); C. P. Stacey, "Rogers, Robert," in *Dictionary of Canadian Biography*, vol. 4.
116. General Thomas Gage to Sir William Johnson, January 13, 1766, *Sir William Johnson Papers*, 13:380.
117. Sir William Johnson to General Thomas Gage, January 25, 1766, *Sir William Johnson Papers*, 12:9.
118. General Thomas Gage's Instruction to Major Robert Rogers, January 10, 1766, *Sir William Johnson Papers*, 12:1.
119. General Thomas Gage to Sir William Johnson, February 3, 1766, *Sir William Johnson Papers*, 5:30.
120. Askin's Memorandum Book.
121. Ibid.
122. Ibid.
123. Ibid.
124. See Record of Manette's Manumission, *Early Land Transfers: Detroit and Wayne County, Michigan*, 1703–1796, vol. A (Detroit: Louisa St. Clair Chapter, Daughters of the American Revolution, 1936), 9. Sterling served as the witness for the manumission of Manette; historians have interpreted his manumission as evidence of a potential relationship. It is impossible to tell without further detail or context.
125. Askin's Memorandum Book.

126. For a list of Askin's creditors, see John Askin's Discharge from Bankruptcy, December 24, 1771, *Askin Papers*, 1:43–45.
127. Askin's Memorandum Book.

Chapter Three. Sound as a Roach and as Full of Intrigue: Michilimackinac, the Hudson's Bay Company, and John Askin's Fur Trade, 1767–1774

1. John Porteous to an unknown recipient, March 8, 1767, John Porteous Letter Book, 1767–1769, William Clements Library, University of Michigan, Ann Arbor, Michigan (hereafter referred to as Porteous Letter Book).
2. See Stefan Bielinski, "Abraham Douw," *The Colonial Albany Social History Project*, http://www.nysm.nysed.gov/albany/bios/d/abdouw2052.html.
3. John Porteous to an unknown recipient, March 8, 1767, Porteous Letter Book.
4. For the early years and history of Phyn, Ellice and Company, see R. H. Fleming, "Phyn, Ellice and Company of Schenectady," *Contributions to Canadian Economies* 4 (1932): 7–41; Thomas Elliot Norton, *The Fur Trade in Colonial New York, 1686–1776* (Madison: University of Wisconsin Press, 1974), 204–219.
5. Sir William Johnson to Secretary Henry Seymour Conway, June 28, 1766, *Documents Colonial History New York*, 836. For a detailed discussion of British policy in the Great Lakes, see Jack M. Sosin, *Whitehall and the Wilderness: The Middle West in British Colonial Policy, 1760–1775* (Lincoln: University of Nebraska Press, 1961), 99–164.
6. Sir William Johnson to Secretary Henry Seymour Conway, June 28, 1766, *Documents Colonial History New York*, 835.
7. For a discussion of how British capital tied together the Great Lakes fur trade, see Harry W. Duckworth, "British Capital in the Fur Trade: John Strettell and John Fraser," in *The Fur Trade Revisited: Selected Papers of the Sixth North American Fur Trade Conference, Mackinac Inland, Michigan, 1991*, ed. Jennifer S. H. Brown, W. J. Eccles, and Donald P. Heldman (East Lansing: Michigan State University Press, 1994).
8. See Duckworth, "British Capital," 39; Fleming, "Phyn, Ellice, and Company," 13.
9. Fleming, "Phyn, Ellice, and Company," 28.
10. For a discussion of the merchandise that frequently showed up in these "outfits" and their frequency at fur trade posts in the Great Lakes, see Dean L. Anderson, "The Flow of European Trade Goods into the Western Great Lakes, Region, 1715–1760," in Brown, Eccles, and Heldman, *The Fur Trade Revisited*.
11. Alexander Henry, *Alexander Henry's Travels and Adventures in the Years 1760–1776*, ed.

Milo M. Quaife (Chicago: R. R. Donnelley & Sons, 1921), 183–185.

12. For a biography of Cadot and a discussion of his importance in the upper Great Lakes, see David A. Armour, "Cadot, Jean-Baptiste," *Dictionary of Canadian Biography*, vol. 5 (Toronto: University of Toronto Press, 1983); Theresa M. Schenck, "The Cadottes: Five Generations of Fur Traders on Lake Superior," in Brown, Eccles, and Heldman, *The Fur Trade Revisited.*
13. Engagé were salaried men employed to transport, portage, interact, and trade with Indian communities; they helped preform the tremendous physical labor necessary for the movement of furs into the North American interior.
14. Henry, *Alexander Henry's Travels*, 187–188.
15. For a discussion of Native Americans as consumers within the Great Lakes fur trade, see Bruce M. White, "Encounters with Spirits: Ojibwa and Dakota Theories about the French and Their Merchandise," *Ethnohistory* 41 (1994): 369–405; Arthur J. Ray, "Indians as Consumers in the Eighteenth Century," in *Old Trails and New Directions: Papers of the Third North American Fur Trade Conference*, ed. Carol M. Judd and Arthur J. Ray (Toronto: University of Toronto Press, 1980), 255–271.
16. Henry, *Alexander Henry's Travels*, 188.
17. For a list of Askin's creditors, see John Askin's Discharge from Bankruptcy, December 24, 1771, *Askin Papers*, 1:43–45.
18. Letter of License to John Askin to transact his business without molestation by his creditors for twelve months, signed March 11, 1769, New York, Rogers Manuscripts.
19. See James Phyn and Alexander Ellice to John Porteous, January 4, 1772, Letterbooks of Phyn and Ellice, Merchants, at Schenectady, New York, 1767–1776, vol. 2, Buffalo Historical Society, Buffalo, New York, microfilmed by the Buffalo Historical Society, copy on file at the Colonial Michilimackinac Archives, Petersen Center Library, Mackinaw City, Michigan (hereafter cited as Letterbooks of Phyn and Ellice); James Phyn and Alexander Ellice to John Askin, April 4, 1772, Letterbooks of Phyn and Ellice, vol. 2.
20. John Porteous to Robert Ellice, August 10, 1767, Porteous Letter Book.
21. For a detailed discussion of the conflict between Major Robert Rogers and Commissary Benjamin Roberts, see Peter Marshall, "The Michilimackinac Misfortunes of Commissary Roberts," in Brown, Eccles, and Heldman, *The Fur Trade Revisited.*
22. Major Robert Rogers to Sir William Johnson, September 23, 1766, *Sir William Johnson Papers*, 12:194.
23. For a detailed discussion of Rogers's efforts to find the Northwest Passage, see Keith

R. Widder, "The 1767 Maps of Robert Rogers and Jonathan Carver: A Proposal for the Establishment of the Colony of Michilimackinac," *Michigan Historical Review* 30 (2004): 35–75.

24. Lieutenant Christian Daniel Claus to Sir William Johnson, October 16, 1766, *Sir William Johnson Papers*, 12:212. See Douglas Leighton, "Claus, Christian Daniel," in *Dictionary of Canadian Biography*, vol. 4 (Toronto: University of Toronto Press, 1979).
25. Major Robert Rogers to Sir William Johnson, September 23, 1766, *Sir William Johnson Papers*, 12:194.
26. See Plan of Major Robert Rogers, 1767, *Sir William Johnson Papers*, 13:452, 454, 458, 460.
27. Sir William Johnson to the Earl of Shelburne, December 3, 1767, *Journals of Major Robert Rogers: An Account of the Several Excursions He Made under the Generals Who Commanded upon the Continent of North America During the Late War* (Albany: Joel Munsell's Sons, 1883), 243.
28. See Major Robert Rogers' Account of the Distribution of Indian Presents, August 10, 1766 to December 5, 1767, in David A. Armour, ed., *Treason at Michilimackinac: The Proceedings of a General Court Martial Held at Montreal in October 1768 for the Trial of Major Robert Rogers* (Mackinac Island, MI: Mackinac Island State Park Commission, 1972), 83–87, 92.
29. General Thomas Gage to Sir William Johnson, May 11, 1767, *Sir William Johnson Papers*, 5:549. For a biography of Benjamin Roberts, see Douglas Leighton, "Roberts, Benjamin," in *Dictionary of Canadian Biography*, vol. 4. For key documents related to the conflict between Major Robert Rogers and Lieutenant Benjamin Roberts at Michilimackinac, and Rogers's arrest and trial, see Schedule of Papers transmitted by General Gage to Mr. Francis, Deputy Solicitor of the Treasury, copy on file at the Colonial Michilimackinac Archives, Petersen Center Library, Mackinaw City, Michigan (hereafter cited as Schedule of Papers).
30. Sir William Johnson to General Thomas Gage, January 25, 1766, *Sir William Johnson Papers*, 12:9.
31. Sir William Johnson to John Brown, October 31, 1766, *Sir William Johnson Papers*, 5:404.
32. Ibid.
33. Robert Rogers, *Journal of Major Robert Rogers*, ed. William L. Clements (Worcester: American Antiquarian Society, 1918), 33, 35.
34. See John F. Ross, *War on the Run: The Epic Story of Robert Rogers and the Conquest of America's First Frontier* (New York: Bantam Books, 2011), 392.

35. Rogers, *Journal*, 33.
36. Major Robert Rogers to Sir William Johnson, August 14, 1767, *Sir William Johnson Papers*, 5:615–616.
37. Benjamin Roberts to Sir William Johnson, August 12, 1767, *Sir William Johnson Papers*, 5:614.
38. Benjamin Roberts to Lieutenant Christian Daniel Claus, August 20, September 21, 1767, *Sir William Johnson Papers*, 5:692.
39. Memorial of Benjamin Roberts, August 21, 1767, *Sir William Johnson Papers*, 5:633.
40. Benjamin Roberts to Captain Christopher Spiesmacher, August 20, 1767, *Sir William Johnson Papers*, 5:629.
41. Benjamin Roberts to Lieutenant Christian Daniel Claus, August 20, September 21, 1767, *Sir William Johnson Papers*, 5:692.
42. See Proceedings of a Court of Inquiry, August 22, 1767, *Sir William Johnson Papers*, 5:638–640.
43. Captain Christopher Spiesmacher to Sir William Johnson, September 22, 1767, *Sir William Johnson Papers*, 5:696.
44. A Deposition made by Nathanl Potter, late of Michilimackina taken before the Honble William Hay, His Majesty's Chief Justice of the Province of Quebec, September 28, 1767, *Documents Colonial History New York*, 990–991.
45. See Ross, *War on the Run*, 396–397, 399–400.
46. General Thomas Gage to Sir William Johnson, November 9, 1767, *Sir William Johnson Papers*, 12:377.
47. Deposition of Joseph Ainsse, in Armour, *Treason at Michilimackinac*, 38.
48. Captain Christopher Spiesmacher to General Thomas Gage, February 24, 1768, Gage Papers, vol. 78.
49. Captain Frederick Spiesmacher to General Thomas Gage, May 26, 1768, Schedule of Papers.
50. Ibid. Spiesmacher complained bitterly to Gage: "I could not help often refusing them the liberty [of being sole executors of his property], and at last positively refus'd them not to visite the major, however . . . [they] got an assignment from him, in theire name, which they look upon as good, and all the rest of the Creditors as unjust unlawfull, and Fradulent."
51. Captain Frederick Spiesmacher to Major Robert Rogers, February 2, 1769, Schedule of Papers.
52. John Askin to Sir William Johnson, September 22, 1767, *Sir William Johnson Papers*, 5:693–694.

53. See Benjamin Roberts to Captain Christopher Daniel Claus, September 21, 1767, *Sir William Johnson Papers*, 5:692 n. 2.
54. John Askin to Sir William Johnson, September 22, 1767, *Sir William Johnson Papers*, 5:694.
55. See Ross, *War on the Run*, 448–449.
56. General Thomas Gage to Sir William Johnson, August 7, 1768, *Sir William Johnson Papers*, 6:313–314.
57. For the history and development of the York Factory, see Arthur J. Ray and Donald B. Freeman, *"Give Us Good Measure": An Economic Analysis of Relations between the Indians and the Hudson's Bay Company before 1763* (Toronto: University of Toronto Press, 1978), 181, 190–191, 194–197. For broader discussions of the history of the Hudson's Bay Company, see Douglas MacKay, *The Honourable Company* (Toronto: McClelland & Stewart, 1936); Barry M. Gough, "The 'Adventurers of England Trading into Hudson's Bay': A Study of the Founding Members of the Hudson's Bay Company, 1665–1670," *Albion* 2 (1970): 35–47; James G. E. Smith, "Chipewyan, Cree and Inuit Relations West of Hudson Bay, 1714–1955," *Ethnohistory* 28 (1981): 133–156.
58. Andrew Graham to the Governor and Committee of the Hudson's Bay Company, August 1772, in *Documents Relating to the North West Company*, ed. William Stewart Wallace (Toronto: Champlain Society, 1934), 39 (hereafter cited as *Documents North West Company*). For biographical information related to Andrew Graham, see Glyndwr Williams, "Graham, Andrew," in *Dictionary of Canadian Biography*, vol. 5.
59. Andrew Graham to the Governor and Committee of the Hudson's Bay Company, August 26, 1772, *Documents North West Company*, 39–41.
60. Ibid.
61. John Porteous to Sampson Fleming, May 26, 1768, Porteous Letter Book.
62. For a history of Grand Portage, see Carolyn Gilman, *The Grand Portage Story* (St. Paul: Minnesota Historical Society Press, 1992); Solon J. Buck, "The Story of the Grand Portage," *Minnesota History* 5 (1923): 14–27; Grace Lee Nute, "A British Legal Case and Old Grand Portage," *Minnesota History* 21 (1940): 117–148.
63. In a legal deposition, Maurice Blondeau noted that he "went up to Grand Portage the first time in 1766. That he knows the fort where the bourgeois were, which was not then cleared and was not cleared for two or three years thereafter and then by a man named [Askin]." Askin was far from the first merchant to utilize Grand Portage for trade purposes. However, Blondeau's testimony shows Askin's early interest in Hudson's Bay. See Nute, "British Legal Case," 134.
64. Andrew Graham to the Governor and Committee of the Hudson's Bay Company,

August 26, 1772, *Documents North West Company*, 40. For a biography of Forrest Oakes, see George E. Thorman, "Oakes, Forrest," in *Dictionary of Canadian Biography*, vol. 4. For biographies of the persons named, see the following: François Béland, "Blondeau, Maurice-Régis"; J. I. Cooper, "McGill, James"; Myron Momryk, "Todd, Isaac"; and Fernand Ouelett, "McBeath, George," all in *Dictionary of Canadian Biography*, vol. 5.

65. Ross, *War on the Run*, 401–402.
66. John Askin's Inventory, 1778. National Archives of Ontario, Toronto, microfilmed by Toronto Public Libraries, copy on file at the Colonial Michilimackinac Archives, Petersen Center Library, Mackinaw City, Michigan. See also Captain Beamsley Glazier's Receipt to John Askin for Governmental Service, May 15, 1770, Gage Papers, vol. 92. For a discussion of the iron industry at Michilimackinac, see Lynn L. Morand, *Craft Industries at Fort Michilimackinac, 1715–1781* (Mackinac Island, MI: Mackinac State Historic Parks, 1994), 17–25.
67. John Gram, *John Askin at Michilimackinac*, unpublished manuscript, June 1995, Mackinac State Historic Parks Library, Mackinac City, MI, 15.
68. For early Quebec- and Montreal-based fur trade efforts in Hudson's Bay, see W. Stewart Wallace, "The Pedlars from Quebec," in *The Pedlars from Quebec and Other Papers on the Nor' Westers* (Toronto: Ryerson Press, 1954), 1–18.
69. See MacKay, *The Honourable Company*, 47–56.
70. For an overview of the Hudson's Bay Company, see MacKay, *The Honourable Company*; Peter C. Newman, *Company of Adventurers: How the Hudson's Bay Empire Determined the Destiny of a Continent* (Toronto: Penguin Canada, 2004); Paul Phillips, *The Fur Trade*, vol. 1 (Norman: University of Oklahoma Press, 1961), 266–287; Harold A. Innis, *The Fur Trade in Canada* (Toronto: University of Toronto Press, 1967), 84–145.
71. For a discussion of Made Beaver, see Ann M. Carlos and Frank D. Lewis, "Trade, Consumption, and the Native Economy: Lessons from York Factory, Hudson's Bay," *Journal of Economic History* 61, no. 4 (December 2001): 1043–1047.
72. See James G. E. Smith, "Chipewyan, Cree and Inuit Relations West of Hudson Bay, 1714–1955," *Ethnohistory* 28 (Spring 1981): 134–135. For an overview of the Hudson's Bay Company and its relationship to the Indian peoples of the Hudson's Bay, see Arthur J. Ray, *I Have Lived Here since the World Began: An Illustrated History of Canada's Native People* (Toronto: Key Porter Books, 1996), 78–111. See also I. Irma Eckert, "The Early Fur Trade at York and Churchill: Implications for the Native People of the North Central Subarctic," *"Castor Fait Tout": Selected Papers of the Fifth*

North American Fur Trade Conference, 1985, ed. Bruce G. Trigger, Toby Morantz, and Louise Dechene (St. Louis: Lake St. Louis Historical Society, 1987), 223–235.

73. For a discussion of Indians as intermediaries in the Hudson's Bay Company, and the important and pivotal roles women played in the fur trade process, see Sylvia Van Kirk, *Many Tender Ties: Women in Fur-Trade Society, 1670–1870* (Norman: University of Oklahoma Press, 1980).
74. For a comprehensive discussion of the rivalry and competition between the French Empire and the Hudson's Bay Company, see Innis, *Fur Trade in Canada*, 84–145.
75. Andrew Graham to the Governor and Committee of the Hudson's Bay Company, August 26, 1772, *Documents North West Company*, 40–41, 43.
76. Ibid., 40–42.
77. W. J. Eccles, "The Fur Trade and Eighteenth-Century Imperialism," *William and Mary Quarterly* 40, no. 3 (1983): 350–351.
78. For the destructive effects of alcohol within Indian communities, see Peter C. Mancall, *Deadly Medicine: Indians and Alcohol in Early America* (Ithaca, NY: Cornell University Press, 1995).
79. Andrew Graham to the Governor and Committee of the Hudson's Bay Company, August 26, 1772, *Documents North West Company*, 41–42.
80. John Askin's Discharge from Bankruptcy, December 24, 1771, *Askin Papers*, 1:69.
81. James Phyn and Alexander Ellice to John Porteous. January 4, 1772, Letterbooks of Phyn and Ellice, vol. 2.
82. James Phyn and Alexander Ellice to John Porteous, January 4, 1772, Letterbooks of Phyn and Ellice, vol. 2.
83. Andrew Graham to the Governor and Committee of the Hudson's Bay Company, August 26, 1772, *Documents North West Company*, 43.
84. For a discussion of the North West Company, see *Documents North West Company*; Marjorie Wilkins Campbell, *The North West Company* (Toronto: Macmillan Company of Canada, 1957); Van Kirk, *Many Tender Ties*.
85. See Entry for October 3, 1775, *Wisconsin Historical Collections*, vol. 19 (Madison: State Historical Society of Wisconsin, 1910), 77 (hereafter cited as *WHC*). A priest from the Illinois Country wrote: "Baptized archange, born the same day Of the Lawful Marriage of Sieur Jean Askin, King's Commissioner at this post, and Of Dame Archange Berthe, his Wife." This cryptic entry references the marriage between Marie Archange Barthe and Askin, and suggests that Askin may have consorted with Marie before their marriage.
86. Milo M. Quiafe, "Introduction," Askin Papers, 1:34, 12n. The complex familial

network of the Barthe family can be pieced together and traced across the Great Lakes; see Christian Denissen, *The Genealogy of the French Families of the Detroit River Region, 1701–1936*, 2 vols. (Detroit: Detroit Society for Genealogical Research, 1987); Judy Jacobson, *Detroit River Connections: Historical and Biographical Sketches of the Eastern Great Lakes Border Region* (Baltimore: Clearfield Company, 1994), 44–48.

87. Karen L. Marrero, *Founding Families: Power and Authority of Mixed French and Native Lineages in Eighteenth-Century Detroit* (New Haven: Yale University Press, 2011), 199–201.
88. For the role the silver trade played in French diplomacy and the fur trade, see David A. Baerreis, "Trade Silver and Indian Silversmiths," *Wisconsin Magazine of History* 34 (1950): 76–82.
89. Marrero, *Founding Families*, 227.
90. Barthe seems to have had numerous dealings with the Jesuit missionaries and the Catholic Church in the Detroit River region. For example, in *The Jesuit Relations*, the priests refer to him as Barte. In 1748, Father de la Richardie notes that "Barte owes . . . a livre of vermilion and 3 pairs of mitasses." Two years later, Richardie records that he "received from sieur barte, armorer, at detroit, The sum of 312 livres in discharge of sieur duouchel, blacksmith, to whom The said barte owed That sum and more for the house in the fort that I sold him last year, 1759." See *The Jesuit Relations and Allies Documents: Trade and Explorations of the Jesuit Missionaries in New France, 1610–1791*, vol. 70, ed. Reuben Gold Thwaites (Cleveland: Burrows Brothers, 1891), 40, 46; John Askin to Commodore Alexander Grant, April 28, 1778, *Askin Papers*, 1:77.
91. Marrero, *Founding Families*, 276.
92. For the role French and Indian women like Marie Angélique Cuillerier played in the Great Lakes fur trade, see Clara Sue Kidwell, "Indian Women as Cultural Negotiators," *Ethnohistory* 39 (1992), 97–107; Susan Sleeper-Smith, "Women, Kin, and Catholicism: New Perspectives on the Fur Trade," *Ethnohistory* 47 (2000), 423–452.
93. James Sterling to John Duncan, February 26, 1765, James Sterling Letterbook.
94. Marrero, *Founding Families*, 280–284. However, as Karen Marrero points out, the marriage proved less beneficial to Marie Angelique Cuillerier, who found Sterling's expectations of her limiting and controlling. In a letter to John Porteous, Sterling informed him that "Mrs. Sterling will answer the end of an interpreter, tho' not to ride after the Indians which is now the mode here." She could translate, but could not trade and winter among her Indigenous kin. James Sterling to John Porteous, September 4, 1765, James Sterling Letterbook.

95. John Askin to Commodore Alexander Grant, April 28, 1778, *Askin Papers*, 1:77.
96. Marrero, *Founding Families*, 228.
97. For a discussion of how trade, family, and imperial work interconnected and reinforced each other, see Bruce M. White, "Balancing the Books: Trader Profits in the British Lake Superior Fur Trade," in *New Faces of the Fur Trade: Selected Papers of the Seventh North Fur Trade Conference, Halifax, Nova Scotia, 1995*, ed. Jo-Anne Fiske, Susan Sleeper-Smith, and William Wicken (East Lansing: Michigan State University Press, 1998), 184–191. This article offers additional insight into the life and trade of Jean-Baptiste Cadott in the mid-1780s.

Chapter Four. One Should Never Give Offence in Trade: Michilimackinac, the American Revolution, and John Askin's Network of Exchange, 1774–1779

1. John Askin to Thomas McMurry, April 28, 1778, *Askin Papers*, 1:69. For a discussion of community surrounding Fort Michilimackinac, see J. Mark Williams and Gary Shapiro, *A Search for the Eighteenth Century Village at Michilimackinac* (Mackinac Island, MI: Mackinac Island State Park Commission, 1982), 1–9, 23.
2. John Askin to Commodore Alexander Grant, April 28, 1778, *Askin Papers*, 1:78.
3. John Askin to Sampson Fleming, June 4, 1778, *Askin Papers*, 1:105.
4. John Askin to John Hay, April 27, 1778, *Askin Papers*, 1:67.
5. Robert Ellice to John Askin, August 13, 1774, Letterbooks of Phyn and Ellice, vol. 3.
6. See Phyn and Ellice to John Askin, January 3, 1775, Letterbooks of Phyn and Ellice, vol. 3.
7. John Askin to James Sterling, May 8, 1778, *Askin Papers*, 1:80.
8. See Record of Archange Askin's Baptism, October 3, 1775, "The Mackinac Register, 1695–1821: Register of Baptisms of the Mission of St. Ignace de Michilimakinak," ed. Reuben Gold Thwaites, *WHC*, 19:77. Curiously, perhaps as a result of the lack of a permanent priest at Michilimackinac, John Askin and Marie Archange Barthe were officially married on the day of their daughter's birth. For a discussion of the importance of baptism and kinship in the Great Lakes fur trade society, see Susan Sleeper-Smith, *Indian Women and French Men: Rethinking Cultural Encounter in the Western Great Lakes* (Amherst: University of Massachusetts Press, 2001).
9. For a discussion of McKee, his family, and their importance in the Ohio Valley, see Larry L. Nelson, *A Man of Distinction among Them: Alexander McKee and British-Indian Affairs along the Ohio Country Frontier, 1754–1799* (Kent, OH: Kent State University Press, 1999).

10. John Askin's inventories of his household reveal a staggering degree of personal and familial wealth brought on by their participation in the Great Lakes fur trade. For example, see John Askin's Inventory, 1776, 1778, National Archives of Ontario, Toronto, microfilmed by Toronto Public Libraries, copy on file at the Colonial Michilimackinac Archives, Petersen Center Library, Mackinaw City, Michigan (hereafter cited as Askin Inventory). The following percentages are not part of the original documents, but represent analysis completed by the author.
11. Askin Inventory, 1776.
12. Askin Inventory, 1776. For a detailed examination of the ship *Welcome*, the conditions it experienced, and the duties it performed on the Great Lakes, see Log-Book of the Welcome, 1779–1782, from the Alexander Harrow Papers in the Burton Historical Collections, microfilmed, copy on file at the Colonial Michilimackinac Archives, Petersen Center Library, Mackinaw City, Michigan (hereafter cited as Welcome Log-Book).
13. Askin Inventory, 1778.
14. Askin Inventory, 1776, 1778.
15. For the most detailed account of Michilimackinac during the American Revolution, see David A. Armour and Keith R. Widder, *At the Crossroads: Michilimackinac during the American Revolution* (Mackinac Island, MI: Mackinac Island State Park Commission, 1978). For further discussion of the American Revolution and the Great Lakes fur trade, see Keith Widder, "Effects of the American Revolution on Fur-Trade Society at Michilimackinac," in *The Fur Trade Revisited: Selected Papers of the Sixth North American Fur Trade Conference, Mackinac Island, Michigan, 1991*, ed. Jennifer S. H. Brown, W. J. Eccles, and Donald P. Heldman (East Lansing: Michigan State University Press, 1994), 285–316; Harold A. Innis, *The Fur Trade in Canada: An Introduction to Canadian Economic History* (New Haven, CT: Yale University Press, 1962), 180–188. For an overview of the American Revolution from the perspective of the British Empire, see Nelson Vance Russell, *The British Regime in Michigan and the Old Northwest, 1760–1796* (Philadelphia: Porcupine Press, 1978), 185–216.
16. Askin Inventory, 1776, 1778.
17. John Askin to Sampson Fleming, April 28, 1778, *Askin Papers*, 1:79. For an account of Askin's farm produce, see Diary of John Askin at Mackinac, 1774, *Askin Papers*, 1:50–58.
18. Askin Inventory. For a discussion of Askin's library and literate life in a fur-trade community, see Agnes Widder, "The John Askin Family Library: A Fur-Trading Family's Book," *Michigan Historical Review* 33 (2007): 27–58.

19. Askin Inventory, 1776, 1778.
20. John Askin to Issac Todd and James McGill, May 8, 1778, *Askin Papers*, 1:84.
21. John Askin to Mr. Beausoleil, May 18, 1778, *Askin Papers*, 1:98.
22. Askin Inventory, 1776.
23. John Askin to John Hay, April 27, 1778, *Askin Papers*, 1:68.
24. John Askin to Sampson Fleming, May 10, 1778, *Askin Papers*, 1:86.
25. Askin Inventory, 1778.
26. For a biography or account of Major Arent Schuyler de Peyster's life, see David A. Armour, "DePeyster, Arent Schuyler," in *Dictionary of Canadian Biography*, vol. 6 (Toronto: University of Toronto Press, 1987); Armour and Widder, *At the Crossroads*, 7–8; Major Arent Schuyler de Peyster to Gentlemen Traders of Michilimackinac, September 20, 1779, *Miscellanies by an Officer* (Dumfries, Scotland: C. Monro, 1888), 4–5. While mostly a book of poems written by de Peyster, *Miscellanies* also reprinted a series of letters from his command at Michilimackinac and Detroit.
27. For an account of this council, see Paul L. Stevens, "Wabasaha Visits Governor Carleton, 1776: New Light on a Legendary Episode of Dakota-British Diplomacy on the Great Lakes Frontier," *Michigan Historical Review* 16 (1990): 21–48.
28. For a discussion of France and the American Revolution, see Ronald Hoffman and Peter J. Albert, eds., *Diplomacy and Revolution: The Franco-American Alliance of 1778* (Charlottesville: University of Virginia Press, 1981); Frank W. Brecher, *Securing American Independence: John Jay and the French Alliance* (Westport, CT: Praeger, 2003); James Pritchard, "French Strategy and the American Revolution: A Reappraisal," *Naval War College Review* 48, no. 4 (1994): 83–108.
29. For a discussion of the material prosperity of the British Empire and its effect on British identity in North America, see T. H. Breen, "An Empire of Goods: The Anglicization of Colonial America," *Journal of British Studies* 25, no. 4 (October 1986): 467–499; T. H. Breen, *The Marketplace of Revolution: How Consumers Politics Shaped American Independence* (Oxford: Oxford University Press, 2005).
30. See Michael J. Braddick, "Civility and Authority," in *The British Atlantic World, 1500–1800*, ed. David Armitage and Michael J. Braddick (New York: Palgrave Macmillan, 2002). Braddick writes that "the Movement of goods and people around the British Atlantic world created a shared material culture which reflected common assumptions about status distinctions," and, accordingly, authority, or conflicts over authority, often manifested themselves within the context of "living appropriately," or, in other words, "bear[ing] the port, charge and countenance of a gentleman." See Braddick, "Civility and Authority," 93–94.

31. Askin Inventory, 1776, 1778; John Baptiste Barthe Manuscripts, 1775–1780, microfilm, Burton Historical Collection, Detroit Public Library, Detroit, Michigan (hereafter cited as Barthe Manuscripts).
32. Askin Inventory, 1778. See also Captain Beamsley Glazier's Receipt to John Askin for Governmental Service, May 15, 1770, Gage Papers, vol. 92. For a discussion of the iron industry at Michilimackinac, see Lynn L. Morand, *Craft Industries at Fort Michilimackinac, 1715–1781* (Mackinac Island, MI: Mackinac State Historic Parks, 1994), 17–25.
33. Captain Patrick Sinclair to General Frederick Haldimand, July–August 1780, *MPHC*, 9:564.
34. John Askin to Philip Dejean, June 4, 1778, *Askin Papers*, 1:107.
35. Lieutenant Governor Henry Hamilton to General Frederick Haldimand, [1778?], *MPHC*, 9:518.
36. John Askin to Isaac Todd and James McGill, May 8, 1778, *Askin Papers*, 1:84.
37. See Edmund Morgan and Helen Morgan, *The Stamp Act Crisis: Prologue to Revolution* (Chapel Hill: University of North Carolina Press, 1995); Charles R. Ritcheson, "The Preparation of the Stamp Acts," *William and Mary Quarterly* 10, no. 4 (October 1953): 543–559.
38. For a discussion of the political debates and origins of the American Revolution, see Bernard Bailyn, *The Ideological Origins of the American Revolution* (Cambridge: Harvard University Press, 1967); Robert R. Palmer, *The Age of the Democratic Revolution: A Political History of Europe and America, 1760–1800*, vol. 1 (Princeton, NJ: Princeton University Press, 1959); Gordon S. Wood, *The Radicalism of the American Revolution* (New York: A. A. Knopf, 1992). For the ways in which the American Revolution cut across race, class, and gender lines, see Gary B. Nash, *The Unknown American Revolution: The Unruly Birth of Democracy and the Struggle to Create America* (New York: Viking, 2005).
39. For a discussion of British colonial protests in response to these acts, see Nash, *The Unknown American Revolution.*
40. See An Act for the better securing the Dependency of His Majesty's Dominions in America upon the Crown and Parliament of Great Britain, *The Statutes: Revised Edition*, vol. 15 (London: George Edward Eyre and William Spottiswoode, 1878), 1291.
41. For a detailed discussion of the New York fur trade during the buildup to the American Revolution, see Thomas Elliot Norton, *The Fur Trade in Colonial New York, 1686–1776* (Madison: University of Wisconsin Press, 1974), 215–220.

42. Phyn and Ellice to James Cassity, August 26, 1769, Letterbooks of Phyn and Ellice, vol. 1.
43. Phyn and Ellice to John Porteous, August 23, 1770, Letterbooks of Phyn and Ellice, vol. 1.
44. Phyn, Ellice, and Company to Piqou and Booth, May 19, 1770, Letterbooks of Phyn and Ellice, vol. 1.
45. On Johnson's sickness and death, see Fintan O'Toole, *White Savage: William Johnson and the Invention of America* (London: Faber, 2005), 321–325.
46. See Further Debates in the Commons on the Bill for regulating the Government of Massachuset's Bay, April 22, 1774, *The Parliamentary History of England from the Earliest Period to This Year, 1803*, vol. 18 (London: T. C. Hansard, Peterborough-Court, Fleet-Street, 1813), 1280. During the debate, Lord North, the prime minister, argued: "The Americans have tarred and feathered your subjects, plundered your merchants, burnt your ships, denied all obedience to your laws and authority; yet so clement, and so long forbearing has our conduct been, that it is incumbent on us now to take a different course. Whatever may be the consequence, we must risk something; if we do not, all is over."
47. An Act for making more effectual Provision for the Government of the Province of Quebec in North America, *The Statutes at Large from the Seventh Year of the Reign of King George the Third to the Eighteenth Year of the Reign of King George the Third*, vol. 8 (London: Carles Eyre and Andrew Strahan, 1786), 405–407. See also Russell, *British Regime in Michigan*, 71–74; Jack M. Sosin, *Whitehall and the Wilderness: The Middle West in British Colonial Policy, 1760–1775* (Lincoln: University of Nebraska Press, 1961), 239–249.
48. Norton, *Fur Trade*, 219.
49. Phyn and Ellice to James Phyn, January 5, 1778, Letterbooks of Phyn and Ellice, vol. 3.
50. Phyn and Ellice to Isaac Todd, November 24, 1774, Letterbooks of Phyn and Ellice, vol. 2.
51. Ibid. See also Phyn and Ellice to John Askin, August 13, 1774, Letterbooks of Phyn and Ellice, vol. 2; Phyn and Ellice to John Askin, January 3, 1775, Letterbooks of Phyn and Ellice, vol. 2.
52. Norton, *Fur Trade*, 219–220.
53. For a biography of Guy Carleton, see G. P. Browne, "Carleton, Guy, 1st Baron Dorchester," in *Dictionary of Canadian Biography*, vol. 5 (Toronto: University of Toronto Press, 1983).

54. See Russell, *British Regime in Michigan*, 74–77.
55. General Guy Carleton to Lieutenant Henry Hamilton, February 2, 1777, *MPHC*, 9:345–346. For an account of Hamilton's life, see Elizabeth Arthur, "Hamilton, Henry," in *Dictionary of Canadian Biography*, vol. 4 (Toronto: University of Toronto Press, 1979). See also *Henry Hamilton and George Rogers Clark in the American Revolution and the Unpublished Journal of Lieut. Gov. Henry Hamilton*, ed. John D. Barnhart (Crawfordsville, IN: R. E. Banta, 1951).
56. Lieutenant Governor Henry Hamilton to the Earl of Dartmouth, August 29–September 1776, *MPHC*, 10:264–270.
57. See David A. Armour, "DePeyster, Arent Schuyler," in *Dictionary of Canadian Biography*, vol. 6; Armour and Widder, *At the Crossroads*, 7–8; Major Arent Schuyler de Peyster to Gentlemen Traders of Michilimackinac, September 20, 1779, *Miscellanies by an Officer*, 4–5.
58. In 1781, after his transfer to Detroit, de Peyster wrote to Askin: "As to your Loyalty I have experienced it upon several essential occasions . . . [and] that the Service has often been greatly forwarded by the assistance you had in your power to give, which you always did most cheerfully, and with disinterestedness. . . . I have ever found you, and know you to be esteemed an Honest man." See Major Arent Schuyler de Peyster to John Askin, May 10, 1781, *MPHC*, 10:479.
59. See Armour and Widder, *At the Crossroads*, 19–23.
60. See Sleeper-Smith, *Indian Women*, 65–66.
61. As historian Karen Marrero notes, "Members of . . . métis family networks understood that many different levels of national identity operated in tandem in the pays d'en haut [Great Lakes]. The ease with which they moved between these nationalities made them both ideal vehicles for the propagation of imperial presence in the pays d'en haut, and conversely and ironically, a persistent threat to its continued existence. As the eighteenth century unfolded, imperial representatives of Native and Euro-American nations of the pays d'en haut would single out members of the [*sic*] these networks as the reason for the various ills that plagued their increasingly complex relationship." See Marrero, *Founding Families*, 219.
62. Ibid.
63. See Paul L. Stevens, "Wabasaha Visits Governor Carleton, 1776: New Light on a Legendary Episode of Dakota-British Diplomacy on the Great Lakes Frontier," *Michigan Historical Review* 16 (1990): 21–48; Armour and Widder, *At the Crossroads*, 27, 44.
64. For a discussion of the early military expeditions of the American Revolution, see

Arthur Tourtellot, *Lexington and Concord: The Beginning of the War of the American Revolution* (New York: Norton, 2000); Mark R. Anderson, *The Battle for the Fourteenth Colony: America's War of Liberation in Canada, 1774–1776* (Hanover, NH: University Press of New England, 2013).

65. See Articles of Capitulation, November 12, 1775, *American Archives*, series 4, vol. 3, ed. Peter Force (Washington, DC: M. St. Clair Clarke, P. Force, 1848–1853), 1597.
66. Armour and Widder, *At the Crossroads*, 54–56.
67. Ibid., 62; Major Arent Schuyler de Peyster to General Guy Carleton, June 29, 1778, *MPHC*, 9:366.
68. For a discussion of the Philadelphia campaign of 1777, see Stephen R. Taaffe, *The Philadelphia Campaign, 1777–1778* (Lawrence: University Press of Kansas, 2003).
69. Lord George Germain to General Guy Carleton, March 26, 1777, *MPHC*, 9:346.
70. General Guy Carleton to Lieutenant Governor Henry Hamilton, February 2, 1777, *MPHC*, 9:345.
71. Council held at Detroit June 14th 1778 with the Ottawas, Chippoweys Hurons, Poutconatamies, Delwares, Shawanese, Miamis, Mingoes, Mohawks and the Tribes of Ouashtanon, Saguinan &c. Delawares Sencas, *MPHC*, 9:445.
72. Lieutenant Governor Henry Hamilton to General Guy Carleton, April 25, 1778, *MPHC*, 9:435.
73. For a biography of George Rogers Clark, see William R. Nester, *George Rogers Clark: "I Glory in War"* (Norman: University of Oklahoma Press, 2012); Barnhart, *Henry Hamilton*.
74. As quoted in Ronald N. Satz, *Tennessee's Indian Peoples: From White Contact to Removal, 1540–1840* (Knoxville: University of Tennessee Press, 1979).
75. General Edward Hand to General Horatio Gates, February 12, 1778, *Frontier Defense on the Upper Ohio, 1777–1778*, ed. Reuben Gold Thwaites and Louise Phelps Kellogg (Madison: Wisconsin Historical Society, 1912), 203.
76. John Askin to Jean Baptiste Barthe, June 21, 1778, *Askin Papers*, 1:141.
77. In a letter from July 8, 1780, Patrick Sinclair, the lieutenant governor of Michilimackinac, described Samuel Robertson as "a Sailor, a Merchant & Carpenter—he managed the Private Vessels in Lake Superior & [Lake Huron]." See Lieutenant Governor Patrick Sinclair to General Frederick Haldimand, July 8, 1780, *MPHC*, 9:577. For Robertson's marriage to Catherine, see John Askin to John Hay, April 27, 1778, *Askin Papers*, 1:68; John Askin to Alexander Henry, June 23, 1778, *Askin Papers*, 1:145; John Askin to Isaac Todd and James McGill, June 14, 1778, *Askin Papers*, 1:128.

78. For a discussion of Cadot's trade activities during the early years of the American Revolution, see David A. Armour, "Cadot, Jean-Baptiste," in *Dictionary of Canadian Biography*, vol. 5; Theresa M. Schenck, "The Cadottes: Five Generations of Fur Traders on Lake Superior," in Brown, Eccles, and Heldman, *The Fur Trade Revisited*, 192–194.
79. See Ledger Sales Book, Barthe Manuscripts; Captain Patrick Sinclair to General Frederick Haldimand, February 1780, *MPHC*, 9:545.
80. John Askin to Jean Baptiste Barthe, June 6, 1778, *Askin Papers*, 1:114.
81. John Askin to Jean Baptiste Barthe, May 9, 1778, *Askin Papers*, 1:103.
82. See John Askin to Isaac Todd and James McGill, July 2, 1778, *Askin Papers*, 1:159.
83. Askin Inventory, 1776. For a discussion of the industries related to lumber and wood at Michilimackinac, see Morand, *Craft Industries at Fort Michilimackinac*, 61–66.
84. Askin Inventory, 1776. For a discussion of food production and processing at Michilimackinac, see Morand, *Craft Industries at Fort Michilimackinac*, 71–73.
85. Askin Inventory, 1776.
86. John Askin to Isaac Todd and James McGill, June 23, 1778, *Askin Papers*, 1:143. See also Welcome Log-Book, June 25, 1780.
87. Askin Inventory, 1776.
88. Askin Inventory, 1778.
89. See Handwritten Tabulations and Summaries of Fur Trade Licenses, 1775, copy on file at the Colonial Michilimackinac Archives, Petersen Center Library, Mackinaw City, Michigan (hereafter cited as Tabulated Returns).
90. See Consolidated Returns of Trade Licenses, 1777, copy on file at the Colonial Michilimackinac Archives, Petersen Center Library, Mackinaw City, Michigan (hereafter cited as: Consolidated Returns); Tabulated Returns, 1777.
91. Consolidated Returns, 1777; Tabulated Returns, 1777.
92. Consolidated Returns, 1778; Tabulated Returns, 1778.
93. Askin Inventory, 1776.
94. Ibid., 1778.
95. Ibid., 1776, 1778.
96. For the cloth trade and dress as cross-cultural negotiation, see Timothy Shannon, "Dressing for Success on the Mohawk Frontier: Hendrick, William Johnson, and the Indian Fashion," *William and Mary Quarterly* 53, no. 1, 3rd ser. (January 1996): 13–42. For a discussion of Indians as consumers, see Arthur J. Ray, "Indians as Consumers in the Eighteenth Century," in *Old Trails and New Directions: Papers of the Third North American Fur Trade Conference*, ed. Carol M. Judd and Arthur J. Ray (Toronto:

University of Toronto Press, 1980), 255–271.

97. For a biography of Alexander Grant, see Carol Whitfield, "Grant, Alexander," in *Dictionary of Canadian Biography*, vol. 5.
98. See General Thomas Gage to Unknown Recipient, April 8, 1771, *MPHC*, 10:246; Russell, *British Regime in Michigan*, 169–170; R. H. Fleming, "Phyn, Ellice and Company of Schenectady," *Contributions to Canadian Economies* 4 (1932): 13–14.
99. Fleming, "Phyn, Ellice and Company," 14–15, 23; Whitfield, "Grant, Alexander."
100. See Diary of John Askin at Mackinac, 1774, *Askin Papers*, 1:53.
101. For a list of vessels operating in the Great Lakes, see Return of all the Vessels upon Lake George, Champlain, Ontario in the year 1759 till this date, Excepting those employed at present, July 1778, *WHC*, 11:198–199. References abound to these ships in Askin's letters from 1778, for example, see John Askin to James Sterling, June 4, 1778, *Askin Papers*, 1:103; John Askin to Jean Baptiste Barthe, June 18, 1778, *Askin Papers*, 1:139.
102. John Askin to Jean Baptiste Barthe, June 8, 1778, *Askin Papers*, 1:118.
103. See Sales Book, Barthe Manuscripts, 1775–1780.
104. See Remarks on Board his Majestys Sloop Felicity by Samuel Roberts on Piloting her on Lake Michigon, 1779, *WHC*, 11:207.
105. John Askin to Jean Baptiste Barthe, June 8, 1778, *Askin Papers*, 1:119.
106. Memorial of the Merchants of Detroit to Frederick Haldimand, August 21, 1781, *MPHC*, 19:654.
107. *Documents North West Company*, 4–6; Marjorie Wilkins Campbell, *The North West Company* (Toronto: Macmillan Company of Canada, 1957), 1–12.
108. See *Documents North West Company*, 11–24.
109. See *Documents North West Company*, 11–13; Campbell, *The North West Company*, 49–51.
110. Fleming, "Phyn, Ellice and Company," 13–14.
111. John Askin to Isaac Todd and James McGill, June 14, 1778, *Askin Papers*, 1:125.
112. John Askin to Benjamin Frobisher, June 6, 1778, *Askin Papers*, 1:109.
113. John Askin to Joseph Frobisher and John McGill, June 13, 1778, *Askin Papers*, 1:124, 125.
114. John Askin to Isaac Todd and James McGill, June 22, 1778, *Askin Papers*, 1:142.
115. See John Askin to Isaac Todd and James McGill, May 8, 1778, *Askin Papers*, 1:84; John Askin to Jean Baptiste Barthe, June 8, 1778, *Askin Papers*, 1:118.
116. See Deposition of Samuel Robertson, August 21, 1789, *MPHC*, 9:626.
117. Articles Relative to the Establishment of a General Store at Michilimackinac, signed July 1, 1779, *MPHC*, 9:305, 305–307.

118. Ibid., 306.
119. Captain Patrick Sinclair to General Frederick Haldimand, August 22, 1780, *MPHC*, 9:571.
120. Major Arent Schuyler de Peyster to General Guy Carleton, May 30, 1778, *MPHC*, 9:366.
121. Lieutenant Governor Henry Hamilton to General Guy Carleton, April 25, 1778, *MPHC*, 9:437.
122. General Guy Carleton to Lieutenant Governor Henry Hamilton, May 22, 1777, *MPHC*, 9:348.
123. John Askin to Isaac Todd and James McGill, May 8, 1778, *Askin Papers*, 1:84.
124. John Askin to Charles Chaboillez, May 18, 1778, *Askin Papers*, 1:95.
125. John Askin to Mr. Beausoleil, May 18, 1778, *Askin Papers*, 1:98.
126. John Askin to James Sterling, April 18, 1778, *Askin Papers*, 1:71.
127. John Askin to Commodore Alexander Grant, April 28, 1778, *Askin Papers*, 1:77.
128. John Askin to the North West Company, May 8, 1778, *Askin Papers*, 1:83.
129. John Askin to Charles Chaboillez, June 27, 1778, *Askin Papers*, 1:151.
130. John Askin to Sampson Fleming, June 4, 1778, *Askin Papers*, 1:105.
131. John Askin to Charles Chaboillez, June 30, 1778, *Askin Papers*, 1:153.
132. John Askin to Jean Baptiste Barthe, June 30, 1778, *Askin Papers*, 1:156.
133. John Askin to James McGill and Joseph Frobisher, June 30, 1778, *Askin Papers*, 1:154–155.
134. John Askin to the North West Company, July 2, 1778, *Askin Papers*, 1:160.
135. John Askin to James McGill and Joseph Frobisher, June 30, 1778, *Askin Papers*, 1:155.
136. John Askin to Jean Baptiste Barthe, June 26, 1778, *Askin Papers*, 1:149.
137. John Askin to Isaac Todd and James McGill, July 2, 1778, *Askin Papers*, 1:159.
138. John Askin to the North West Company, July 2, 1778, *Askin Papers*, 1:160.
139. John Askin to Alexander Henry, June 23, 1778, *Askin Papers*, 1:145.
140. John Askin to Sampson Fleming, June 4, 1778, *Askin Papers*, 1:105.
141. John Askin to Richard Dobie, June 15, 1778, *Askin Papers*, 1:131.
142. For a discussion of the New York campaign and its effects on the American Revolution, see Max Mintz, *The Generals of Saratoga: John Burgoyne and Horatio Gates* (New Haven, CT: Yale University Press, 1990); Richard M. Ketchum, *Saratoga: Turning Point of America's Revolutionary War* (New York: Holt, 1999).
143. For a discussion of Spain and the Dutch Republic's involvement in the American Revolution, see Thomas E. Chávez, *Spain and the Independence of the United States* (Albuquerque: University of New Mexico Press, 2002); Friedrich Edler, *The Dutch*

Republic and the American Revolution (New York: AMS Press, 1971).

144. In a letter to General Frederick Haldimand, Captain Dietrich Brehm discussed the disruption caused by the spreading news of French, Spanish, and Dutch involvement in the American Revolution. He writes, "The Rebells having spread among all the Western or Wabash or Illinois Indians by some disaffected savages that French spain even germans & americans are all Joined together, to drive the English out of America, has not only effect among the Indians, but likewise among the French from the Illinois and Wabash through this whole settlement." See Captain Dietrich Brehm to General Frederick Haldimand, May 28, 1779, *MPHC*, 9:411.
145. Major Arent Schuyler de Peyster to General Frederick Haldimand, July 24, 1778, *MPHC*, 9:368.
146. Major Arent Schuyler de Peyster to General Frederick Haldimand, August 31, 1778, *MPHC*, 9:369.
147. Major Arent Schuyler de Peyster to General Frederick Haldimand, August 31, 1778, *MPHC*, 9:369–370.
148. Lieutenant Governor Henry Hamilton to General Guy Carleton, August 11, 1778, *MPHC*, 9:460.
149. Major Arent Schuyler de Peyster to General Frederick Haldimand, September 21, 1778, *MPHC*, 9:371.
150. Lieutenant Governor Henry Hamilton to General Frederick Haldimand, September 22, 1778, *MPHC*, 9:477.

Chapter Five. The Key of Canada in His Pocket: Michilimackinac, the British Empire, and John Askin's Banishment, 1779–1781

1. For a biography or account of Major Arent Schuyler de Peyster's life, see David A. Armour, "DePeyster, Arent Schuyler," in *Dictionary of Canadian Biography*, vol. 6 (Toronto: University of Toronto Press, 1987); David A. Armour and Keith R. Widder, *At the Crossroads: Michilimackinac during the American Revolution* (Mackinac Island, MI: Mackinac Island State Park Commission, 1978), 7–8.
2. Major Arent Schuyler de Peyster to Gentlemen Traders of Michilimackinac, September 20, 1779, *Miscellanies by an Officer* (Dumfries, Scotland: C. Monro, 1888), 4–5. While mostly a book of poems written by de Peyster, *Miscellanies* also reprinted a series of letters from his command at Michilimackinac and Detroit.
3. Instructions for Captain Patrick Sinclair, Lieut. Governor & Superintendent of Indians at Missilc, July 1779, *MPHC*, 9:517.

4. Susan Sleeper-Smith, *Indian Women and French Men: Rethinking Cultural Encounter in the Western Great Lakes* (Amherst: University of Massachusetts Press, 2001), 65.
5. See Paul L. Stevens, "Wabasaha visits Governor Carleton, 1776: New Light on a Legendary Episode of Dakota-British Diplomacy on the Great Lakes Frontier," *Michigan Historical Review* 16 (1990): 21–48; Armour and Widder, *At the Crossroads*, 96–97.
6. See Armour and Widder, *At the Crossroads*, 105–116.
7. De Peyster, *Miscellanies by an Officer*, 16.
8. Ibid., 16–17.
9. Ibid., 4.
10. James Gordon, "The Reminiscences of James Gordon," ed. Josephine Mayer, *Quarterly Journal of the New York State Historical Association* 17, nos. 3–4 (1936): 430.
11. John Askin to Jean Baptiste Barthe, June 6, 1778, *Askin Papers*, 1:86.
12. For the everyday nature of the fur trade, long-term financing, how goods moved, how profits were made, and other practical concerns, see Harry W. Duckworth, "British Capital in the Fur Trade: John Strettell and John Fraser," in *The Fur Trade Revisited: Selected Papers of the Sixth North American Fur Trade Conference, Mackinac Island, Michigan, 1991*, ed. Jennifer S. H. Brown, W. J. Eccles, and Donald P. Heldman (East Lansing: Michigan State University Press, 1994); Bruce M. White, "Balancing the Books: Trader Profits in the British Lake Superior Fur Trade," in *New Faces of the Fur Trade: Selected Papers of the Seventh North American Fur Trade Conference, Halifax, Nova Scotia, 1995*, ed. Jo-Anne Fiske, Susan Sleeper-Smith, and William Wicken (East Lansing: Michigan State University Press, 1998); Dean L. Anderson, "The Flow of European Trade Goods into the Western Great Lakes Region, 1715–1760," in *Rethinking the Fur Trade: Cultures of Exchange in an Atlantic World*, ed. Susan Sleeper-Smith (Lincoln: University of Nebraska Press, 2009).
13. John Askin to Jean Baptiste Barthe, May 29, 1778, *Askin Papers*, 1:103.
14. For an account of Benjamin Lyon's life and the Jewish community in the Great Lakes fur trade, see Sheldon J. Godfrey and J. C. Godfrey, *Search Out the Land: The Jews and the Growth of Equality in British Colonial America, 1740–1867* (Montreal: McGill-Queen's University Press, 1995).
15. For an account of Patrick Sinclair's life, see William Jenks, *Patrick Sinclair* (Lansing: Wynkoop Hallenbeck Crawford, 1914); Armour and Widder, *At the Crossroads*; H. B. Eaton, "Lieutenant-General Patrick Sinclair: An Account of his Military Career," *Journal of the Society for Army Historical Research* 56 (Autumn–Spring 1978–1979): 128–142, 215–232, 45–55.

16. For the most detailed account of Michilimackinac during the American Revolution, see Armour and Widder, *At the Crossroads*. Armour and Widder's work has been especially helpful in contextualizing and exploring the conflict between Sinclair and Askin, and the role that de Peyster played in it. For an overview of the American Revolution from the perspective of the British Empire, see Nelson Vance Russell, *The British Regime in Michigan and the Old Northwest, 1760–1796* (Philadelphia: Porcupine Press, 1978), 185–216.
17. Captain Patrick Sinclair to General Frederick Haldimand, August 19, 1779, *MPHC*, 9:518. For the orders that drew Sinclair's ire, see Instructions for Captain Patrick Sinclair, Lieut. Governor & Superintendent of Indians at Missilc, July 1779, *MPHC*, 9:518.
18. For an account of Clark's campaign, see *Henry Hamilton and George Rogers Clark in the American Revolution and the Unpublished Journal of Lieut. Gov. Henry Hamilton*, ed. John D. Barnhart (Crawfordsville, IN: R. E. Banta, 1951).
19. For an account of Hamilton's life, and his countercampaign, see Elizabeth Arthur, "Henry Hamilton," in *Dictionary of Canadian Biography*, vol. 4 (Toronto: University of Toronto Press, 1979); "Account of the Expedition of Lieutenant Governor Hamilton," *MPHC*, 9:489–516.
20. For a detailed account of the myriad and multifaceted roles Indian peoples in the Ohio Valley and the Great Lakes played in the American Revolution, see Colin G. Calloway, *The American Revolution in Indian Country: Crisis and Diversity in Native American Communities* (Cambridge: Cambridge University Press, 1995). Calloway's discussion of Fort Niagara as a refugee center for Native American communities during the American Revolution, and the "politics of hunger" that came from competition between Indian chiefs and British imperial officials for "power and patronage," using each other "to validate [their] positions, legitimize [their] actions, and bolster [their] support" helped inform this chapter, especially in considering the activities of de Peyster and Sinclair when they occupied the roles of commandant of Michilimackinac. See Calloway, *American Revolution in Indian Country*, 129–157.
21. Instructions for Captain Patrick Sinclair, Lieut. Governor & Superintendent of Indians at Missilc, July 1779, *MPHC*, 9:517.
22. General Frederick Haldimand to Captain Patrick Sinclair, August 17, 1779, *MPHC*, 9:519–520.
23. As quoted in Jenks, *Patrick Sinclair*, 9, 10.
24. Armour and Widder, *At the Crossroads*, 49.
25. General Frederick Haldimand to Captain Patrick Sinclair, August 20, 1779, *MPHC*,

9:521.

26. Captain Patrick Sinclair to Lieutenant Dietrich Brehm, October 7, 1779, *MPHC*, 9:526.
27. Captain Patrick Sinclair to General Frederick Haldimand, October 1780, *MPHC*, 9:564.
28. Captain Patrick Sinclair to Lieutenant Dietrich Brehm, October 7, 1779, *MPHC*, 9:523, 525.
29. Captain Patrick Sinclair to Lieutenant Dietrich Brehm, February 15, 1780, *MPHC*, 9:538.
30. For a detailed discussion of this campaign, see Armour and Widder, *At the Crossroads*, 129–131, 137–140.
31. Captain Patrick Sinclair to Lieutenant Dietrich Brehm, February 15, 1780, *MPHC*, 9:542.
32. Captain Patrick Sinclair to General Frederick Haldimand, July/August 1780, *MPHC*, 9:563.
33. Captain Patrick Sinclair to Lieutenant Dietrich Brehm, February 15, 1780, *MPHC*, 9:541.
34. Captain Patrick Sinclair to General Frederick Haldimand, May 29, 1780, *MPHC*, 9:548, 548–549.
35. For more detailed discussions of the Anglo-Spanish conflicts along the Mississippi River, see Clarence W. Alford, "The Conquest of St. Joseph, Michigan, by the Spaniards in 1781," *Michigan History* 14 (1930): 398–414; A. P. Nasatir, "The Anglo-Spanish Frontier in the Illinois Country during the American Revolution, 1779–1783," *Journal of the Illinois State Historical Society* 21 (1928): 291–358.
36. Captain Patrick Sinclair to General Frederick Haldimand, July 8, 1780, *MPHC*, 9:558–560.
37. Captain Patrick Sinclair to General Frederick Haldimand, July 8, 1780, *MPHC*, 9:558–560.
38. For a more detailed discussion of the St. Joseph Potawatomi, see Sleeper-Smith, *Indian Women*, 64–72. For a detailed discussion of the Potawatomi during the American Revolution, see R. David Edmunds, *The Potawatomis: Keepers of the Fire* (Norman: University of Oklahoma Press, 1978), 97–115.
39. Lieutenant Governor Henry Hamilton to General Frederick Haldimand, April 1776, *MPHC*, 9:466.
40. Major Arent Schuyler de Peyster to Unnamed, June 13, 1777, *MPHC*, 10:277.
41. Major Arent Schuyler de Peyster to General Frederick Haldimand, August 31, 1778,

MPHC, 9:369–370.

42. Captain Patrick Sinclair to General Frederick Haldimand, May 29, 1780, *MPHC*, 9:554.
43. Sleeper-Smith, *Indian Women*, 67–69.
44. See David A. Armour, "Ainsse, Joseph-Louis," in *Dictionary of Canadian Biography*, vol. 5 (Toronto: University of Toronto Press, 1983).
45. Captain Patrick Sinclair to General Frederick Haldimand, August 2, 1780, *MPHC*, 9:569.
46. Sleeper-Smith, *Indian Women*, 67.
47. Captain Patrick Sinclair to General Frederick Haldimand, August 2, 1780, *MPHC*, 9:569–570.
48. Petition of Louis Chevalier to General Frederick Haldimand, August 1789, *MPHC*, 10:440.
49. Major Arent Schuyler de Peyster to Lieutenant Colonel Mason Bolton, July 6, 1780, *MPHC*, 19:540.
50. Major Arent Schuyler de Peyster to Captain Patrick Sinclair, September 17, 1780, *MPHC*, 9:617.
51. Captain Patrick Sinclair to General Frederick Haldimand, February 1780, *MPHC*, 9:545.
52. Ibid. See also Sales Book, Barthe Manuscripts. The sales book shows numerous French engagés employed by Sinclair, Barthe, Cadot, and Askin.
53. Captain Patrick Sinclair to General Frederick Haldimand, July 8, 1780, *MPHC*, 9:577.
54. Deposition of Samuel Robertson, August 21, 1780, *MPHC*, 9:625.
55. Samuel Robertson to Captain Patrick Sinclair, April 28, 1780, *MPHC*, 9:620–621.
56. Lieutenant Dietrich Brehm to Captain Patrick Sinclair, April 17, 1780, *MPHC*, 9:536.
57. Ibid.
58. For the records and lists of the following figures related to Askin's inventorying of the King's Storehouse, see Return of Provisions & Liquors; Account of all the Provisions & Rum; Chart of Deficiencies, *MPHC*, 9:656.
59. Captain Patrick Sinclair to General Frederick Haldimand, May 29, 1780, *MPHC*, 9:554. In 1776, David Mitchell married Elizabeth Bertrand Mitchell, a very influential multiethnic fur trader and landowner from the Odawa community of Arbre Croche; together, they would play an increasingly important and increasingly contested economic, social, and political role at Michilimackinac and Mackinac Island after the Revolution. See Susan Sleeper-Smith, "[A]n Unpleasant Transaction on This Frontier": Challenging Autonomy and Authority at Michilimackinac," *Journal of the*

Early Republic 25, no. 3 (Fall 2005): 417–443.

60. Captain Patrick Sinclair to General Frederick Haldimand, May 29, 1780, *MPHC*, 9:555.
61. Deposition of Samuel Robertson, August 21, 1780, *MPHC*, 9:625.
62. Major Arent Schuyler de Peyster to Captain Patrick Sinclair, May 26, 1780, *MPHC*, 9:584.
63. Deposition of Samuel Robertson, August 21, 1780, *MPHC*, 9:626.
64. Captain Patrick Sinclair to Lieutenant Dietrich Brehm, May 29, 1780, *MPHC*, 9:552; Captain Patrick Sinclair to General Frederick Haldimand, July–August 1780, *MPHC*, 9:564.
65. General Frederick Haldimand to Captain Patrick Sinclair, August 10, 1780, *MPHC*, 9:567.
66. Captain Patrick Sinclair to General Frederick Haldimand, July 8, 1780, *MPHC*, 9:577.
67. Soldier's Petition to Major Arent Schuyler de Peyster, July 30, 1780, *MPHC*, 9:588.
68. Ibid.
69. Major Arent Schuyler de Peyster to the Petitioners at Michilimackinac, August 1780, *MPHC*, 9:588–589.
70. Major Arent Schuyler de Peyster to General Frederick Haldimand, August 13, 1780, *MPHC*, 9:599.
71. Major Arent Schuyler De Peyster's Regimental Order, August 22, 1780, *MPHC*, 9:591–592.
72. Captain John Mompesson to General Frederick Haldimand, August 22, 1780, *MPHC*, 9:589.
73. Captain Patrick Sinclair to General Frederick Haldimand, August 1780, *MPHC*, 9:591.
74. Major Arent Schuyler de Peyster to General Frederick Haldimand, August 13, 1780, *MPHC*, 9:599.
75. Captain Patrick Sinclair to Lieutenant Dietrich Brehm, August 23, 1780, *MPHC*, 9:610–611.
76. Major Arent Schuyler de Peyster to General Frederick Haldimand, August 13, 1780, *MPHC*, 9:598.
77. Captain Patrick Sinclair to Major Arent Schuyler de Peyster, September 13, 1780, *MPHC*, 9:616.
78. Major Arent Schuyler de Peyster to Captain Patrick Sinclair, September 17, 1780, *MPHC*, 9:617.
79. Major Arent Schuyler de Peyster to General Frederick Haldimand, October 1, 1780, *MPHC*, 9:615.

80. General Frederick Haldimand to Captain Patrick Sinclair, August 21, 1780, *MPHC*, 9:621–622.
81. Captain Patrick Sinclair to General Frederick Haldimand, August 3, 1780, *MPHC*, 9:572–573; General Frederick Haldimand to Captain Patrick Sinclair, August 21, 1780, *MPHC*, 9:573–574; General Arent Schuyler de Peyster to General Frederick Haldimand, August 13, 1780, *MPHC*, 9:598–599.
82. General Frederick Haldimand to Major Arent Schuyler de Peyster, January 6, 1781, *MPHC*, 9:628; Memorial of Louis Joseph Ainsse to General Frederick Haldimand, August 5, 1780, *MPHC*, 10:434–438; Petition of Louis Chevalier to General Frederick Haldimand, August 1789, *MPHC*, 10:438–440.
83. John Askin to Nathaniel Day, July 29, 1780, *MPHC*, 9:551.
84. Captain Patrick Sinclair to Captain Alexander Harrow, July 19, 1780, *MPHC*, 9:602.
85. General Frederick Haldimand to Brigadier General Howell, June 24, 1781, *MPHC*, 10:492–493.
86. General Frederick Haldimand to Major Arent Schuyler de Peyster, June 24, 1781, *MPHC*, 10:491.
87. General Frederick Haldimand to Brigadier General Howell, June 24, 1781, *MPHC*, 10:493.
88. Captain Patrick Sinclair to General H. Watson Powell, June 6, 1781, *MPHC*, 19:638–639.
89. Captain Patrick Sinclair to Unaddressed, July 31, 1781. *MPHC*, 10:503–504.
90. See Armour and Widder, *At the Crossroads*, 171.
91. Captain Patrick Sinclair to Unaddressed, July 31, 1781, *MPHC*, 10:504.
92. Captain Patrick Sinclair to General Frederick Haldimand, September 26, 1781, *MPHC*, 10:514–515.
93. For a detailed account of the postrevolutionary violence of the Ohio Valley, see Patrick Griffin, *American Leviathan: Empire, Nation, and Revolutionary Frontier* (New York: Hill and Wang, 2007). Griffin casts the postwar landscape as akin to Thomas Hobbes's "state of nature," where war existed unfettered by the constraints of civilization. Between 1763 and 1794, American settlers and their Indian counterparts lived lives defined by violence and uncertainty, as each side struggled to maintain or achieve mastery. See Griffin, *American Leviathan*, 10–16.
94. Captain Patrick Sinclair to Lieutenant Dietrich Brehm, August 23, 1780, *MPHC*, 9:611.
95. Captain Patrick Sinclair to Major Arent Schuyler de Peyster, October 17, 1780, *MPHC*, 9:618.

96. Captain Patrick Sinclair to Major Arent Schuyler de Peyster, October 15, 1780, *MPHC*, 9:618.
97. Benjamin Lyon to John Askin (?), December 27, 1780, *MPHC*, 9:627.
98. For an account of British and American efforts to control the Great Lakes and the Ohio Valley, see Alan Taylor, *The Civil War of 1812: American Citizens, British Subjects, Irish Rebels, and Indian Allies* (New York: Knopf, 2010), 27–33. Taylor argues that in the aftermath of the American Revolution, many European observers believed the new United States' nation-state "would collapse, leaving the forts, the Indians, and the fur trade in the British orbit." For the quote, see Taylor, *Civil War of 1812*, 28.
99. For the active role that Askin played in the establishment of the Miami Company, see Divisions of Debts of the Miami Company, September 9, 1789, *Askin Papers*, 1:325–330; Power of Attorney from the Miami Company to John Askin, September 22, 1789, *Askin Papers*, 1:331–332; Assignment of Claims of the Miami Company, September 22, 1789, *Askin Papers*, 1:332–334.
100. See Eric Hinderaker, *Elusive Empires: Constructing Colonialism in the Ohio Valley, 1673–1800* (Cambridge: Cambridge University Press, 1997), 236–244.
101. Louis Lorimier to John Askin, November 24, 1786, *Askin Papers*, 1:271.
102. James McGill to John Askin, January 10, 1794, *Askin Papers*, 1:487.
103. For a discussion of Askin's land speculation within the early American Republic, see John Askin to Major Vigo, July 2, 1795, *Askin Papers*, 1:549; Syndicate for the Promotion of Cuyahoga Purchase, June 17, 1795, *Askin Papers*, 1:546; Power of Attorney to Alexander Henry, August 8, 1795, *Askin Papers*, 1:556–558. For a map of Askin and company's speculation in northern Ohio, see Folder 9: 1796, Cuyahoga Purchase, Wallets, John Askin Manuscripts, Burton Historical Collection, Detroit Public Library, Detroit, Michigan.
104. John Askin Jr. to Colonel Richard England, August 19, 1795, *Askin Papers*, 1:560.
105. John Askin to John Askin Jr., July 5, 1795, *Askin Papers*, 1:550.
106. John Askin Jr. to Colonel Richard England, August 19, 1795, *Askin Papers*, 1:564.
107. For an account of this postwar controversy, see Jenks, *Patrick Sinclair*, 33–37.
108. Orders as quoted by Lieutenant Colonel Henry Hope in a letter to General Fredrick Haldimand, October 19, 1782, *MPHC*, 10:656.
109. Ibid.; Report of the State & Condition of the Works of Fort Michilimackinac, prepared by Lieutenant Richard Hockings, September 20, 1782, *MPHC*, 10:642–645; Lieutenant Colonel Henry Hope, et al. to Captain Daniel Robertson, September 20, 1782, *MPHC*, 10:638–640; Lieutenant Colonel Henry Hope to General Frederick Haldimand, September 21, 1782, *MPHC*, 10:645.

110. General Frederick Haldimand to Captain Patrick Sinclair, October 21, 1782, *MPHC*, 10:61.

Epilogue. A Drink Generally Closes the Scene: Alexander Henry's Lament and John Askin's Death

1. Alexander Henry, May 16, 1809, *Askin Papers*, 2:625.
2. Ibid.
3. For a discussion of Great Britain's efforts to maintain control over the Great Lakes after the American Revolution, see Alan Taylor, *The Civil War of 1812: American Citizens, British Subjects, Irish Rebels, and Indian Allies* (New York: Knopf, 2010), 3–74.
4. James McGill to John Askin, January 6, 1811, *Askin Papers*, 2:667.
5. John Askin to Colonel Arent Schuyler de Peyster, August 30, 1805, *Askin Papers*, 2:479.
6. Ibid.
7. John Askin to Isaac Todd, September 13, 1809, *Askin Papers*, 2:643. For a discussion of Askin Jr.'s command of Indians during the capture of Mackinac Island from the Americans in 1812, see John Askin Jr. to John Askin, July 19, 1812, *MPHC*, 32:482–483.
8. John Askin to Isaac Todd, September 13, 1809, *Askin Papers*, 2:642. For a short biography of John Richardson, see David R. Beasley, "John Richardson," in *Dictionary of Canadian Biography*, vol. 8 (Toronto: University of Toronto Press, 1985).
9. John Askin to John Askin Jr., July 5, 1809, *Askin Papers*, 2:626; Charles Askin's Journal of the Detroit Campaign, July 24–September 12, 1812, *Askin Papers*, 2:711–729.
10. For a discussion of the War of 1812 in the Great Lakes, see Taylor, *Civil War of 1812*; Donald R. Hickey, *The War of 1812: A Forgotten Conflict* (Urbana: University of Illinois Press, 1995). For the diary that John Askin kept during the War of 1812, see Extracts from the diary of John Askin, *MPHC*, 32:468–473.
11. See David Curtis Skaggs, *Oliver Hazard Perry: Honor, Courage, and Patriotism in the Early U. S. Navy* (Annapolis, MD: Naval Institute Press, 2006), 78–119.
12. See John Sugden, *Tecumseh: A Life* (New York: Holt Paperbacks, 1999), 279–382.
13. Alexander Henry to John Askin, May 9, 1815, *Askin Papers*, 2:782.
14. Madeleine Askin to Marie Archange Askin, no date included, *Askin Papers*, 2:785.
15. Will of John Askin, signed November 11, 1808, Amended in 1811, *Askin Papers*, 2:785, 786.

Bibliography

Manuscripts and Primary Sources

Archives and Manuscripts, New York Public Library, New York City, New York

Papers Concerning Robert Rogers and Rogers' Rangers, 1760–1763

Burton Historical Collection, Detroit Public Library, Detroit, Michigan

John Askin Papers, 1701–1891

John Porteous Manuscripts, 1760–1767

Jean Baptiste Barthe Manuscripts, 1775–1780

Colonial Michilimackinac Archives, Petersen Center Library, Mackinac City, Michigan

Letterbooks of Phyn and Ellice, Merchants, at Schenectady, New York, 1767–1773

John Askin Papers, 1766–1835

Handwritten Tabulations and Summaries of Fur Trade Licenses, 1774–1776

Consolidated Returns of Licenses, 1777–1790

Log-Book of the Welcome, 1779–1782

William L. Clements Library, University of Michigan, Ann Arbor, Michigan

James Sterling Letterbook, 1761–1765

John Porteous Letterbook, 1767–1769

Thomas Gage Papers, American Series, 1754–1783

Books, Articles, and Dissertations

Adelman, Jeremy, and Stephen Aron. "From Borderlands to Borders: Empires, Nation-States, and the Peoples in Between in North America." *American Historical Review* 104 (1999): 814–841.

———. "Of Lively Exchanges and Larger Perspectives." *American Historical Review* 104 (1999): 1235–1239.

Alden, John. *General Gage in America.* Baton Rouge: Louisiana State University Press, 1948.

———. *John Stuart and the Southern Colonial Frontier: A Study of Indian Relations, War, Trade, and Land Problems in the Southern Wilderness, 1755–1775.* Ann Arbor: University of Michigan Press, 1944.

Alford, Clarence W. "The Conquest of St. Joseph, Michigan, by the Spaniards in 1781." *Michigan History* 14 (1930): 398–414.

Allen, Robert S. *His Majesty's Indian Allies: British Indian Policy in the Defense of Canada, 1774–1815.* Toronto: Dundurn Press, 1992.

American State Papers: Documents, Legislative and Executive, of the Congress of the United States. 9 vols. Greenville, SC: Southern Historical Press, 1994.

Amherst, Jeffery. *The Journal of Jeffery Amherst: Recording the Military Career of General Amherst in America from 1758–1763.* Edited by J. Clarence Webster. Chicago: University of Chicago Press, 1931.

Anderson, Dean L. "The Flow of European Trade Goods into the Western Great Lakes Region, 1715–1760." In *The Fur Trade Revisited: Selected Papers of the Sixth North American Fur Trade Conference, Mackinac Island, Michigan, 1991,* edited by Jennifer S. H. Brown, W. J. Eccles, and D. P. Heldman, 93–115. East Lansing: Michigan State University Press, 1994.

Anderson, Fred. *Crucible of War: The Seven Years' War and the Fate of Empire in British North America, 1754–1766.* New York: Alfred A. Knopf, 2000.

Anderson, Gary Clayton. *Kinsmen of Another Kind: Dakota-White Relations in the Upper Mississippi Valley, 1650–1862.* Lincoln: University of Nebraska Press, 1984.

Anderson, Mark R. *The Battle for the Fourteenth Colony: America's War of Liberation in Canada, 1774–1776.* Hanover, NH: University Press of New England, 2013.

Anderson, Virginia DeJohn. *Creatures of Empire: How Domestic Animals Transformed Early America.* Oxford: Oxford University Press, 2004.

Armitage, David. *The Ideological Origins of the British Empire.* Cambridge: Cambridge University Press, 2000.

———. "Three Concepts of Atlantic History." In *The British Atlantic World, 1500–1800*, edited by David Armitage and Michael J. Braddick, 11–30. New York: Palgrave Macmillan, 2002.

Armour, David A. "Ainsse, Joseph-Louis." In *Dictionary of Canadian Biography*. Vol. 5. Toronto: University of Toronto Press, 1983.

———. "Bourassa, René." In *Dictionary of Canadian Biography*. Vol. 4. Toronto: University of Toronto Press, 1979.

———. "Cadot, Jean-Baptiste." In *Dictionary of Canadian Biography*. Vol. 5. Toronto: University of Toronto Press, 1983.

———. "DePeyster, Arent Schuyler." In *Dictionary of Canadian Biography*. Vol. 6. Toronto: University of Toronto Press, 1987.

———. "Du Jaunay, Pierre." In *Dictionary of Canadian Biography*. Vol. 4. Toronto: University of Toronto Press, 1979.

———. "Mineweh." In *Dictionary of Canadian Biography*. Vol. 3. Toronto: University of Toronto Press, 1974.

———. "Nissowaquet." In *Dictionary of Canadian Biography*. Vol. 4. Toronto: University of Toronto Press, 1979.

———, ed. *Treason? At Michilimackinac: The Proceedings of a General Court Martial Held at Montreal in October 1768 for the Trial of Major Robert Rogers*. Mackinac Island, MI: Mackinac Island State Park Commission, 1967.

———. "Untitled Work on John Askin, 1778." Unpublished Manuscript, Mackinac State Historic Parks Library, Mackinac City, MI.

Armour, David A., and Keith R. Widder. *At the Crossroads: Michilimackinac during the American Revolution*. Mackinac Island, MI: Mackinac Island State Park Commission, 1978.

Arthur, Elizabeth, "Hamilton, Henry." In *Dictionary of Canadian Biography*. Vol. 4. Toronto: University of Toronto Press, 1979.

Askin, John. *The John Askin Papers*. Edited by Milo Quiafe. 2 vols. Detroit: Detroit Library Commission, 1928–1931.

Axtell, James. "The White Indians of Colonial America." *William and Mary Quarterly* 32 (1975): 55–88.

Bailyn, Bernard. "The First British Empire: From Cambridge to Oxford." *William and Mary Quarterly* 57, no. 3 (July 2000): 647–660.

———. *The Ideological Origins of the American Revolution*. Cambridge: Harvard University Press, 1967.

———. *The New England Merchants in the Seventeenth Century*. Cambridge: Harvard

University Press, 1955.

———. *The Origins of American Politics*. New York: Knopf, 1968.

———. *The Peopling of British North America: An Introduction*. New York: Knopf, 1986.

———. *Voyagers to the West: A Passage in the Peopling of America on the Eve of the Revolution*. New York: Knopf, 1986.

Baerreis, David A. "Trade Silver and Indian Silversmiths." *Wisconsin Magazine of History* 34 (1950): 76–82.

Barr, Juliana. *Peace Came in the Form of a Woman: Indians and Spaniards in the Texas Borderlands*. Chapel Hill: University of North Carolina Press, 2007.

Baugh, Daniel. *The Global Seven Years' War, 1754–1763*. New York: Pearson Press, 2011.

Bauman, Zygmunt. *Liquid Modernity*. Cambridge: Polity Press, 2000.

Beasley, David R. "Richardson, John." In *Dictionary of Canada Biography*. Vol. 13. Toronto: University of Toronto Press, 1984.

Beck, Ulrich. *Risk Society: Towards a New Modernity*. London: Sage, 1992.

Bedford-Jones, H. *L'Arbre Croche Mission*. Santa Barbara: printed by author, 1917.

Beland, Francois. "Blondeau, Maurice." In *Dictionary of Canadian Biography*. Vol. 5. Toronto: University of Toronto Press, 1983.

Berkeley, Edmund C. *Dr. John Mitchell: The Man Who Made the Map of North America*. Chapel Hill: University of North Carolina Press, 1974.

Berkhofer, Robert F. *The White Man's Indian: Images of the American Indian from Columbus to the Present*. New York: Knopf, 1978.

Blackbird, Andrew J. *History of the Ottawa and Chippewa Indians of Michigan: A Grammar of Their Language, and Personal and Family History of the Author*. Ypsilanti, MI: Ypsilantian Job Printing House, 1887.

Bohaker, Heidi. "Anishinaabe Toodaims: Contexts for Politics, Kinship, and Identity in the Eastern Great Lakes." In *Gathering Places: Aboriginal and Fur Trade Histories*, edited by Carolyn Podruchny and Laura Peers, 93–118. Vancouver: University of British Columbia Press, 2010.

———. "Nindoodemag: The Significance of Algonquian Kinship Networks in the Eastern Great Lakes, 1600–1701." *William and Mary Quarterly* 63, no. 1 (January 2006): 23–56.

Bouquet, Henry. *The Papers of Colonel Henry Bouquet*. Edited by Sylvester K. Stevens and Donald H. Kent. 6 vols. Harrisburg: Pennsylvania Historical Commission, 1951–1994.

Bowen, H. V. "British Conceptions of Global Empire, 1756–83." *Journal of Imperial and Commonwealth History* 26 (1998): 1–27.

———. *Elites, Enterprise, and the Making of the British Overseas Empire, 1688–1775*. New

York: Palgrave Macmillan, 1996.

Boynton, James. *Fishers of Men: The Jesuit Mission at Mackinac, 1670–1765*. Mackinac Island, MI: Ste. Anne's Church, 1996.

Braddick, Michael J. "Civility and Authority." In *The British Atlantic World, 1500–1800*, edited by David Armitage and Michael J. Braddick, 93–112. New York: Palgrave Macmillan, 2002.

Brecher, Frank W. *Securing American Independence: John Jay and the French Alliance*. Westport, CT: Praeger, 2003.

Breen, T. H. "An Empire of Goods: The Anglicization of Colonial America." *Journal of British Studies* 25, no. 4. (October 1986): 467–499.

———. *The Marketplace of Revolution: How Consumer Politics Shaped American Independence*. New York: Oxford University Press, 2004.

Brewer, John. *The Sinews of Power: War, Money, and the English State, 1688–1783*. New York: Knopf, 1989.

Brodine, Charles E. "Henry Bouquet and British Infantry Tactics on the Ohio Frontier, 1758–1764." In *The Sixty Years' War for the Great Lakes, 1754–1814*, edited by David Curtis Skaggs and Larry L. Nelson, 43–61. East Lansing: Michigan State University Press, 2001.

Broshar, Hellen. "The First Push Westward of the Albany Traders." *Mississippi Valley Historical Review* 7 (1920): 228–241.

Brown, Kathleen M. *Good Wives, Nasty Wenches, and Anxious Patriarchs: Gender, Race, and Power in Colonial Virginia*. Chapel Hill: University of North Carolina Press, 1996.

Brown, Jennifer S. H. *Strangers in Blood: Fur Trade Company Families in Indian Country*. Vancouver: University of British Columbia Press, 1980.

Browne, G. P. "Carleton, Guy, 1st Baron Dorchester." In *Dictionary of Canadian Biography*. Vol. 5. Toronto: University of Toronto Press, 1983.

Browning, William. "The Early History of Jonathan Carver." *Wisconsin Magazine of History* 3 (1920): 291–305.

Buck, Solon J. "The Story of the Grand Portage." *Minnesota History* 5 (1923): 14–27.

Buffington, Arthur H. "The Policy of Albany and English Westward Expansion." *Mississippi Valley Historical Review* 8 (1922): 327–366.

Bukowczyk, John J. "The Production of History, the Becoming of Place." In *Permeable Border: The Great Lakes Basin as Transnational Region, 1650–1990*, by John J. Bukowczyk, Nora Faires, David Smith, and Randy Widdis, 1–9. Pittsburgh: University of Pittsburgh Press, 2005.

———. "Trade, War, Migration, and Empire in the Great Lakes Basic, 1650–1815." In

Permeable Border: The Great Lakes Basin as Transnational Region, 1650–1990, by John J. Bukowczyk, Nora Faires, David Smith, and Randy Widdis, 10–28. Pittsburgh: University of Pittsburgh Press, 2005.

Burnard, Trevor. "Empire Matters? The Historiography of Imperialism in Early America, 1492–1830." *History of European Ideas* 33 (2007): 87–107.

Burton, Clarence Monroe, William Stocking, and Gordon K. Miller. *The City of Detroit, Michigan, 1701–1922.* Detroit: S.J. Clarke, 1922.

Burton Historical Collection Staff. "Sterling, James." In *Dictionary of Canadian Biography.* Vol. 4. Toronto: University of Toronto Press, 1979.

Bushman, Richard L. *The Refinement of America: Persons, Houses, Cities.* New York: Knopf, 1992.

Calloway, Colin G. *The American Revolution in Indian Country: Crisis and Diversity in Native American Communities.* Cambridge: Cambridge University Press, 1995.

———. *Crown and Calumet: British-Indian Relations, 1783–1815.* Norman: University of Oklahoma Press, 1987.

———. *The Scratch of a Pen: 1763 and the Transformation of North America.* Oxford: Oxford University Press, 2006.

Campbell, Marjorie Wilkins. *The North West Company.* New York: St. Martin's Press, 1957.

Canny, Nicholas P. "The Ideology of English Colonization: From Ireland to America." *William and Mary Quarterly* 30 (1973): 575–598.

Carlos, Ann, and Frank Lewis. "Trade, Consumption, and the Native Economy: Lessons from York Factory, Hudson Bay." *Journal of Economic History* 61 (2001): 1037–1064.

Carlson, Jenna K. *Culinary Creolization: Subsistence and Cultural Interaction at Fort Michilimackinac, 1730–1761.* Mackinac Island, MI: Mackinac Island State Park Commission, 2012.

Carstens, Kenneth Charles, and Nancy Carstens, eds. *The Life of George Rogers Clark, 1752–1818: Triumphs and Tragedies.* Westport, CT: Praeger, 2004.

Carter, Clarence E., ed. *The Territorial Papers of the United States.* 28 vols. Washington, DC: United States Government Printing Office, 1934.

Carver, Jonathan. *The Journals of Jonathan Carver and Related Documents, 1766–1770.* Edited by John Parker. St. Paul: Minnesota Historical Society, 1976.

———. *Travels through the Interior Parts of North America in the Years 1766, 1767, and 1768.* London: J. Walter and S. Crowder, 1778.

Chavez, Thomas E. *Spain and the Independence of the United States.* Albuquerque: University of New Mexico Press, 2002.

Clarke, John. *Land, Power and Economics on the Frontier of Upper Canada.* Montreal:

McGill-Queen's University Press, 2001.

Cleland, Charles E. *Rites of Conquest: The History and Culture of Michigan's Native Americans*. Ann Arbor: University of Michigan Press, 1992.

Clifton, James A, ed. *Being and Becoming Indian: Biographical Studies of North American Frontiers*. Chicago: Dorsey Press, 1989.

Collections of the Illinois State Historical Library. 38 vols. Springfield: Illinois State Historical Library, 1903–1978.

Collections of the New York Historical Society. 85 vols. New York City: New York Historical Society, 1868–1975.

Colley, Linda. *Britons: Forging the Nation, 1707–1837*. New Haven, CT: Yale University Press, 1992.

Cooper, J. I. "McGill, James." In *Dictionary of Canadian Biography*. Vol. 5. Toronto: University of Toronto Press, 1983.

Countryman, Edward. "Indians, the Colonial Order, and the Social Significance of the American Revolution." *William and Mary Quarterly* 53 (1996): 342–362.

Creighton, D. G. *The Commercial Empire of the St. Lawrence, 1760–1860*. Toronto: Macmillan, 1956.

Croghan, George. "Croghan's Journal: October 21, 1760–January 7, 1761." In *Early Western Journals, 1748–1765*, edited by Reuben Gold Thwaites, 100–125. Lewisburg, PA: Wennawoods Publishing, 1998.

Cronon, William. *Changes in the Land: Indians, Colonists, and the Ecology of New England*. New York: Hill and Wang, 1983.

Cuneo, John R. *Robert Rogers of the Rangers*. New York: Oxford University Press, 1959.

Curtis, Edward E. *The Organization of the British Army in the American Revolution*. New Haven, CT: Yale University Press, 1926.

Davis, Natalie Zemon. *The Return of Martin Guerre*. Cambridge: Cambridge University Press, 1983.

Darwin, John. "Imperialism and the Victorians: The Dynamics of Territorial Expansion." *English Historical Review* 112 (June 1997): 614–642.

Del Papa, Eugene M. "The Royal Proclamation of 1763: Its Effect upon Virginia Land Companies." *Virginia Magazine of History and Biography* 83 (1975): 406–411.

Denissen, Christian, ed. *Genealogy of the French Families of the Detroit River Region: 1701–1936*. 2 vols. Detroit: Detroit Society for Genealogical Research, 1987.

Dennis, Matthew. *Cultivating a Landscape of Peace: Iroquois-European Encounters in Seventeenth Century America*. Ithaca, NY: Cornell University Press, 1993.

Densmore, Frances. *Chippewa Customs*. St. Paul: Minnesota Historical Society Press, 1979.

De Peyster, Arent Schuyler. *Miscellanies by an Officer*. Dumfries, Scotland: C. Munro, 1888.

Dixon, David. *Never Come to Peace Again: Pontiac's Uprising and the Fate of the British Empire in North America*. Norman: University of Oklahoma Press, 2005.

Documents Relative to the Colonial History of the State of New York. 15 vols. Albany: Weed, Parsons and Company, 1853–1887.

Dowd, Gregory Evans. *A Spirited Resistance: The North American Indian Struggle for Unity, 1745–1815*. Baltimore: Johns Hopkins University Press, 1992.

———. *War under Heaven: Pontiac, the Indian Nations, and the British Empire*. Baltimore: Johns Hopkins University Press, 2002.

Draper, Lyman Copeland, Reuben Gold Thwaites, Milo M. Quaife, and Joseph Schafer, eds. *Collections of the State Historical Society of Wisconsin*. 20 vols. Madison: Wisconsin Historical Society, 1855–1915.

Duckworth, Harry W. "British Capital in the Fur Trade: John Strettell and John Fraser." In *The Fur Trade Revisited: Selected Papers of the Sixth North American Fur Trade Conference, Mackinac Island, Michigan, 1991*, edited by Jennifer S. H. Brown, W. J. Eccles, and Donald P. Heldman, 39–56. East Lansing: Michigan State University Press, 1994.

Dunn, Walter S. *Choosing Sides on the Frontier in the American Revolution*. Westport, CT: Praeger, 2007.

———. *The New Imperial Economy: The British Army and the American Frontier*. Westport, CT: Praeger, 2001.

———. *Opening New Markets: The British Army and the Old Northwest*. Westport, CT: Praeger, 2002.

Dunnigan, Brian Leigh. "Fortress Detroit, 1701–1826." In *The Sixty Years' War for the Great Lakes, 1754–1814*, edited by David Curtis Skaggs and Larry L. Nelson, 167–185. East Lansing: Michigan State University Press, 2001.

———. *Frontier Metropolis: Picturing Early Detroit, 1701–1838*. Detroit: Wayne State University Press, 2001.

———. *The Necessity of Regularity in Quartering Soldiers: The Organization, Material Culture and Quartering of the British Soldier at Michilimackinac*. Mackinac Island, MI: Mackinac State Historic Parks, 1999.

DuVal, Kathleen. *The Native Ground: Indians and Colonists in the Heart of the Continent*. Philadelphia: University of Pennsylvania Press, 2006.

Eaton, H. B. "Lieutenant-General Patrick Sinclair: An Account of His Military Career." *Journal of the Society for Army Historical Research* 56 (Autumn–Spring 1978–1979): 45–55, 128–142, 215–232.

Eccles, W. J. *The Canadian Frontier, 1534–1760.* New York: Holt, Rinehart and Winston, 1969.

———. *The French in North America, 1500–1783.* East Lansing: Michigan State University Press, 1998.

———. "The Fur Trade and Eighteenth-Century Imperialism." *William and Mary Quarterly* 40 (1983): 342–362.

Eckert, I. Irma. "The Early Fur Trade at York and Churchill: Implications for the Native People of the North Central Subarctic." In *"Castor Fait Tout": Selected Papers of the Fifth North American Fur Trade Conference, 1985*, edited by Bruce G. Trigger, Toby Morantz, and Louise Dechene, 223–235. St. Louis: Lake St. Louis Historical Society, 1987.

Edler, Friedrich. *The Dutch Republic and the American Revolution.* New York: AMS Press, 1971.

Edmunds, R. David. *The Potawatomis: Keepers of the Fire.* Norman: University of Oklahoma Press, 1978.

Edmunds, R. David, and Joseph L. Peyser. *The Fox Wars: The Mesquakie Challenge to New France.* Norman: University of Oklahoma Press, 1993.

Ekberg, Carl J. *French Roots in the Illinois Country: The Mississippi Frontier in Colonial Times.* Urbana: University of Illinois Press, 1998.

———. *Stealing Indian Women: Native Slavery in the Illinois Country.* Urbana: University of Illinois Press, 2007.

Evans, Lynn L. M. *House D of the Southeast Row House: Excavations at Fort Michilimackinac, 1989–1997.* Mackinac Island, MI: Mackinac State Historic Parks, 2001.

Farnie, D. A. "The Commercial Empire of the Atlantic, 1607–1783." *Economic History Review* 15 (1962): 205–218.

Farrell, David R. "Askin, John." In *Dictionary of Canadian Biography.* Vol. 5. Toronto: University of Toronto Press, 1983.

Fenn, Elizabeth A. *Pox Americana: The Great Smallpox Epidemic of 1775–82.* New York: Hill and Wang, 2001.

Fleming, R. H. "Phyn, Ellice and Company of Schenectady." *Contributions to Canadian Economics* 4 (1932): 7–41.

Force, Peter, ed. *American Archives.* 9 vols. Washington, DC: St. Clair Clarke and Peter Force, 1837–1853.

Gallay, Alan. *The Indian Slave Trade: The Rise of the English Empire in the American South, 1670–1717.* New Haven, CT: Yale University Press, 2002.

Games, Alison. "Atlantic History: Definitions, Challenges, and Opportunities." *American Historical Review* 111 (2006): 741–757.

Gates, Charles M., ed. *Five Fur Traders of the Northwest.* St. Paul: Minnesota Historical Society Press, 1965.

Gilman, Carolyn. *The Grand Portage Story*. St. Paul: Minnesota Historical Society Press, 1992.

———. *Where Two Worlds Meet: The Great Lakes Fur Trade*. St. Paul: Minnesota Historical Society, 1982.

Ginzburg, Carlo. *The Cheese and the Worms: The Cosmos of a Sixteenth-Century Miller*. Baltimore: Johns Hopkins University Press, 1980.

Gitlin, Jay. *The Bourgeois Frontier: French Towns, French Traders, and American Expansion*. New Haven, CT: Yale University Press, 2010.

Gladwin, Henry. *The Gladwin Manuscripts*. Lansing, MI: Robert Smith Printing Company, 1897.

Godfrey, Sheldon J., and J. C. Godfrey. *Search Out the Land: The Jews and the Growth of Equality in British Colonial America, 1740–1867*. Montreal: McGill-Queen's University Press, 1995.

Gordon, James. "The Reminiscences of James Gordon." Edited by Josephine Mayer. *Quarterly Journal of the New York State Historical Association* 17 (1936): 423–439.

Gough, Barry M. "The 'Adventurers of England Trading into Hudson's Bay': A Study of the Found Members of the Hudson's Bay Company, 1665–1670." *Albion* 2 (1970): 35–47.

Gram, John. "John Askin at Michilimackinac." Unpublished manuscript, June 1995, Mackinac State Historic Parks Library, Mackinac City, MI.

Greene, Jack P. *Pursuits of Happiness: The Social Development of Early Modern British Colonies and the Formation of American Culture*. Chapel Hill: University of North Carolina Press, 1988.

———. *The Quest for Power: The Lower Houses of Assembly in the Southern Royal Colonies, 1689–1776*. Chapel Hill: University of North Carolina Press, 1963.

———. "Transatlantic Colonization and the Redefinition of Empire in the Early Modern Era: The British-American Experience." In *Negotiated Empires: Centers and Peripheries in the Americas, 1500–1820*, edited by Christine Daniels and Michael V. Kennedy, 269–282. New York: Routledge, 2002.

Griffin, Patrick. *American Leviathan: Empire, Nation, and Revolutionary Frontier*. New York: Hill and Wang, 2007.

Guy, Alan J. *Oeconomy and Discipline: Officership and Administration in the British Army,*

1714–63. Manchester, UK: Manchester University Press, 1985.

Haefeli, Evan. "A Note on the Use of North American Borderlands." *American Historical Review* 104 (1999): 1222–1225.

Haeger, John D. *John Jacob Astor: Business and Finance in the Early Republic*. Detroit: Wayne State University Press, 1991.

Halchin, Jill Yvonne. *Excavations at Fort Michilimackinac, 1983–1985: House C of the Southeast Row House, the Solomon-Levy-Parant House*. Mackinac Island, MI: Mackinac Island State Park Commission, 1985.

Hamilton, Henry. *Henry Hamilton and George Rogers Clark in the American Revolution: With the Unpublished Journal of Lieut. Gov. Henry Hamilton*. Edited by John D. Barnhart. Crawfordsville, IN: R.E. Banta, 1951.

Hamilton, Milton W. *Sir William Johnson, Colonial American, 1715–1763*. New York: Kennikat Press, 1976.

Hamlin, Marie C. W. *Legends of Le Detroit*. Detroit: Thorndike Nourse, 1884.

Hancock, David. *Citizens of the World: London Merchants and the Integration of the British Atlantic Community, 1735–1785*. Cambridge: Cambridge University Press, 1995.

Harlow, Vincent T. *The Founding of the Second British Empire, 1763–1793*. London: Longmans, Green, 1952.

Harrington, Virginia D. *The New York Merchant on the Eve of the Revolution*. Gloucester, MA: Peter Smith, 1964.

Hauser, Judith Ann. *Jesuit Rings from Fort Michilimackinac and Other European Contact Sites*. Mackinac Island, MI: Mackinac Island State Park Commission, 1982.

Havard, Gilles. *The Great Peace of Montreal of 1701: French-Native Diplomacy in the Seventeenth Century*. Montreal: McGill-Queen's University Press, 2001.

Heldman, Donald P. *Archaeological Investigations at French Farm Lake in Northern Michigan, 1981–1982: A British Colonial Farm Site*. Mackinac Island, MI: Mackinac Island State Park Commission, 1983.

Henry, Alexander. *Alexander Henry's Travels and Adventures in the Years, 1760–1776*. Edited by Milo M. Quaife. Chicago: The Lakeside Press, 1921.

Hinderaker, Eric. *Elusive Empires: Constructing Colonialism in the Ohio Valley, 1673–1800*. New York: Cambridge University Press, 1997.

Hinderaker, Eric, and Peter C. Mancall. *At the Edge of Empire: The Backcountry in British North America*. Baltimore: Johns Hopkins University Press, 2003.

Hoffman, Ronald, and Peter J. Albert, eds. *Diplomacy and Revolution: The Franco-American Alliance of 1778*. Charlottesville: University of Virginia Press, 1981.

Humphreys, David A. "Lord Shelburne and the Proclamation of 1763." *English Historical*

Review 49 (1934): 241–264.

Ingram, Daniel. *Indians and British Outposts in Eighteenth-Century America*. Gainesville: University Press of Florida, 2012.

Innis, Harold A. *The Fur Trade in Canada: An Introduction to Canadian Economic History*. New Haven, CT: Yale University Press, 1962.

Jackson, Marjorie Gordon. "The Beginning of British Trade at Michilimackinac." *Minnesota History* 11 (1930): 231–270.

Jacobson, Judy. *Detroit River Connections: Historical and Biographical Sketches of the Eastern Great Lakes Border Region*. Baltimore: Clearfield, 1994.

Jenks, William Lee. *Patrick Sinclair*. Lansing: Wynkoop Hallenbeck Crawford Company, State Printers of Michigan, 1914.

Jennings, Francis. *Empire of Fortune: Crowns, Colonies, and Tribes in the Seven Years War in America*. New York: Norton, 1988.

Johnson, William. *The Papers of Sir William Johnson*. 14 vols. Albany: State University of New York, 1921–1963.

Kammen, Michael G. "The Colonial Agents, English Politics and the American Revolution." *William and Mary Quarterly 22* (1965): 244–263.

Ketchum, Richard M. *Saratoga: Turning Point of America's Revolutionary War*. New York: Holt, 1999.

Karras, Alan L. *Smuggling: Contraband and Corruption in World History*. Lanham, MD: Rowman & Littlefield, 2010.

Kelley, Sharon A., ed. *Marriage Records, Ste. Anne Church, Detroit, 1701–1850*. Detroit: Detroit Society for Genealogical Research, 2001.

Kellogg, Louise Phelps, ed. *Early Narratives of the Northwest, 1634–1699*. New York: C. Scribner's Sons, 1917.

Kidwell, Clara Sue. "Indian Women as Cultural Negotiators." *Ethnohistory* 39 (1992): 97–107.

Kinietz, W. Vernon. *The Indians of the Western Great Lakes, 1615–1760*. Ann Arbor: University of Michigan Press, 1965.

Krum, Gracie B., ed. *Early Land Transfers, Detroit and Wayne County, Michigan*. Vols. A–C, 1703–1793. Detroit: Louisa St. Clair Chapter, Daughters of the American Revolution, 1936.

Lafitau, Joseph. *Rare of Unpublished Documents, or the Aulneau Collection, 1734–1745*. 2 vols. Montreal: Archives of St. Mary's College, 1893.

Lajeunesse, Ernest J., ed. *The Windsor Border Region: Canada's Southernmost Frontier: A Collection of Documents*. Toronto: Champlain Society, 1960.

Leighton, Douglas. "Claus, Christian Daniel." In *Dictionary of Canadian Biography*. Vol. 4. Toronto: University of Toronto Press, 1979.

Lepore, Jill. "Historians Who Love Too Much: Reflections on Microhistory and Biography." *Journal of American History* 88 (2001): 129–144.

MacKay, Douglas. *The Honourable Company: A History of the Hudson's Bay Company*. Indianapolis: Bobbs-Merrill, 1936.

MacLeitch, Gail. "'Red' Labor: Iroquois Participation in the Atlantic Economy." *Labor* 1 (2004): 69–90.

Magnaghi, Russell M. "Red Slavery in the Great Lakes Country during the French and British Regimes." *Old Northwest* 12 (1996): 201–217.

Mancall, Peter C. *Deadly Medicine: Indians and Alcohol in Early America*. Ithaca, NY: Cornell University Press, 1995.

Mancke, Elizabeth. "Negotiating an Empire: Britain and Its Overseas Peripheries, 1550–1780." In *Negotiated Empires: Centers and Peripheries in the Americas, 1500–1820*, Edited by Christine Daniels and Michael V. Kennedy, 269–282. New York: Routledge, 2002.

Marrero, Karen L. *Founding Families: Power and Authority of Mixed French and Native Lineages in Eighteenth-Century Detroit*. New Haven, CT: Yale University Press, 2011.

Marshall, P. J. *The Making and Unmaking of Empires: Britain, India, and America, 1750–1783*. Oxford: Oxford University Press, 2005.

———, ed. *The Oxford History of the British Empire*. Vol. 2, *The Eighteenth Century*. Oxford: Oxford University Press, 1998.

Marshall, Peter. "The Michilimackinac Misfortunes of Commissary Roberts." *The Fur Trade Revisited: Selected Papers of the Sixth North American Fur Trade Conference, Mackinac Inland, Michigan, 1991*, edited by Jennifer S. H. Brown, W. J. Eccles, and Donald P. Heldman, 285–298. East Lansing: Michigan State University Press, 1994.

Matson, Cathy D. *Merchants and Empire: Trading in Colonial New York*. Baltimore: Johns Hopkins University Press, 1998.

Mayer, Josephine Jane. "Major Robert Rogers, Trader." *Quarterly Journal of the New York State Historical Association* 15 (1934): 388–397.

Mayo, Lawrence Shaw. *Jeffery Amherst: A Biography*. London: Longmans, Green, 1916.

McClurken, James. "Augustin Hamlin Jr.: Odawa Identity and the Politics of Persistence." In *Being and Becoming Indian: Biographical Studies of North American Frontiers*, edited by James A. Clifton, 82–111.

———. *Our People, Our Journey: The Little River Band of Ottawa Indians*. East Lansing: Michigan State University Press, 2009.

McConnell, Michael N. *Army and Empire: British Soldiers on the American Frontier, 1758–1775*. Lincoln: University of Nebraska Press, 2004.

———. *A Country Between: The Upper Ohio Valley and Its Peoples, 1724–1774*. Lincoln: University of Nebraska Press, 1992.

McCullough, A. B. "Currency Conversion in British North America, 1760–1900." *Archivaria* 16 (1983): 83–94.

McCusker, John J., and Kenneth Morgan, eds. *The Early Modern Atlantic Economy*. Cambridge: Cambridge University Press, 2000.

McDonnell, Michael A. "Charles-Michel Mouet de Langlade: Warrior, Soldier, and Intercultural 'Window' on the Sixty Years' War for the Great Lakes." In *The Sixty Years' War for the Great Lakes, 1754–1814*, edited by David Curtis Skaggs and Larry L. Nelson, 79–103. East Lansing: Michigan State University Press, 2001.

———. *Masters of Empire: Great Lakes Indians and the Making of America*. New York: Hill and Wang, 2015.

McDowell, John E. "Therese Schindler of Mackinac: Upward Mobility in the Great Lakes Fur Trade." *Wisconsin Magazine of History* 61 (1977–1978): 125–143.

Merrell, James Hart. *The Indians' New World: Catawbas and Their Neighbors from European Contact through the Era of Removal*. Chapel Hill: University of North Carolina Press, 1989.

———. *Into the American Woods: Negotiators on the Pennsylvania Frontier*. New York: Norton, 1999.

Michigan Pioneer and Historical Collection. 40 vols. Lansing: Michigan Pioneer and Historical Society, 1874–1929.

Miller, Cary. *Ogimaag: Anishinaabeg Leadership, 1760–1845*. Lincoln: University of Nebraska Press, 2010.

Mintz, Max. *The Generals of Saratoga: John Burgoyne and Horatio Gates*. New Haven, CT: Yale University Press, 1990.

Momryk, Myron, "Todd, Isaac." In *Dictionary of Canadian Biography*. Vol. 5. Toronto: University of Toronto Press, 1983.

Montresor, John. "The Montresor Journals." In *Collections of the New York Historical Society for the Year 1881*, edited by G. D. Scull. New York: New York Historical Society, 1882.

Moodie, D. W. "Agriculture and the Fur Trade." In *Old Trails and New Directions: Papers of the Third North American Fur Trade Conference*, edited by Carol M. Judd and Arthur J. Ray, 272–290. Toronto: University of Toronto Press, 1980.

Moogk, Peter N. *La Nouvelle France: The Making of French Canada; A Cultural History*. East Lansing: Michigan State University Press, 2000.

Morand, Lynn L. *Craft Industries at Fort Michilimackinac: An Eighteenth Century Fur Trade Outpost*. Mackinac Island, MI: Mackinac State Historic Parks, 1993.

Morgan, Edmund S., and Helen M. Morgan. *The Stamp Act Crisis: Prologue to Revolution*. Chapel Hill: University of North Carolina Press, 1995.

Morison, Daniel. *The Doctor's Secret Journal*. Edited by George May. Mackinac Island, MI: Mackinac Island State Park Commission, 1960.

Morris, Thomas. "Journal of Captain Thomas Morris of His Majesty's XVII Regiment of Infantry." In *Early Western Journals, 1748–1765*, edited by Reuben Gold Thwaites, 301–328. Lewisburg, PA: Wennawoods Publishing, 1998.

Murphy, Lucy Eldersveld. *A Gathering of Rivers: Indians, Metis, and Mining in the Western Great Lakes, 1737–1832*. Lincoln: University of Nebraska Press, 2000.

Namias, June. *White Captives: Gender and Ethnicity on the American Frontier*. Chapel Hill: University of North Carolina Press, 1993.

Nasatir, A. P. "The Anglo-Spanish Frontier in the Illinois Country during the American Revolution, 1779–1783." *Journal of the Illinois State Historical Society* 21 (1928): 291–358.

Nash, Gary B. *The Unknown American Revolution: The Unruly Birth of Democracy and the Struggle to Create America*. New York: Viking, 2005.

Nelson, Larry L. *A Man of Distinction among Them: Alexander McKee and the Country Frontier, 1754–1799*. Kent, OH: Kent State University Press, 1999.

Nester, William R. *George Rogers Clark: "I Glory in War"*. Norman: University of Oklahoma Press, 2012.

Nettels, Curtis. "The Place of Markets in the Old Colonial System." *New England Quarterly* 6 (1933): 491–512.

Norton, Thomas Elliot. *The Fur Trade in Colonial New York, 1686–1776*. Madison: University of Wisconsin Press, 1974.

Nute, Grace Lee. "A British Legal Case and Old Grand Portage." *Minnesota History* 21 (1940): 117–148.

Olson, Alison G. "The London Mercantile Lobby and the Coming of the American Revolution." *Journal of American History* 69 (1982): 21–41.

O'Toole, Fintan. *White Savage: William Johnson and the Invention of America*. London: Faber and Faber, 2005.

Ouelett, Fernand. "McBeath, George." In *Dictionary of Canadian Biography*. Vol. 5. Toronto: University of Toronto Press, 1983.

Palmer, Robert R. *The Age of the Democratic Revolution: A Political History of Europe and America, 1760–1800*. Princeton, NJ: Princeton University Press, 1959.

Pare, George, and Milo M. Quiafe, eds. "The St. Joseph Baptismal Register." *Mississippi*

Valley Historical Review 13, no. 2 (September 1926): 201–239.

Parkman, Francis. *The Conspiracy of Pontiac and the Indian War after the Conquest of Canada*. Lincoln: University of Nebraska Press, 1994.

The Parliamentary History of England from the Earliest Period to This Year 1803. Vol. 18. London: T. C. Hansard, 1813.

Peckham, Howard H. *Pontiac and the Indian Uprising*. Princeton, NJ: Princeton University Press, 1947.

Peckham, Howard H., and Charles Gibson, eds. *Attitudes of Colonial Powers toward the American Indian*. Salt Lake City: University of Utah Press, 1969.

Petersen, Eugene T. *Gentlemen on the Frontier: A Pictorial Record of the Culture of Michilimackinac*. Mackinac Island, MI: Mackinac Island State Park Commission, 1964.

Peterson, Jacqueline. "Prelude to Red River: A Social Portrait of the Great Lakes Metis." *Ethnohistory* 25 (1978): 41–67.

Peterson, Jacqueline, and Jennifer S. H. Brown, eds. *The New Peoples: Being and Becoming Métis in North America*. St. Paul: Minnesota Historical Society Press, 1985.

Peyser, Joseph L., and Jose Antonio Brandao, eds. *Edge of Empire: Documents of Michilimackinac, 1671–1716*. East Lansing: Michigan State University Press, 2008.

Philips, Paul. *The Fur Trade*. Norman: University of Oklahoma Press, 1961.

Philips, Ruth B. *Patterns of Power: The Jasper Grant Collection and Great Lakes Indian Art of the Early Nineteenth Century*. Kleinburg, Ontario: McMichael Canadian Collection, 1984.

Podruchny, Carolyn. *Making the Voyageur World: Travelers and Traders in the North American Fur Trade*. Lincoln: University of Nebraska Press, 2006.

Porter, Bernard. *The Absent-Minded Imperialists: Empire, Society, and Culture in Britain*. Oxford: Oxford University Press, 2004.

Pound, Arthur, and Richard Edwin Day. *Johnson of the Mohawks: A Biography of Sir William Johnson, Irish Immigrant, Mohawk War Chief, American Soldier, Empire Builder*. New York: Macmillan, 1930.

Pritchard, James. "French Strategy and the American Revolution: A Reappraisal." *Naval War College Review* 47, no. 4 (1994): 83–108.

Putnam, Lara. "To Study the Fragments/Whole: Microhistory and the Atlantic World." *Journal of Social History* 39 (2006): 615–630.

Quaife, Milo M. "Detroit Biographies: Alexander Macomb." *Burton Historical Collections Leaflet* 10 (1931): 1–16.

Radin, Paul, and A. B. Reagan. "Ojibwa Myths and Tales: The Manabozho Cycle." *Journal of American Folklore* 41 (1928): 61–146.

Ray, Arthur J. *I Have Lived Here since the World Began: An Illustrated History of Canada's Native People*. Toronto: Key Porter Books, 2010.

———. "Indians as Consumers in the Eighteenth Century." In *Old Trails and New Directions: Papers of the Third North American Fur Trade Conference*, edited by Carol M. Judd and Arthur J. Ray, 255–271. Toronto: University of Toronto Press, 1980.

Ray, Arthur J., and Donald B. Freeman. *"Give Us Good Measure": An Economic Analysis of Relations between the Indians and the Hudson's Bay Company before 1763*. Toronto: University of Toronto Press, 1978.

Richter, Daniel K. *Facing East from Indian Country: A Native History of Early America*. Cambridge: Harvard University Press, 2001.

———. *The Ordeal of the Longhouse: The Peoples of the Iroquois League in the Era of European Colonization*. Chapel Hill: University of North Carolina Press, 1992.

———. "War and Culture: The Iroquois Experience." *William and Mary Quarterly* 40, no. 4. (October 1983): 537–544.

Ritcheson, Charles R. "The Preparation of the Stamp Acts." *William and Mary Quarterly* 10, no. 4 (October 1953): 543–559.

Rogers, Robert. *Journal of Major Robert Rogers*. Edited by William L. Clements. Worcester: American Antiquarian Society, 1918.

———. *Journals of Major Robert Rogers: An Account of the Several Excursions He Made under the Generals Who Commanded upon the Continent of North America, during the Late War*. Edited by Franklin B. Hough. Albany: Joel Munsell's Sons, 1883.

Ross, Frank E. "The Fur Trade of the Western Great Lakes Region." *Minnesota History* 19 (1938): 271–307.

Ross, John F. *War on the Run: The Epic Story of Robert Rogers and the Conquest of America's First Frontier*. New York: Bantam Books, 2011.

Rushforth, Brett. *Bonds of Alliance: Indigenous and Atlantic Slaveries in New France*. Chapel Hill: University of North Carolina Press, 2012.

———. "'A Little Flesh We Offer You': The Origins of Indian Slavery in New France." *William and Mary Quarterly* 60 (2003): 781–783.

Russell, Nelson Vance. *The British Regime in Michigan and the Old Northwest*. Philadelphia: Porcupine Press, 1978.

Rutherfurd, John. *The Siege of Detroit in 1763: The Journal of Pontiac's Conspiracy and John Rutherfurd's Narrative of a Captivity*. Edited by Milo M. Quaife. Chicago: R. R. Donnelley & Sons, 1958.

Salisbury, Neal. "The Indians' Old World: Native Americans and the Coming of the

Europeans." *William and Mary Quarterly* 53 (1996): 435–458.

Sarson, Steven. *British America, 1500–1800: Creating Colonies, Imagining an Empire.* London: Hodder Arnold, 2005.

Satz, Ronald N. *Tennessee's Indian Peoples: From White Contact to Removal, 1540–1840.* Knoxville: University of Tennessee Press, 1979.

Schenck, Theresa M. "The Cadottes: Five Generations of Fur Traders on Lake Superior." In *The Fur Trade Revisited: Selected Papers of the Sixth North American Fur Trade Conference, Mackinac Island, Michigan, 1991*, edited by Jennifer S. H. Brown, W. J. Eccles, and Donald P. Heldman, 189–197. East Lansing: Michigan State University Press, 1994.

Schmidt-Nowara, Christopher Ebert. "Borders and Borderlands of Interpretation." *American Historical Review* 104 (1999): 1226–1228.

Shannon, Timothy. "Dressing for Success on the Mohawk Frontier: Hendrick, William Johnson, and the Indian Fashion." *William and Mary Quarterly* 53, no. 1 (January 1996): 13–42.

———. *Iroquois Diplomacy on the Early American Frontier.* New York: Penguin, 2008.

Shields, David S. *Civil Tongues and Polite Letters in British America.* Chapel Hill: University of North Carolina Press, 1997.

Shoemaker, Nancy. *A Strange Likeness: Becoming Red and White in Eighteenth-Century North America.* Oxford: Oxford University Press, 2004.

Simcoe, Elizabeth. *Mrs. Simcoe's Diary.* Edited by Mary Quayle Innis. Toronto: Dundurn, 2007.

Simcoe, John. *The Correspondence of Lieutenant Governor John Graves Simcoe.* Edited by E. A. Cruikshank. 5 vols. Toronto: Ontario Historical Society, 1923–1926.

Skaggs, David C. *Oliver Hazard Perry: Honor, Courage, and Patriotism in the Early U. S. Navy.* Annapolis, MD: Naval Institute Press, 2006.

Skinner, Claiborne A. *The Upper Country: French Enterprise in the Colonial Great Lakes.* Baltimore: Johns Hopkins University Press, 2008.

Sosin, Jack M. *Whitehall and the Wilderness: The Middle West in British Colonial Policy, 1760–1775.* Lincoln: University of Nebraska Press, 1961.

Silver, Peter. *Our Savage Neighbors: How Indian War Transformed Early America.* New York: Norton, 2008.

Sleeper-Smith, Susan. "Forum Introduction: *The Middle Ground* Revisited." *William and Mary Quarterly* 63, no. 1 (January 2006): 3–8.

———. "'Ignorant Bigots and Busy Rebels': The American Revolution in the Western Great Lakes." In *The Sixty Years' War for the Great Lakes, 1754–1814*, edited by

David Curtis Skaggs and Larry L. Nelson, 145–165. East Lansing: Michigan State University Press, 2001.

———. *Indian Women and French Men: Rethinking Cultural Encounter in the Western Great Lakes*. Amherst: University of Massachusetts Press, 2001.

———. "'[A]n Unpleasant Transition on This Frontier': Challenging Female Autonomy and Authority at Michilimackinac." *Journal of the Early Republic* 25 (2005): 417–443.

———. "Women, Kin, and Catholicism: New Perspectives of the Fur Trade." *Ethnohistory* 47, no. 2 (Spring 2000): 423–452.

Smith, James G. E. "Chipewyan, Cree and Inuit Relations West of Hudson Bay, 1714–1955." *Ethnohistory* 28 (1981): 133–156.

Stacey, C. P. "Rogers, Robert." In *Dictionary of Canadian Biography*. Vol. 4. Toronto: University of Toronto Press, 1979.

The Statues: Revised Edition. Vol. 15. London: George Edward Erye and William Spottiswoode, 1878.

The Statues at Large from the Seventh Year of the Reign of King George the Third to the Eighteenth Year of the Reign of King George the Third. Vol. 13. London: Charles Erye and Andrew Strahan, 1786.

Steele, Ian Kenneth. *Warpaths: Invasions of North America*. New York: Oxford University Press, 1994.

Stevens, Paul L. "The Indian Diplomacy of Capt. Richard B. Lernoult, British Military Commandant of Detroit, 1774–1775." *Michigan Historical Review* 13 (1987): 47–82.

———. "Wabasaha Visits Governor Carleton, 1776: New Light on a Legendary Episode of Dakota-British Diplomacy on the Great Lakes Frontier." *Michigan Historical Review* 16 (1990): 21–48.

Stevens, Wayne Edson. *The Northwest Fur Trade*. Urbana: University of Illinois, 1928.

Stone, Lawrence. *An Imperial State at War: Britain from 1689 to 1815*. London: Routledge, 1994.

Sugden, John. *Tecumseh: A Life*. New York: Holt Paperbacks, 1999.

Taaffe, Stephen R. *The Philadelphia Campaign, 1777–1778*. Lawrence: University Press of Kansas, 2003.

Tanner, Helen Hornbeck. "The Glaize in 1792: A Composite Indian Community." *Ethnohistory* 25 (1978): 15–39.

Tanner, Helen Hornbeck, and Miklos Pinther, eds. *Atlas of Great Lakes Indian History*. Norman: University of Oklahoma Press, 1987.

Taylor, Allen. *The Civil War of 1812: American Citizens, British Subjects, Irish Rebels, and Indian Allies*. New York: Alfred A. Knopf, 2010.

———. *The Divided Ground: Indians, Settlers and the Northern Borderland of the American Revolution*. New York: Alfred A. Knopf, 2006.

Thomas, Charles M. "Successful and Unsuccessful Merchants in the Illinois Country." *Journal of the Illinois State Historical Society* 30 (1938): 429–440.

Thomas, Peter D. G. "The Cost of the British Army in North America, 1764–1775." *William and Mary Quarterly* 45 (1988): 510–516.

Thorman, George E. "Oakes, Forrest." In *Dictionary of Canadian Biography*. Vol. 4. Toronto: University of Toronto Press, 1979.

Thorne, Tanis C. *The Many Hands of My Relations: French and Indians on the Lower Missouri*. Columbia: University of Missouri Press, 1996.

Thwaites, Reuben Gold, ed. *The Jesuit Relations and Allies Documents: Trade and Explorations of the Jesuit Missionaries in New France, 1610–1791*. 71 vols. Cleveland: Burrows Brothers, 1898–1901.

Thwaites, Reuben Gold, and Louise Phelps Kellogg, eds. *Frontier Defense on the Upper Ohio, 1777–1778*. Madison: Wisconsin Historical Society, 1912.

Tourtellot, Arthur. *Lexington and Concord: The Beginning of the War of the American Revolution*. New York: Norton, 2000.

Trigger, Bruce G. *The Children of Aataentsic: A History of the Huron People to 1660*. Montreal: McGill-Queen's University Press, 1976.

Trudel, Marcel. *L'esclavage au Canada Français: Histoire et Conditions de L'esclavage*. Quebec: Les Presses Universitaires Lava, 1960.

Ulrich, Laurel. *A Midwife's Tale: The Life of Martha Ballard, Based on Her Diary, 1785–1812*. New York: Vintage Books, 1991.

Usner, Daniel H. *Indians, Settlers and Slaves in a Frontier Exchange Economy: The Lower Mississippi Valley before 1783*. Chapel Hill: University of North Carolina Press, 1992.

Van Kirk, Sylvia. "From 'Marrying-In' to 'Marrying-Out': Changing Patterns of Aboriginal/Non-aboriginal Marriage in Colonial Canada." *Frontiers* 23 (2002): 1–11.

———. *Many Tender Ties: Women in Fur-Trade Society, 1670–1870*. Norman: University of Oklahoma Press, 1983.

Wainwright, Nicholas B. *George Croghan, Wilderness Diplomat*. Chapel Hill: University of North Carolina Press, 1959.

Wallace, W. S., ed. *Documents Relating to the North West Company*. Toronto: Champlain Society, 1934.

———. "The Pedlars from Quebec." *Canadian Historical Review* 13 (1932): 387–402.

———. *The Pedlars from Quebec, and Other Papers on the Nor' Westers*. Toronto: Ryerson Press, 1954.

Wheeler, Robert C. *A Toast to the Fur Trade: A Picture Essay on Its Material Culture*. St. Paul: Wheeler Productions, 1985.

White, Bruce M. "Balancing the Books: Trader Profits in the British Lake Superior Fur Trade." In *New Faces of the Fur Trade: Selected Papers of the Seventh North American Fur Trade Conference, Halifax, Nova Scotia, 1995*, edited by Jo-Anne Fiske, Susan Sleeper-Smith, and William Wicken, 175–192. East Lansing: Michigan State University Press, 1998.

———. "Encounters with Spirits: Ojibwa and Dakota Theories about the French and Their Merchandise." *Ethnohistory* 41 (1994): 369–405.

———. "'Give Us a Little Milk': The Social and Cultural Meanings of Gift Giving in the Lake Superior Fur Trade." *Minnesota History* 48 (Summer 1982): 66–67.

———. "The Woman Who Married a Beaver: Trade Patterns and Gender Roles in the Ojibwa Fur Trade." *Ethnohistory* 46, no. 1 (Winter 1999): 109–147.

White, Richard. "Creative Misunderstandings and New Understandings." *William and Mary Quarterly* 63, no. 1 (January 2006): 9–14.

———. *The Middle Ground: Indians, Empires, and Republics in the Great Lakes Region, 1650–1815*. Cambridge: Cambridge University Press, 1991.

Whitfield, Carol. "Grant, Alexander." In *Dictionary of Canadian Biography*. Vol. 5. Toronto: University of Toronto Press, 1983.

Widder, Agnes Haigh. "The John Askin Family Library: A Fur-Trading Family's Book." *Michigan Historical Review* 33 (2007): 27–58.

Widder, Keith R. *Beyond Pontiac's Shadow: Michilimackinac and the Anglo-Indian War of 1763*. East Lansing: Michigan State University Press, 2013.

———. "Effects of the American Revolution on Fur-Trade Society at Michilimackinac." In *The Fur Trade Revisited: Selected Papers of the Sixth North American Fur Trade Conference, Mackinac Island, Michigan, 1991*, edited by Jennifer S. H. Brown, W. J. Eccles, and Donald P. Heldman, 285–316. East Lansing: Michigan State University Press, 1994.

———. "The French Connection: The Interior French and Their Role in the French-British Relations in the Western Great Lakes Region, 1760–1775." In *The Sixty Years' War for the Great Lakes, 1754–1814*, edited by David Curtis Skaggs and Larry L. Nelson, 125–143. East Lansing: Michigan State University Press, 2001.

———. "The 1767 Maps of Robert Rogers and Jonathan Carver: A Proposal for the Establishment of the Colony of Michilimackinac." *Michigan Historical Review* 30 (2004): 35–75.

William L. Clements Library. *Old Fort Michilimackinac: Reproductions of Two Maps from the Papers of General Thomas Gage in the William L. Clements Library, with a Reconstruction Drawing of the Fort.* Ann Arbor: University of Ann Arbor Press, 1938.

Williams, J. Mark, and Gary Shapiro. *A Search for the Eighteenth-Century Village at Michilimackinac: A Soil Resistivity Survey.* Mackinac Island, MI: Mackinac Island State Park Commission, 1982.

Wilson, Kathleen. "Introduction: Histories, Empires, Modernities." In *A New Imperial History: Culture, Identity and Modernity in and the Empire, 1660–1840*, edited by Kathleen Wilson, 1–28. Cambridge: Cambridge University Press, 2004.

Wise, S. F. "Gage, Thomas." In *Dictionary of Canadian Biography.* Vol. 4. Toronto: University of Toronto Press, 1979.

Witgen, Michael J. *An Infinity of Nations: How the Native New World Shaped Early North America.* Philadelphia: University of Pennsylvania Press, 2012.

Wood, Gordon S. *The Creation of the American Republic, 1776–1787.* Chapel Hill: University of North Carolina Press, 1969.

———. *The Radicalism of the American Revolution.* New York: A. A. Knopf, 1992.

Wright, J. C. *Stories of the Crooked Tree.* Harbor Springs, MI: Lakeside Press, 1915.

Wunder, John R., and Pekka Hamalainen. "Of Lethal Places and Lethal Essays." *American Historical Review* 104 (1999): 1229–1234.

Zahedieh, Nuala. *The Capital and the Colonies: London and the Atlantic Economy, 1660–1700.* Cambridge: Cambridge University Press, 2010.

Index

A